Windows on the Sixties

WINDOWS ON THE SIXTIES

EXPLORING KEY TEXTS OF MEDIA AND CULTURE

Edited by

Anthony Aldgate
James Chapman
Arthur Marwick

I.B.Tauris *Publishers*
LONDON • NEW YORK

Published in 2000 by I.B.Tauris & Co Ltd

Victoria House, Bloomsbury Square, London WC1B 4DZ

175 Fifth Avenue, New York NY 10010

Website: http://www.ibtauris.com

In the United States and Canada distributed by St. Martin's Press

175 Fifth Avenue, New York NY 10010

ISBN 1 86064 383 3

A full CIP record for this book is available from the British Library

A full CIP record for this book is available from the Library of Congress

Library of Congress catalog card: available

Typeset by Dexter Haven, London

Printed and bound in Great Britain

Contents

Contributors

ROWANA AGAJANIAN is a research assistant for the Sixties Research Group at The Open University. She has recently published an article on the Children's Film Foundation in the *Historical Journal of Film, Radio and Television*.

ANTHONY ALDGATE is Reader in Film and History at The Open University and Co-Director of the Sixties Research Group. He has published extensively on British cinema history, including *Cinema and History: British Newsreels and the Spanish Civil War* (1979), *Censorship and the Permissive Society: British Cinema and Theatre 1955–1965* (1995), *Britain Can Take It: The British Cinema in the Second World War*, with Jeffrey Richards (second edition 1994) and *Best of British: Cinema and Society from 1930 to the Present* (second edition 1999). He is also Associate Tutor at Kellogg College, Oxford, and Director of the Oxford Undergraduate Certificate in Film Studies.

JAMES CHAPMAN is Lecturer in Film and Television History at The Open University and a member of the Sixties Research Group. He is the author of *The British at War: Cinema, State and Propaganda, 1939–1945* (1998) and *Licence to Thrill: A Cultural History of the James Bond Films* (1999), both published by I.B.Tauris. In addition he has written various essays on aspects of British cinema history and has published articles in the *Historical Journal of Film, Radio and Television* and the *Journal of Popular British Cinema*. He is also a member of the management committee of the Society for the Study of Popular British Cinema (SSPBC).

MICHAEL COYNE is a writer and film historian, and author of *The Crowded Prairie: American National Identity in the Hollywood Western* (1997), published by I.B. Tauris. He is currently working on a study of the films of David Lean.

DANIEL J. LEAB is Professor of History at Seton Hall University, New Jersey, and is a Visiting Fellow with the Sixties Research Group at The Open University. His published works include *From Sambo to Superspade: The Black Experience in Motion Pictures* (1975), *The Labor History Reader* (1987) and the forthcoming *I Was a Communist for the FBI: The Unhappy Life and Times of Matt Cvetic*. He is Editor of the journal *Labor History*, General Secretary of the Historians of American Communism, and Treasurer of the International Association for Media and History (IAMHIST).

ARTHUR MARWICK was appointed founding Professor of History at The Open University in 1969 and is Co-Director of the Sixties Research Group. He has held visiting professorships at the State University of New York at Buffalo, Stanford University, Rhodes College in Memphis, l'École des Hautes études en Sciences Sociales in Paris, and the University of Perugia. His many publications include *The Nature of History* (third edition 1989), *Beauty in History: Society, Politics and Personal Appearance c.1500 to the Present* (1988) and *British Society Since 1945* (third edition 1996). His most recent books are *A History of the Modern British Isles 1914–1999: Circumstances, Events and Outcomes* (2000), and the major survey *The Sixties: Cultural Revolution in Britain, France, Italy and the United States, c.1958–c.1974* (1998).

ALLAN F. MOORE is Reader in Music in the School of Performing Arts at the University of Surrey and is a founder member of the Critical Musicology Forum. His previous publications include *Rock: the Primary Test* and a monograph on the Beatles' Sgt Pepper album. He has contributed to such publications as *Popular Music*, *Contemporary Music Review*, *Music and Letters* and *Grove's Dictionary of Music and Musicians*, and he is also active as a composer of concert music.

ROBERT ROWLAND is an independent documentary film producer and a Visiting Fellow with the Sixties Research Group at The Open University. He was film producer of the BBC's *Panorama* programme from 1962 to 1969. He was the first Deputy Editor of *Nationwide* in 1969, Editor of *The Money Programme* 1970–1 and Editor of *Panorama* 1972–3.

Preface

Windows on the Sixties is the first joint publication arising from the work of the Sixties Research Group in the History Department of The Open University. The aim of the group is to foster rigorous scholarly research into, especially, social and cultural developments in Europe and the United States during the period between the late 1950s and the early 1970s. Since 1992 the Sixties Research Group has been holding a series of seminars in which scholars have presented the fruits of their research into the 1960s alongside participants who have shared memories of their own experiences during the decade of 'cultural revolution'. Our thanks are due in the first instance to all the participants in our seminars, and to the Arts Faculty Research Committee which has generously funded these events.

The editors would like to extend their sincere thanks to Philippa Brewster at I.B.Tauris, who was quick to offer her support to this project and exceptionally patient as the hand-over date was constantly pushed back. A special note of appreciation should also be recorded for Margaret Marchant, who prepared the manuscript on disk, coped stoically with numerous revisions of earlier drafts, and generally managed the entire production process. Authors' personal acknowledgements can be found at the end of their respective chapters.

For permission to quote from unpublished archival materials, grateful acknowledgements are extended to: the British Board of Film Classification for censors' reports relating to *This Sporting Life*; the British Film Institute Library for publicity material on *The Avengers*; Alison Lurie and the Rare Books and Manuscripts Library, Cornell University, for extracts from Alison Lurie's papers; and the BBC Written Archives Centre at Caversham for production documentation relating to *Panorama*. Our thanks also to Alison Lurie for permission to quote extensively from her novels.

Illustrations from *The Apartment* are from the author's personal collection. Other illustrations from film and television texts were provided by BFI Stills, Posters and Designs. Stills from *This Sporting Life* appear by courtesy of Carlton International Media Limited, from *The Avengers* by courtesy of Canal+ Image International, and from *A Hard Day's Night* by courtesy of Walter Shenson. The picture of Cornell University in chapter 6 appears by courtesy of Cornell University Photography.

While every effort has been made to secure the necessary permissions, we may have failed in a few cases to trace the copyright holder. We apologise for any apparent negligence. Should the copyright holders contact us after publication, we would be happy to include a suitable acknowledgement in any future edition of the work.

Introduction

Locating Key Texts Amid the Distinctive Landscape of the Sixties

Arthur Marwick

The jumble of metaphors – 'windows', 'key', 'landscape' – should arouse instant suspicion, and can only be justified by the need, in titles, to say much in little. This book sets out to discuss certain texts, for the most part readily accessible to readers, which do in a significant way contribute to our understanding of, or at the very least raise questions about, some of the social and cultural changes of the 1960s. This Introduction seeks to explicate what I, as one of the two co-directors of the Open University History Department's Sixties Research Group, take to be the characteristic features which identify the 'long sixties' (c.1958–c.1974) as a period of distinctive, and long-lasting, change. The contributors to this book, of course, are not specifically asked to endorse, or elaborate, these views (though some may do so), though they are asked to test them, qualify them, or reject them if that seems necessary. And, while each individual contributor will handle his or her text, or texts, in the manner which to them seems most appropriate, this Introduction seeks also to establish the basic questions which each contributor is expected to address.

Other writers on the sixties have presented views very different from my own, so the opening paragraphs of this Introduction will focus on both discussing alternative views of the sixties, and why I disagree with them, and on summarising my main contentions. My starting point is that periodisation is an analytical device of historians, who, depending upon their particular specialism, perceive certain chunks of the past as having a kind of internal coherence, or unity, or even identity, these 'periods' being divided from other 'periods' by what may be loosely termed 'points of change' or 'turning points', though 'turning points' are seldom abrupt, and no period is hermetically sealed from the one which precedes it or the one which follows it. There is much *prima facie* evidence that, for good or ill, there were important movements of change in the sixties. But decades as defined by the calendar do not usually coincide with the analytical periods of the historian. In any case an economic historian (as distinct from a social and cultural one) could well argue that it is appropriate to speak of one continuous period from the end of World War II till the world oil crisis of 1973, Eric Hobsbawm's 'Golden Age, 1945-73' or 'les trentes glorieuses' (of the French historians).[1] My researches as a social and cultural historian, however, have led me to identify the beginnings of certain important cultural and social changes around 1958–9, while recognising, with Hobsbawm, a further 'turning point' in 1973–4. Thus, I present 'the long sixties', a distinctive and influential period of change running from c.1958 to c.1974. Others, with interests akin to my own, have disagreed. Some, overawed perhaps by a famous Philip Larkin poem, have seen the sixties as only 'beginning' in 1963; many have seen the sixties as having 'ended' by 1968. Many problems, I believe, are resolved if we divide our 'long sixties' into three sub-periods: 'The First Stirrings of a Cultural Revolution, c.1958–c.1963'; 'The High Sixties, c.1964–c.1968/9'; 'Everything Goes, and Catching Up, c.1969–c.1974'.[2]

A large proportion of books on the sixties concentrate on individuals and minorities, on the icons of pop-rock groups, designers, models, photographers, on hippie communes and on the various branches of the underground: all of these have their importance, and, indeed, were responsible for creating some of the most significant 'texts' of the time.[3] But it is my contention, secondly, that the really historically significant feature of the sixties was what happened to majorities – the changes in status and living standards of ordinary people of all races, the changes in personal relationships, between men and women, between children and adults, the changes in relationships between social classes and between races, the new freedoms, the new empowerment, the new participation involving people of all social groups. In a simple, but I think telling, phrase, the working class, women, provincials, young people, blacks, became visible as never before. This is what I mean by the 'cultural revolution' which I mentioned earlier, though I accept that the term may seem over-rhetorical and that indeed others have used it in the entirely different sense of an existing culture (usually defined as 'bourgeois culture') being replaced by an 'alternative culture' or 'counter-culture'. For the phrase 'cultural revolution' I would quite happily substitute 'social and cultural transformation', save that, of course, that does not have quite the same ring to it. The important thing is not the fancy phrase one uses, but the actuality of the changes one is identifying.

Actually, to move to my third proposition, I totally reject the idea of there having been one unified, cohesive, 'counter-culture' in the sixties, as I reject the notion of there having been any dialectical process whereby one type of culture or society was in direct confrontation with, and about to take the place of, another. The essence of sixties developments, it seems to me, is the coming into being of a large number of subcultures and movements, all in some way or another critical of the established order of things, all expanding and interacting, and ultimately permeating society. This process of permeation, fourthly, was greatly assisted by what I term measured judgement, that is to say the flexible, tolerant, liberal responses to the new developments of many of those in positions of authority. I believe Marcuse to have been completely in error when he spoke of 'repressive tolerance' to describe the reactions of establishment figures.[4] We come much nearer to understanding what was really happening in the sixties, I would maintain, if we substitute the phrase 'measured judgement' for 'repressive tolerance'.

That is not in any way to deny the continuing operation within society of forces of extreme reaction (in making this fifth point, I refer in particular to the various police forces above all, but also to some sections of the judiciary, usually the lower ones, to elements in the Catholic and fundamentalist Protestant churches, and to right-wing, racist and extreme nationalist groups). There was much violence in the sixties, throughout the decade, not just in 1968–9. The most frequent single cause of riots, whether in urban ghettos or on university campuses, was provocative action by the police. Police forces in all the Western countries tended to operate as states within the state, usually left, even by liberal politicians, to get on with what they saw as their job in whatever way they chose.

A relatively unnoticed feature of the subcultures, movements and new institutions of the sixties is their pronounced entrepreneurial character: some enterprises – experimental theatres, for instance – did get subsidies from local or national authorities, but many were also involved in lucrative transfers from the original little theatre to a mainstream stage (the musical *Hair* is a classic instance of this); rock bands, obviously, were closely integrated with major commercial interests; but design studios, photographic and model agencies, underground, listings and pornographic magazines, head shops and paperback bookshops were all money-spinning enterprises (and none the worse for that). The major implication of this sixth proposition, perhaps, is ratification of the point that there was no sharp, dialectical divide between a commercialised, mainstream culture and a socialistic, non-profit-making alternative culture. Andy Warhol, maker of underground movies, was an important figure in New York high society; Marcuse's *One-Dimensional Man*, calling upon students to act as the revolutionary leaders of what he identified as the revolutionary class, the rootless, the misfortunate, the racial minorities (what others were terming the 'under-class'), was subsidised by a government-funded research council, and by a number of private foundations; the Arts Lab in London was an essential spot for foreign dignitaries and wealthy foreigners.[5]

My seventh proposition is that the relationship between the arts and sixties society is not well represented by the cultural theorists who see cultural artefacts and practices merely as the embodiment of ideologies, whether dominant or alternative. In the first place, the arts (this is particularly true of novels and films, but may also be true of music – élite as well as popular – painting, poetry and sculpture) can be vehicles for presenting new values and new modes of behaviour to larger or smaller sections of the public, and, still more, can serve to legitimate new modes (I am thinking particularly of sexual behaviour here). That apart, the arts and entertainments in the sixties have a number of distinctive characteristics (not individually new, but significant in the sixties because of the way in which they converge and reinforce each other). Not every cultural product revealed all of these characteristics, but I believe the following list of eight headings does capture the essence of artistic endeavours which were not only striking in themselves, but which affected the wider society.

1. Cross-Over: the mixing of élite and popular cultural forms; the attempts to break down the barriers between the two.

2. Obliteration of Boundaries between different art forms: between painting and sculpture, between music and speech, between film and drama; the advent of 'concrete poetry', the extended and intensified use of music in the theatre.

3. Conceptualism: the privileging of the idea, the concept, the message at the expense of aesthetic or formal elements (at the extreme, you didn't actually have to view a painting, or a film, or read a book, to be shocked by it: you only needed to have the concept reported to you).

4. Indeterminacy or the Aleatoric: ensuring that chance plays an important part in the creation of the cultural artefact.

5. Participation: the notion that the reader, the viewer, the audience should play a part in determining the meaning of a cultural product (this took its most extreme form in the theory put forward by the French post-structuralists, particularly Barthes, of 'the death of the author').

6. Use of Technology: seen in the use of photographic techniques in creating paintings, in the use of electrical power in elaborate mobiles and constructions, and also in the creation of artistic products under the influence of drugs.

7. Radicalism: many artists of the time espoused some form of Marxism, entertained some notion, however vague, of 'revolution', or, at the very least, felt bound to express rejection of 'bourgeois' standards and modes; the influence of Situationism (a movement with strong resemblances to the earlier Dadaism) was strong; 'consumer culture' was a frequent target; the *nouveau roman* was an explicit attack on the conventions of the 'bourgeois novel' (stable characterisation, linear story line etc); art was used to advocate a variety of radical causes, including feminism and gay liberation.

8. Cultural Practices as Spectacle: we must never lose sight of the entrepreneurial element which I have already mentioned, nor the influence of television in rendering the private quickly public, creating, with other factors, an ambience in which nothing succeeded like excess, and in which society more and more expected to be entertained by spectacle.

Sixties changes, not just, or even most importantly, in the arts, were long-lasting; they, if I may permit myself a cliché, set the social and cultural agenda for the rest of the century. Now that eighth proposition contradicts a deeply cherished view of the sixties, one nurtured above all by certain of the cultural icons of the time, who like to tell us what a wonderful time the sixties was, what a wonderful time they personally had, and, indeed, what wonderful people they themselves were, before going on to insist that this wonderful era was necessarily short-lived, that its ideals quickly evaporated and had no lasting effects, concluding with commiserations for those not fortunate enough to have had direct experience of the sixties – this was very much the attitude of Jim Haynes, founder of the Traverse Theatre in Edinburgh and the Arts Lab in London, in the autobiography which he published in the late eighties, and also of George Melly in the new material created for the recent second edition of his *Revolt Into Style*.[6] A stronger version of the rather self-indulgent, nostalgic Haynes-Melly view is that of what I term the 'sour left'. The view that there ought to have been a revolution in 1968-9, but that due to the feebleness of the faithful, and the machinations of the bourgeoisie, this never took place so that all the aspirations, all the efforts, simply collapsed into a continuance of the same bad old capitalist system; some, indeed, simply denounced the whole of sixties culture as totally contaminated with 'bourgeois' commercialism.[7]

Just as I reject that kind of undervaluing of sixties achievements, so also, ninthly, I reject the negative views which have become fairly standard among even liberal American academics, and which are put with great vehemence by conservatives in both Britain and America. The standard American thesis is that of the 'unraveling' (*sic*) of American society in the mid- and later sixties. This thesis posits a consensual society at ease with itself in the fifties and early sixties which, frankly, never existed; and it mistakenly perceives the laudable exposure of, and action against, racism, hypocrisy and inequality as the destruction of the fundamental bases of American society.[8] There was, indeed, appalling, and unnecessary, violence; and some of the actions of the militants were unsavoury and absurd. But, in the upshot, many manifest social evils were removed, as others were revealed, such as the abuses of power by Mayor Daley of Chicago, and Governor Ronald Reagan of California, and the police forces they imperfectly commanded. An American conservative academic, Alan Bloom, likened the aims and actions of the university protest movements of the sixties to those of the Nazis; British Conservative Prime Minister Margaret Thatcher declared that the movements of the sixties destroyed the Victorian virtues of self-discipline and restraint, and were the causes of the near-ruin from which she rescued Great Britain.[9] There are many things to criticise: the spread of drug-taking and the deification of the revelation it was alleged to induce; the early manifestations of what came to be known as 'political correctness'; misconceived housing and redevelopment plans. But the denunciations of conservatives, and the 'unraveling' thesis of liberal academics underestimate the positive long-term outcomes of sixties developments.

Finally, one can just perceive in the sixties the first adumbrations of multiculturalism. Crude manifestations of racism remain to this day in the United

States (and Britain), but it is not an exaggeration to say that in America the crucial moves from segregation to multiculturalism took place during the 1960s. In Britain, and several other European countries, by contrast, tensions between different racial communities only became major issues at the beginning of the sixties, while Italy only acquired a substantial black population in the early seventies (in some ways Italy's race problem was that of tension between self-satisfied Northerners and the immigrants among them who had come from Southern Italy). Anyway, it has to be admitted that racism was very evident in all of the European countries in the early seventies. None the less, some important figures had been putting forward the notion of a multicultural society – for instance, Roy Jenkins, Home Secretary for a time in the Harold Wilson Labour Government of 1966–70, and Giscard d'Estaing, President of France from 1974.[10] The greatest force making for multiculturalism everywhere was, in fact, rock music.

These sweeping and, most certainly, contestable generalisations arise from researches conducted in a very wide range of sources. It is a commonplace to historians that no single source, or 'text', can itself provide any very significant, or secure, knowledge. Historians habitually study large numbers of different sources, seeing how they support, qualify, or contradict each other, producing their conclusions from an evaluation of the whole range of sources, paying par-ticular attention to the 'unwitting testimony' all sources contain, in addition to the 'witting testimony'.[11] But, that said, one can recognise that there are certain cultural artefacts which, provided we take them within a context established by the study of other sources, do have considerable impact in, at the very least, raising questions in the minds of historians, if not in always providing answers to these. The texts discussed in the different chapters of this book fall broadly into that category: treated knowledgeably and circumspectly, their 'unwitting testimony' being carefully winnowed out, they can be said to open 'windows on the sixties'. That is the general orientation of historians, always asking of a text 'what does it tell us about the period in which it was created?'. But it is perfectly legitimate to be interested in the text itself; and then, historians would argue, they have the specialist function of providing the contextual knowledge essential if the text is to be fully understood in all of its ramifications. So the chapters in this book both ask the question, 'What does this text, or this series of texts, tell us about the sixties?' and the question 'What do the sixties tell us about this text?'

This Introduction is written in the manner of what I have elsewhere described as the non-metaphysical, source-based historian.[12] There are, obviously, other approaches to the study of the sixties. For myself, I have no problem with that, provided that the academic concerned does from the outset make his or her approaches and assumptions absolutely explicit. Thus, the first task imposed on the contributors to this volume is, where relevant, to make clear how their approach differs from that of the non-metaphysical historian. There then follow five basic questions which each contributor should be asking with regard to their particular text or series of texts: 'How did the text come into existence?'

('production'); 'What genre and tradition does it belong to, what are its stylistic and technical features?' ('genre, form, aesthetics'); 'How was it received?' ('consumption, status, reception'); 'What does knowledge of the sixties contribute to understanding and using the text?' ('context'); 'What does the text contribute to our knowledge and understanding of particular aspects of the sixties?' ('significance to the historian').

To provide a more substantial framework for the answering of that last complex question, I am now – elaborating greatly on the opening paragraphs of this Introduction – going to list the sixteen features which I take to be most characteristic of the sixties as a period of social and cultural transformation.

1. The formation of new subcultures and movements, generally critical of, or in opposition to, one or more aspects of established society, which expanded, overlapped and interacted, creating conditions of continuous cultural innovation and political ferment. These ranged from experimental theatres and architectural think-tanks to New Left, Civil Rights, anti-war, Child Poverty, Help the Homeless, environmental protection, and feminist and gay-rights groups.

2. Closely associated with the above, a great outburst of initiative, entrepreneuralism, individualism, doing your own thing. Sometimes these initiatives were supported by government or local subsidy (as with some experimental theatres), but in essence they were uninhibited examples of private enterprise, and in no way socialistic. Included here are clubs, boutiques, modelling and photographic agencies, bookshops, cafés, restaurants, art galleries, 'arts labs', pornographic and listings magazines, and design studios.

3. The rise to positions of unprecedented influence of young people, with youth subculture having a steadily greater impact on the rest of society, dictating taste in fashion, music and popular culture generally. It has to be noted that youth subculture was not monolithic: in respect to some developments one is talking of teenagers, with respect to others it may be a question of everyone under thirty or so. Such was the prestige of youth and the appeal of the youthful lifestyle that it became possible to be 'youthful' at much more advanced ages than would ever have been thought proper previously: that again was symbolic of the great power of the very notion of youth. Youth, particularly at the teenage end, created a vast market of its own in the artefacts of popular culture. But with respect to spending patterns and changing lifestyles attention must be given to young married couples, and particularly young wives, who, of course, not many years before had themselves belonged to youth, narrowly defined. We must constantly bear in mind that children quickly become teenagers, teenagers quickly become young adults, young adults quickly become married couples.

4. Important advances in technology, notably in relation to communications and entertainment: television, transistor radios, extended and long-play records, synthesisers, modernised telephone systems (beloved of teenagers), the remarkable expansion in jet travel, as well as the complete substitution of quickly-accelerating electric and diesel locomotives for steam ones. Also, though the effects were not widespread till the end of the decade, the development of the contraceptive pill.

5. The advent, as a consequence in particular of the almost universal presence of television, of 'spectacle' as an integral part of the interface between life and leisure. The most rebellious action, the most obscure theories, the wildest cultural extremism, the very 'underground' itself: all operated as publicly as possible, and all, thanks to the complex interaction with commercial interests and the media, attracted the maximum publicity. Thus one extreme gesture, one breaking of all existing taboos, simply accelerated into the next. Each spectacle had to be more extreme than the previous one.

6. Unprecedented international cultural exchange, in which – along with, for example, espresso machines from Italy, discos from France, and theatrical innovation from America – Britain, particularly with respect to pop music and fashion, film and television, played an unprecedently distinctive role.

7. Massive improvements in material life, so that large sections of society, hitherto excluded, joined the consumer society and acquired 'mod cons'; in many backward areas this involved the arrival, for the first time, of electricity, together with inside lavatories and properly equipped bathrooms. Those who railed, and rail, against the consumer society of the sixties forget how welcome it was to those who were only in the process of joining it.

8. Upheavals in race, class and family relationships. Given the importance of the civil rights movement in America, it may seem inappropriate to run these three categories together. Nonetheless, I believe it is right to see the challenge to established authorities and hierarchies in human relations as one single, though multi-faceted, process, subverting the authority of the white, the upper and middle class, the husband, the father, and the male generally. The working class did not reverse its position in the class hierarchy, and blacks were far from securing the removal of all discrimination. Yet, what happened over the sixties was that blacks and members of the working class became visible in their societies in a way in which they had never been before.

9. 'Permissiveness', that is to say a general sexual liberation, entailing striking changes in public and private morals and, what I am particularly keen to stress, a new frankness, openness and indeed honesty in personal relations and modes of expression.

10. New modes of self-presentation, involving emancipation from the old canons of fashion, and a rejoicing in the natural attributes of the human body. If some of the more fantastic forms of apparel did tend to become a kind of uniform for, say, 'beatniks' or 'hippies', nevertheless it remained true as never before that individuals could dress to please themselves, rather than to meet some convention as to what was suitable to a particular age, class or profession. There was for the first time (something which I also wish to particularly stress) the beginnings of a recognition of the realities of physical beauty (specifically, that only a small minority of both sexes are truly beautiful and that, therefore, this minority have a very high commercial value) as against the traditional polite fictions and evasions.

11. A participatory, innovatory, and uninhibited popular culture, whose central component was rock music, which in effect became a kind of universal language.

12. Original, striking (and sometimes absurd) developments in élite thought – associated with the structuralists and post-structuralists, such as Barthes, Foucault, Althusser and Eco, and also with Marcuse, Marshal McLuhan, R.D. Laing etc – and culture, as seen in pop art, conceptual art, concrete poetry and the privileging of 'chance' in literature, art and music. There was an obsession with language, conceived, along with knowledge, as an instrument of bourgeois oppression. Writers and artists became more 'reflexive', more self-conscious about the nature of their activities. There was a revival of the anti-art notions of Dada. Some commentators describe such trends as 'postmodernist'.

13. The continued existence, and indeed expansion, of a liberal, progressive presence within the institutions of authority the characteristic which I have defined as 'measured judgement'. Many of the exciting developments in the sixties, and much of its unique character, are due to the existence of a genuine liberal tolerance and willingness to accommodate to the new subcultures, permitting them to permeate and transform society.

14. Against that, we must place the continued existence of elements of extreme reaction, concentrated, in particular, in the various police forces, but also in certain religious bodies. While it is clear that some of the protesting movements, particularly in the later stages, deliberately set out to provoke violence, there can be no question that throughout the decade almost all instances of violence and rioting came into being because of the insensitive, or worse, behaviour of the police.

15. New concerns for civil and personal rights, and a new willingness to become involved in often risky action on behalf of these. In presenting this heading, I may seem either to be duplicating part of what is contained under heading 8, or to be crudely running together great human ventures which deserve individual treatment. But it is my belief that the major fact of the changing role and status of the black American relates both to the kind of changing circumstances which were producing modifications in class and family relationships, and to the conscious protest movements against not just segregation and discrimination, but the destruction of the environment, the consumer society and militaristic imperialism. Seeing all of these as parts of one multi-sided characteristic offers a key insight into the nature of what was happening in the sixties. Also involved are the American urban riots of 1965 and afterwards (though these are more spontaneous outbreaks against white, and particularly police, oppression, than components of co-ordinated protest movements), the events of 1968–9, the new feminism, and the beginnings of gay liberation. Some of these developments did lead on to violent confrontations, involving deaths and substantial destruction of property, but much of that, as I have already indicated, only came about because of the provocative actions of the police. The specific events of sixty-eight do not deserve the attention lavished on them at the time and over the following decade, nor do they deserve the oblivion into which they have now fallen (the flood of books on sixty-eight published in 1998 notwithstanding). The cardinal point is that they should not be studied in isolation from

the other developments of the sixties. They did not embody 'a revolution that failed'. They were a product of all the forces developing in the sixties, in their positive and their negative features, in their clarity and in their muddle.

16. The first intimations of the electric challenges implicit in the concept of the entire West as a collection of multicultural societies. Just when formal segregation between black and white was being dismantled in America, Britain and France acquired substantial racial minorities, a process which began in Italy in the early seventies. The greatest single vehicle of multiculturalism was rock/pop music. Of all my assertions this must be the most controversial, given that everywhere today there are frequent and ugly reminders of the persistence of racism.

In concluding this Introduction, I do not intend to follow the tedious custom of unloading a series of microscopic summaries of the specialist chapters which follow. In the Conclusion at the end of the book, however, I shall follow my own best practice in previous books of which I have been an editor[13] and endeavour to assess both what we have learned about the individual texts selected for study and what has been added to our knowledge about social and cultural change in the sixties.

NOTES TO INTRODUCTION

1   Eric Hobsbawm, *The Age of Extremes: The Short Twentieth Century 1914–1991* (London, 1994, Michael Joseph); Jean Fourastié, *Les Trente glorieuses ou la révolution invisible de 1946 à 1975* (Paris, 1976).

2   Arthur Marwick, *The Sixties: Cultural Revolution in Britain, France, Italy and the United States, c.1958–c.1974* (Oxford, 1998, Oxford University Press).

3   See the bibliography in ibid., and the notes to chapter 1. The editors have not compiled a new bibliography for *Windows on the Sixties*: in addition to the notes appended to individual chapters, readers are referred to the one in Arthur Marwick, *The Sixties*, op. cit. The mighty German-American collection, Carole Fink, Philipp Gassert and Detlef Junker (eds), *1968: The World Transformed* (Washington, DC and Cambridge, 1998, German Historical Institute and Cambridge University Press), contains many rich contributions, several of which stress the importance of the cultural revolution of the long sixties rather than the single year of 1968.

4   Herbert Marcuse, 'Repressive Tolerance' in Robert Paul Wolff, Barrington Moore Jr and Herbert Marcuse, *A Critique of Pure Tolerance* (New York and Boston, 1969, Beacon Press) pp 81–123

5   The funding of *One-Dimensional Man* is acknowledged in the Preface to that book. For Andy Warhol see David Bourdon, *Warhol* (New York, 1989, Abrams). For the Arts Lab see Jim Haynes, *Thanks for Coming! An Autobiography* (London, 1984, Faber).

6   Ibid.; George Melly, 'Afterward' in *Revolt into Style* (new edition, Oxford, 1989, Oxford University Press).

7   Marwick, *The Sixties*, op. cit., ch. 1 and notes.

8   Allan J. Matusow, *The Unraveling of America: A History of Liberalism in the 1960s* (New York, 1984, Harper & Row); W.L. O'Neill, *Coming Apart: An Informal History of America in the 1960s* (Chicago, 1971, Quadrangle Books); John M. Blum, *Years of Discord: American Politics and Society 1961–1974* (New York, 1991, W.W. Norton); David Burner, *Making Peace with the Sixties* (Princeton, NJ, 1996, Princeton University Press).

9   Allan Bloom, *The Closing of the American Mind: How Higher Education Has Failed Democracy and Impoverished the Souls of Today's Students* (New York, 1987, Simon & Schuster), pp 313–4, 322; Margaret Thatcher's statement, reported in the *Daily Mail*, 30 March 1982; Brian Masters, *The Swinging Sixties* (London, 1985, Constable), p 14.

10   Gary P. Freeman, *Immigrant Labour and Racial Conflict in Industrial Societies: The French and British Experience 1945–1975* (Princeton, NJ, 1974, Princeton University Press), pp 57, 98.

11   For 'witting and unwitting testimony' see Arthur Marwick, *The Nature of History* (London, 1989, Macmillan), pp 216ff.

12   Arthur Marwick, 'Two Approaches to Historical Study: The Metaphysical (including Postmodernism) and the Historical', *Journal of Contemporary History*, vol. 30, no. 1, January 1995, pp 5–34.

13   See Arthur Marwick (ed.), *Total War and Social Change* (London, 1988, Macmillan) and *The Arts, Literature and Society* (London, 1989, Routledge).

1 A Walk on the Wilder Side

The Apartment as Social Commentary

Daniel J. Leab

The Apartment, which premiered in mid-1960, is a transitional film. This over-two-hour-long movie – in its attitudes, content, decor and style – looks, Janus-like, both back to the recent past preceding its production and forward to the immediate future. *The Apartment*'s approach to the complexity of American society at various levels certainly underscores Arthur Marwick's view that the end of the 1950s (when the film's creators first envisaged *The Apartment*) was a 'point of change', especially with regard to the culture.

More so than most 1960 media artefacts this film incorporates concepts, ideas and views of the controlled, regulated, somewhat conservative, staid 1950s American way of life and previews some of the counter-culture response which would permeate much of the 1960s USA, resulting, for example, in dramatic changes in morality and approaches to sex. In any event, however one analyses *The Apartment* – and much of the film to this day remains poignantly moving as well as splendidly funny – it presents, for all of its varied entertainment values, a mordant view of what then served as 'the American dream'.[1] In the final analysis *The Apartment* presents a less than endearing view of contemporary US life, during what has been dubbed its 'golden age'.

As the presidency of Dwight Eisenhower began to draw to a close in 1960, so too did the golden days of what proved to be a very short-lived 'American century'. As one journalist has perceptively pointed out, 'America had been very lucky... and the luck ran out'. *The Apartment* dwells on that change for people who had seemingly benefited from the American century. The movie never con-descends to its leading characters, but ultimately it does not offer them much in terms of a positive future.[2]

The guiding creative genius behind the film was Billy Wilder, aptly charac-terised as 'one of Hollywood's most accomplished and consistently iconoclastic filmmakers'. Movie production admittedly is a collaborative effort, and in addition to Wilder various other talents, such as art director Alexander Trauner, played significant roles in making *The Apartment* an award-winning film. A variety of restrictions, such as the industry's self-censorship Production Code, obviously also influenced the end result. But Wilder, then approaching the zenith of his Hollywood career, certainly put his particular stamp on *The Apartment*.[3]

Billy Wilder was born Samuel Wilder in 1906 in Suchaz, a small town in Austria-Hungary (now a part of Poland). He enjoyed some success as a journalist in Vienna before moving to Berlin in 1926. There he prospered as a crime reporter before becoming a journeyman screen-writer fashioning zesty comedies and light romances. After the Nazi takeover in early 1933, Wilder, who was Jewish, fled Germany (those of his family who did not leave, including his mother, died in concentration camps, victims of the Holocaust). After a short stay in France, he made his way via Mexico permanently to Hollywood.

He found work as a screen-writer and soon teamed up with Charles Brackett, a more experienced writer and a man of some substance in his own right (Harvard Law School graduate, well-received novelist, and before leaving for Hollywood in the early 1930s, the *New Yorker*'s respected drama critic). Seven Brackett-Wilder scripts were filmed between 1938 and 1942, when Wilder started directing. They included such hits as the Garbo comedy vehicle *Ninotchka* (1939). Wilder then directed the scripts he wrote with Brackett, with the latter generally serving as producer. These films included the Academy-Award-winning *The Lost Weekend* (1945) and the Oscar-nominated *Sunset Boulevard* (1950).

Wilder was not an easy man to work with. He later recalled that 'Brackett was an excellent collaborator', but according to one report Brackett and Wilder 'were known for their screaming matches as well as for their scripts'. The mystery writer Raymond Chandler, who collaborated with Wilder on the script for *Double Indemnity* (an enduring 1944 movie, properly described as 'one of the best and most popular examples of film noir') also had his problems: so much so that he later complained that 'working with Billy Wilder... was an agonising experience and... probably shortened my life'.[4]

Wilder, to Brackett's unhappiness, broke with his talented but somewhat stuffy collaborator after *Sunset Boulevard*. Brackett subsequently expressed some bitterness about the break, and seemingly 'never forgave Wilder' (in the judgment of one biographer).[5] Over the next seven years, Wilder – who seems to have needed collaborators on the screenplays he directed – worked one time only with various talented professionals. These included George Axelrod (*The Seven Year Itch*, 1955), Harry Kurnitz (*Witness for the Prosecution*, 1957), Ernest

Lehman (*Sabrina*, 1954), Wendell Mayes (*The Spirit of St Louis*, 1957) and Lesser Samuels (*Ace in the Hole*, 1951).

The resulting films, while always interesting, had a variegated track record. An attack on the sensationalistic US media failed artistically and commercially; a Marilyn Monroe comedy vehicle dealing with the possibilities of marital infidelity did well at the box office; a fiftieth-anniversary recreation of Charles Lindbergh's pioneering solo 1927 flight across the Atlantic bombed; a screen version of a Broadway hit about World War II American POWs in a German camp won Wilder an Oscar nomination, achieved critical raves, and made a lot of money.

Whatever the subject of a Wilder film – murder, marital infidelity, greed, war, love, or what-have-you – critics invariably espied vulgarity, cynicism, misogyny, contempt, misanthropy and other negative forces. Even the critics who applauded Wilder's films touched on what was dubbed 'the Wilder side of life', on what the noted film critic James Agee called the movie maker's 'rotten taste'. As proved to be the case with *The Apartment*, Wilder, more than most of his contemporaries, continually pushed at the borders of convention while reportedly serving (in one commentator's words) as 'a scathing observer'.[6]

In the late 1950s Wilder began collaborating on screenplays with I.A.L. Diamond. The film-maker found the Jewish Diamond, who stemmed from a similar background, a congenial collaborator. Born Itek Dommnici in a small Rumanian mountain town, and over a decade younger than Wilder, Diamond had come to the US in 1929. While attending school in New York City he became Isidore Diamond. He was graduated from Columbia University in 1941 intent on a writing career; he had been an editor of Columbia's humour magazine, and of the *Columbia Daily Spectator*. Diamond became something of a legend as 'the only man to write four consecutive Varsity Shows' (the college's annual musical comedy revue) and to do it 'solo'. Typical of his efforts for these shows was a pitch for 'Plucky Tripe Cigarettes' and the lyrics, 'Pitching Woo in an Igloo'.[7]

After graduation, Diamond went to Hollywood and became a journeyman screen-writer as I.A.L. Diamond. An erstwhile mathematics whiz, Diamond claimed that the initials stood for 'Interscholastic Algebra League', of which in 1936 and 1937 he had been 'a tristate champion'. In the years before joining up with Wilder he worked at various studios. His credits included an early Doris Day film (*Romance on the High Seas* in 1948) and the adaptation of a successful Broadway comedy for Bob Hope (*That Certain Feeling*, 1956).[8]

Wilder and Diamond complemented each other very well, working together on 12 films over a quarter of a century. During those years Diamond undertook some assignments independently of Wilder, such as the 1969 screen version of the Broadway comedy hit *The Cactus Flower*, but only once early on in their collaboration did Wilder work with a writer other than Diamond. Years after Diamond's death in 1988, Wilder said that he 'still missed him terribly'.[9]

Initially, as with *The Apartment*, Wilder and Diamond did well with their joint efforts, especially at the box office. Two of their most lucrative efforts came out just before and not long after *The Apartment* premiered in 1960. A year earlier, a drag comedy, *Some Like It Hot*, was released. One of Marilyn Monroe's best movies, and considered by some 'probably Wilder's best loved film', it dealt with two musicians who after witnessing a 1920s Chicago gangland execution find refuge posing as women with an all-girl band on its way to Miami. In 1963 came the Wilder/Diamond non-musical version of the Broadway musical *Irma La Douce*, about the redemption of a Paris prostitute through the strenuous but comic efforts of a good man who loves her. It became Wilder's greatest commercial success, apparently in terms of box office 'far surpassing anything else he ever made'.[10]

The duo fared less well in the later 1960s and the 1970s. Their efforts produced a series of clinkers such as *Kiss Me, Stupid* (1964), *The Fortune Cookie* (1966), *The Private Life of Sherlock Holmes* (1970), *Feodora* (1978), and their last film, *Buddy, Buddy* (1981). Some of these films had their defenders (one described the baleful *Feodora* as 'one of the most beautiful of modern films') but these movies could not find an audience. A kind of unredeemed tastelessness marred these films, but that was not their greatest drawback. As one analysis put it, these films demonstrated 'a marked preference for the values of the past' that did not appeal to audiences. These films might deal with sex, but not explicit sex. As in *Kiss Me, Stupid*, the sex lies in double and triple *entendres*; the smut lies in vulgar words, not in the soft-core images found in other movies of the time. Wilder preferred 'the word': such a style did not really appeal in the day of the sexual revolution to the increasingly younger movie audience for whom a dirty picture was paramount.[11]

Wilder later recalled that for him and Diamond 'the inspiration' for *The Apartment* came from the 1945 British movie *Brief Encounter*. This well-received David Lean tearjerker dealt with an unconsummated, tender love affair between a suburban housewife and a local doctor. Wilder considered it to be one of Lean's best films; it won many awards, including first prize at the initial postwar Cannes Film Festival. What particularly struck Wilder was when the doctor at one point borrows a friend's flat so that he and the woman can meet there, a tryst that fails.[12]

The Apartment was released just at the cusp of the changes American society would undergo. This movie could still raise moral questions effectively in that environment, and it could with relative ease be sold as risqué (*vide* the suggestive trailer with its wry comments on infidelity). Yet it could still deal with more traditional values, with what Wilder described later as 'the American sickness' of 'getting ahead' at all costs. *The Apartment*, for all its moral complexity, has a relatively simple plot about 'boy' and 'girl' who meet, part, and finally sort of get together. The plot centres on C.C. Baxter, who has come to New York City from Cincinnati to make his way in the world. Well described by *Variety* as 'a phony Horatio Alger', Baxter is an ambitious, lonely clerk toiling away on the nineteenth floor of the building that houses the thousands of people employed by the insurance company Consolidated Life of New York.[13]

Baxter lives almost anonymously in a small one-bedroom apartment in a brownstone on West 67th Street, 'just half a block from Central Park', and he makes this apartment available to four somewhat minor, philandering Consolidated executives for their amorous trysts. His neighbours, especially Dr Dreyfuss next door, consider Baxter an 'iron man' because of the sexual activity constantly and loudly taking place in the apartment. In reality Baxter leads an isolated life, eating TV dinners and watching old films on television. In the movie's words, Baxter lives 'like Robinson Crusoe – shipwrecked among eight million people'. And four of them have him at their beck and call. They are demanding as well as inconsiderate, so much so that Baxter periodically quite literally is left out in the cold.[14]

The four executives do recommend Baxter for promotion, but J.D. Sheldrake, the Director of Personnel, discovers that the four glowing recommendations have something to do with the apartment. Much to Baxter's surprise, Sheldrake, who 'rates a four-window office', also wants to make use of Baxter's apartment, telling him that 'next month there's going to be a shift in personnel around here – and as far as I am concerned, you're executive material'. Sheldrake wishes to use the apartment, unbeknownst to Baxter, to resume an affair with an elevator operator, Fran Kubelik. Baxter, unbeknownst to Sheldrake, has a crush on Kubelik.[15]

Some weeks pass, and by the beginning of December Baxter has received his promotion and has moved from the sea of desks to a cubicle-like little office similar to, but somewhat smaller than, that of the philandering four. Sheldrake monopolises the apartment, carrying on his affair with Kubelik, who is truly in love with him. During the office Christmas party, Baxter accidentally discovers

Miss Kubelik (Shirley Maclaine) applauds Mr Dobisch (Ray Walston)
and friends during the company Christmas party

that she is the girl whom Sheldrake brings to the apartment; she in turn learns from a former Sheldrake paramour – his secretary, Miss Olsen – that the lecherous executive has had 'a little ring-a-ding-ding' with various women employed by the insurance company, promising them all, as he has Kubelik (and earlier Miss Olsen) that in due course he will divorce his wife. Wilder later recalled that until he and Diamond thought up Miss Olsen, who serves as a kind of *deus ex machina* who periodically advances the plot, 'we were stuck'.[16]

On Christmas Eve, a dejected Baxter drinks at a neighborhood bar while Sheldrake uses the apartment. Baxter picks up the blonde, attractive, articulate wife of a jockey who has been imprisoned in Castro's Cuba for doping a race horse. Taking her back to what he assumes is an empty apartment, Baxter finds in his bed a comatose Kubelik, 'near death from an overdose of sleeping pills', as one review put it. Kubelik is a woman who, ever since her teenage days in Pittsburgh, had 'been jinxed' with men 'from the word go', to use her words. She had confronted Sheldrake with Miss Olsen's comments about his past affairs. He did not deny their truth, but treated the situation with equanimity. Worse, in return for the LP record that Kubelik had purchased for him specially as a Christmas gift, he peeled off a $100 bill from a roll of bills and told her to 'go out and buy yourself something special'.[17]

Baxter, on discovering the near-dead Kubelik, quickly and unceremoniously gets rid of his unaware pickup. He prevails on Dr Dreyfuss to treat Kubelik and subsequently convinces him not to report the suicide attempt. The next day, after her situation has stabilised, Baxter calls Sheldrake at his Westchester home (where the executive is shown with his two young sons as they play with their Christmas gifts). Baxter informs Sheldrake about what has happened and that 'there'll be no trouble, police-wise or newspaper-wise'. Later, at the insistence of Baxter, who wants to buoy Kubelik's spirits, Sheldrake in a subsequent phone conversation reassures her and wishes her well.[18]

While Baxter plays nursemaid to Kubelik, his crush turns to love. They have a good time together. The day after Christmas her concerned brother-in-law, Karl Matuschka, inquires at Consolidated about his missing in-law, who normally lives with him and his wife, her sister. One of the philandering executives directs Matuschka to the apartment. There he misreads the situation on seeing the partially dressed Kubelik. Dr Dreyfuss stops by just then to inquire about her condition. The already irate Matuschka becomes very angry when he learns about the suicide attempt. Baxter accepts responsibility for causing it, and the brother-in-law decks him. She leaves with Matuschka.

A love-stricken Baxter decides to inform Sheldrake that he 'will take Miss Kubelik off his hands'. Too late! An angry Sheldrake had fired Miss Olsen for spilling the beans to Kubelik; the secretary in turn contacted Mrs Sheldrake; the wife, as an annoyed Sheldrake tells Baxter, 'fired me'. Sheldrake has determined for the moment to continue his affair with Kubelik, and he rewards Baxter for the use of the apartment and for hushing up any possible scandal. Baxter is promoted to Assistant Director of Personnel and is moved next door to Sheldrake on the twenty-seventh floor into what the screenplay calls 'a three-window office'. The perks, as Sheldrake points out, include 'lunch in the executive dining room', 'a nice little expense account' and 'use of the executive washroom'. Thus Baxter has leapfrogged the philandering four.[19]

On New Year's Eve Sheldrake – who, having been thrown out by his wife, lives at a club that is 'strictly stag' – asks Baxter for the use of the apartment for an assignation with Kubelik. Because of the holiday Sheldrake has been unable to book a hotel room. Baxter adamantly refuses the request ('Especially not Miss Kubelik'), knowing it means his job. He had already decided to vacate the apartment. Just at midnight as Sheldrake and Kubelik celebrate along with other revelers, Sheldrake apologises for the fact that Baxter would not let them use the apartment: 'that little punk... said I couldn't bring anybody to his apartment, especially not Miss Kubelik'. She learns that Baxter has lost his job. Kubelik, despite her suicide attempt and affection for Baxter, has remained committed to Sheldrake (earlier she had said to Baxter 'why can't I ever fall in love with somebody nice?'). Now, on the spur of the moment, she leaves Sheldrake and races to the apartment, where she joins a stunned but very happy Baxter, who amidst his partially-packed possessions declares his love for her.[20]

The movie on release in mid-1960 did engender some enthusiastic responses. *Time*'s reviewer found the movie 'a peerless comedy'; Bosley Crowther, the *New York Times*'s influential and socially-concerned film critic, maintained that *The*

Dr Dreyfuss (Jack Kruschen) and C.C. Baxter (Jack Lemmon) walk Miss Kubelik around the apartment to keep her awake after she has taken an overdose of sleeping pills

Apartment successfully negotiated 'a line of extremely sophisticated balancing between cynicism and sentiment, between envy and pity'. Overall, most of the daily press reviewers, even if not overwhelmingly favourable, generally responded positively to the movie.[21]

But most of what can be described as 'establishment critics' reacted very negatively. John McCartin, the *New Yorker*'s reviewer, dismissed the film in 55 words as 'an acrid story… that involves… many shades of craven ethics'. Dwight Macdonald, then in his heyday as a commentator on US culture, expressed 'disgust' at the movie, and suggested that Diamond change his name to 'Zircon'. The *New Republic*'s Stanley Kaufman criticised the story line for being 'based on a tasteless gimmick'. The feisty Pauline Kael, then just at the beginning of her career as a reviewer, dismissed *The Apartment* as 'machine-tooled… social consciousness'. The *Saturday Review* critic, Hollis Alpert, who was usually quite easygoing, damned the film as 'a dirty fairy tale…' which argued 'the quickest way up the executive ladder is pimping'.[22]

Such comments notwithstanding, the film achieved commercial success. *The Apartment* cost about $2.9 million to make and to promote, and within two years of its premiere had grossed over $6 million domestically and nearly $3 million abroad. The film also garnered numerous awards, including Oscars for Best Picture, Best Director, Best Original Screenplay, Best Art Direction, and Best Editing. It also won Oscar nominations for two of its stars (Jack Lemmon, who played Baxter, and Shirley Maclaine, who played Kubelik), for its Director of Photography (Joseph La Shelle), and for one of the supporting players (Jack Kruschen, who portrayed Dr Dreyfuss). Among other awards, the New York Film Critics voted *The Apartment* Best Picture, Best Director and Best Screenplay prizes. And the British Film Academy judged it the Best Film From Any Source for 1960 and named Lemmon the Best Foreign Actor.

In reviewing the *melange* that makes up the plot of *The Apartment* it is clear that the storyline and characters allow for several readings, except possibly for Dr Dreyfuss. As has been pointed out by various commentators over the years, Dr Dreyfuss serves as an 'archetypal' sage 'who acts as a moral influence'. His moral homilies include urging Baxter at one point to 'Be a mensch'. And just in case the meaning of this Yiddishism is unclear, Dreyfuss explains to Baxter that the word stands for 'human being'. In terms of analysing the film in its context of as a transitional document the doctor remains a fascinating figure.[23]

Within a few years of the film's release Federal legislation, such as that establishing Medicare, would lead to massive changes in the practice of American medicine. Independent general practitioners such as Dr Dreyfuss would virtually disappear. Stricken people, instead of calling a neighborhood MD, would go to hospital emergency rooms. Moreover, the rapid increase in the use of drugs on all levels of American society, as well as the continued breakdown of that society's norms, meant that doctors would not, as did Dr Dreyfuss, travel the streets with their traditional black bags. The medical bag came to attract the unwanted attention of those who would mug the physician for the bag's contents, however meager. Dr Dreyfuss, the concerned, middle-class, general practitioner, has not totally disappeared, but for viewers of *The Apartment* since a few years after its premiere he has become as much an anachronism as the village blacksmith.

The doctor also pointed to other forthcoming significant social changes in the USA, especially regarding the place of Jews in American life. Antisemitism had been part of the fabric of American society for generations. To use one writer's apt words, 'anti-Semitism... a widespread and to an extent even respectable attitude... was a pervasive and seemingly indisputable fact of American life... Its prominence was indisputable'.[24] Prior to the industry's adoption in 1934 of self-censorship with the implementation of the Production Code, Jews did appear in all genres, usually as secondary characters, often as less than satisfying caricatures.

Thanks to the Code, as well as to the fears and sensitivities aroused among the predominately Jewish production executives by the brutal antisemitism practiced by the Nazis in Germany and elsewhere, Jewish characters received little play on-screen in Hollywood between the mid-1930s and the beginning of the 1960s. Jewish characters almost disappeared from American movies, just as they did from the more visible parts of the industry (thus the actor Jules Garfinkle on joining Warners in 1938 became John Garfield). Jewish characters did appear occasionally, especially during World War II, when Hollywood presented ethnic diversification in its war movies. Jews could also be found in the few movies that made up 1947's limited anti-antisemitism cycle of films, such as the screen version of Laura Z. Hobson's controversial novel, *Gentlemen's Agreement*, in movies so to speak torn from the headlines such as *Sword in the Desert* (1949), dealing with the fight to establish Israel, and in some oddball films such as *The Jolson Story* (a 1946 bio-pic about a star entertainer who was the son of a cantor, it sympathetically but briefly portrayed the Jewish home of the parents).

Suddenly in the 1960s the situation changed with a vengeance. As one Jewish writer somewhat incredulously reported in 1961, 'Jewish characters, Jewish themes, Jewish environments with a sauce of Yiddish, are in style'. On Madison Avenue, the advertising arbiter of American taste, the watchword became 'Dress British, Think Yiddish'. As a famous sales pitch put it, 'You Don't Have To Be Jewish To Love Levy's Jewish Rye'. Over time this philo-semitism would decline, and antisemitism did not fade entirely from American life, but Dr Dreyfuss and his wife (who offers Kubelik 'a little noodle soup with chicken – white meat – and a glass of tea') admittedly are stereotypes. However, *The Apartment* presents them favourably, and the response of a non-Jewish America was good, as such stereotypes became a positive fodder for numerous films.[25]

The Apartment does elicit a very different kind of response in terms of its treatment of Kubelik and the Consolidated Life women employees at the mercy of the company's philandering executives. Especially for such women (working-class even if they held white-collar jobs) the introduction of 'the pill' – announced with little fanfare in May 1960 just weeks before the film's release – made an obvious and important difference. As one history succinctly put it, 'the first oral contraceptive for women... promised at once to save them from unwanted pregnancy and to make them as free about sex as men always had been'. Yet class still shackled them in various ways. For Kubelik and her peers the brouhaha aroused a few years later as a result of *The Feminine Mystique* meant relatively little because it spoke 'primarily to educated suburban women'.[26]

Yet the general attitude towards a Kubelik and her way of life changed remarkably quickly after 1960. Two astute social commentators just a few years later in 1964 pinpointed and summed up these changes in describing the differences between what they called the 'old sentimentality' and the 'new sentimentality': thus adultery was an 'old phrase', while 'affairs... don't destroy the union' of marriage. In taking account of such diverging attitudes for the readers of *Esquire* magazine (which billed itself as a guide to 'the character of America's collective confusion' in the 1960s), these two commentators declared that far-reaching changes had taken place: 'to be a "swinger" is to pat yourself on the back and be glad you're weak... we respect girls who sleep around a little... virgins scare...'[27]

Certainly movies now treated females and sex much more graphically, with little left to the imagination: silicone-enhanced breasts jiggle nakedly all over the place; male and female frontal nudity are less than rare; yesterday's grainy black-and-white porno flick pales besides today's well-made colour movie dealing with all kinds of sex, which in due course cable TV brings into the home. What seems to have outraged *The Apartment*'s vigorous nay-sayers at the time of its release was not any display of flesh or other sexual activity, but the film's less than critical approach to casual sex. The movie flaunted its attitudes and allowed no misunderstanding about the purposes for which various characters utilised Baxter's apartment. Yet already in the 1970s a Wilder biographer understandably declared that 'it seems hard to believe... that anybody... could have been shocked by *The Apartment*'. And in 1994 an unrepentant Wilder remarked that what in 1960 had been called a 'dirty... story... compared to now... was about altar boys'.[28]

Interestingly enough, *The Apartment* did not have much difficulty with the Production Code Administration. For over 20 years after the adoption of the Code in 1934 this body had held a tight rein over the industry. A number of Wilder films had fallen foul of the industry's self-censorship body. But because the industry came to face increasingly successful competition for the American entertainment dollar by the 1950s, censorship relaxed as 'the movie trade' followed 'a natural impulse' and increasingly reverted to 'shock and titillation'. The Code lingered on into the later 1960s, but already by the later 1950s a film that earlier might not have received the 'seal of approval' necessary for widespread distribution did get one. Even the Legion of Decency – the once-potent Catholic organisation dedicated to maintaining movie morality – had found it necessary to make compromises. In 1957 it eased its classifications, adding the rating A3, 'morally acceptable for adults'. The Legion found *The Apartment* 'troubling'; the film 'offended' the group's reviewers. But recognising the temper of the times, the Legion granted *The Apartment* an A3 rating rather than a more censorious one.[29]

Whatever the developments in reel life, a working-class woman such as Kubelik in real life continued to have to battle for survival economically. And she continued on the job to face problems caused by her sex and her vulnerability. A person like her always has faced exploitation and temptation (whether in an 1890s sweatshop or a computer-dominated office a century later). How 'good' a girl such as Kubelik can be depends on many factors, not least the economics of her life and the consequent possibilities of seduction. The relationships that *The Apartment* depicted continue to this day. And so does sexual harassment, despite a plethora of legislation and numerous court decisions. Miss Olsen, if she could afford it or if she could interest a concerned private or government agency, might now have some recourse against her summary dismissal by Sheldrake. But it seems to me that Kubelik would remain a victim. She would not obtain the education, either academically or otherwise, to escape what for women like her has been described accurately as 'the reality of their subordinate status with men... and in jobs'.[30]

The Apartment, in dealing with its milieu, drew on various precedents, most notably and very effectively in its opening sequences. These chillingly portray the corporate anonymity which initially marked Baxter's working life. He labours at his desk alongside dozens of similarly employed paper-pushers amidst a sea of desks, a sight which has been well-described as 'a Kafkaesque structure of... impersonality, a labyrinth... which stretches to infinity'.[31] Various writers over the years have commented on the similarity of these scenes to ones in the very powerful, moving 1928 silent film *The Crowd*, which also dealt very insightfully with the lives and aspirations of white-collar urban workers.

Directed and co-scripted by the durable, eminent, talented King Vidor, *The Crowd*'s plot differs significantly from that of *The Apartment* in dealing at length with the trials and tribulations of the main character after marriage. But Vidor's film, like Wilder's effort, deals with (in his words) 'a sort of nondescript – but not negative – individual, the sort of fellow you could like...' Both *The Crowd*'s protagonist and Baxter come to New York City from elsewhere in America to seek their fortune. Vidor's character, while approaching Manhattan on a ferry, hears 'you've got to be good in that town if you want to beat the crowd'. He does not, and soon becomes what has been aptly described as 'one of the number of faceless employees engulfed by the big office buildings which spot the city like massive beehives'.[32]

Wilder at the time of *The Apartment*'s release 'acknowledged' his debt to *The Crowd*. Years after *The Apartment*'s filming Vidor recalled that Wilder had asked him 'how many desks he had had' in *The Crowd*'s office scenes. It is worth noting that Alexander Trauner, who won an Oscar for his art direction on *The Apartment*, used 'forced perspective' to achieve the design of the Consolidated Life office. He used increasingly shorter extras to sit at the desks which were further away from the cameras: Wilder said the extras farthest away were dwarves, Trauner said they were children. Wilder, who used Trauner on various films, maintained that the art director was 'the best'. Without any doubt the success of the film owes a great deal to Trauner, who managed to make Baxter's apartment believable, to make it look lived-in.[33]

Although admittedly Vidor's film inspired some scenes, Wilder (and Diamond) unmistakably added their own voices. A dry, fascinating narration accompanies the series of images which begin after the titles. The script originally called for the film to begin with 'a man's hand… punching out a series of figures on the keyboard' of a desk calculator. However, the finished film begins with aerial views of New York City followed by such shots as a busy street, an office building and rows of desks, before zeroing in on Baxter at his desk working a giant calculator. A most telling first-person narration places Baxter in context as one among many:

> On November 1st 1959, the population of New York City was 8,024,753. If you laid all these people end to end, figuring an average height of five feet six-and-a-half inches, they would reach from Times Square to the outskirts of Karachi, Pakistan. I know facts like these because I work for an insurance company – Consolidated Life of New York. We are one of the top five companies in the country. Our home office has 31,259 employees, which is more than the entire population of Natchez, Mississippi. I work on the nineteenth floor – Ordinary Policy Department – Premium Accounting division – Section W – desk number 861. My name is C.C. Baxter.[34]

The concept of people as automata – an intrinsic part of Baxter's narration – had been widely bruited about during the 1950s by what historian Paul Johnson has dubbed 'pop sociologists'. Writers and academics such as C. Wright Mills, David Riesman (and his associate Nathan Glazer) and William Whyte expressed serious concern about what they perceived as a dangerous and growing conformity in the United States. For them, the accompanying loss of individuality especially boded ill for the continuation of 'the American dream'. An increasing number of Americans lost the initiative to achieve and settled into passivity. Bestselling novelists such as John Cheever and Sloan Wilson echoed such sentiments in their popular, critically well-received works. Much of what was written concentrated on the burgeoning suburbs, which one book called 'a split-level trap'. But all these commentators also meant their *obiter dicta* to apply to American society in general. The 1960s proved them wrong, and certainly *The Apartment* did not wholly follow their line.[35]

The film's dénouement, with Baxter and Kubelik turning their backs on the goodies available to them, looked to the forthcoming upheaval which marked much of the 1960s. But *The Apartment* did incorporate many of the fears of the 1950s critics. Whyte's *The Organization Man* in effect argued that 'bureaucratic corporations' (presumably companies like Consolidated Life) created 'a dehumanised collective'. Riesman and Glazer maintained that 'the American character' was changing, that Americans had lost their individualistic bent and had become 'other-directed', allowing the opinions and behaviour of their peers to control their actions (certainly a trap that Baxter had fallen into). C. Wright

Mills maintained that Americans lived and worked in 'a benumbing society' from which they needed to escape (an argument not far different from that set forth by Dr Dreyfuss to Baxter, which initially falls on deaf ears). Novelists like Wilson (the title of whose bestseller, *The Man in the Gray Flannel Suit*, became a watchword at the time) and popular fiction in general 'stressed business success, conformity, individual acquisition', according to one critic, a view that has found many echoes. *The Apartment* ultimately did not conform – and its rebellion, albeit a mild one, against then-standard values partakes of the much more vigorous counter-culture which became the norm not too long after the film premiered.[36]

One can read *The Apartment* in various ways: consider its approach to corporate culture or to the treatment of women. If, however, the movie does seem bifurcated in much of its approach to American society, it does not waffle in its view of Consolidated Life's managers. The movie presents them as a rum lot, with nothing likeable or redeeming about them. They are smarmy, abrasive, insensitive, self-centred, immoral. The movie-makers' creation and development of such managerial types goes against the mainstream cultural view at the end of the 1950s. Businessmen did come under attack for their failings, but overall 'the system', whatever the admitted and recognised shortcomings, generally escaped condemnation.

A generation earlier, manifestly in part because of the Great Depression's stultifying impact, many Americans echoed Marxist critiques of business which emphasised its 'drive for monopoly profits', the 'increasing gap between the extremes of wealth and poverty', the 'decaying economic structures', the 'sharpening of class conflict'. These concepts would again come into widespread usage during the 1960s, but in the 1950s commentators on the American scene usually dealt sympathetically with the travails of business: 'the "image" was changing'; the 'Depression-born animus... was disappearing...'[37]

Nothing illustrates this change towards more positive attitudes better than the bestsellers of the day, which when dealing with American businessmen in the main argued that 'their individual efforts redounded to the benefit of their society and, by implication at least to the good of mankind as a whole". Sloan Wilson's *The Man in the Gray Flannel Suit* did contain some serious criticisms of American business life, but at one point a media tycoon passionately and convincingly insists that if he did not do what had to be done, those who depended on his direction of the company would suffer. In the very popular *Marjorie Morningstar* (1955) the eponymous heroine, after a stab at the bohemian life, settles down contentedly with a businessman. Cameron Hawley, whose very popular fiction now has fallen into limbo, wrote eminently readable novels which were sympathetic to American corporate life, while portraying it warts and all. His best-known novels, *Executive Suite* (1952) and *Cash McCall* (1954), included corporate abuses, sharp business practices and infidelity among other drawbacks, but portrayed moral businessmen (who did not cut corners) beating down the corporate sharks.[38]

The makers of *The Apartment* would have none of it. And because they would not, one must also question the ending of the film. Beneath the veneer of comedy – and there are some very funny scenes – its view of American life and the human condition is bleak. To consider the ending satisfactory is acceptable, but to judge it happy is daft. Kubelik and Baxter have each other, but not much more. They are jobless; soon they will be homeless. They obviously come from different ethnic and socioeconomic backgrounds. Can love overcome all obstacles? The movie's trenchant comments on American society would suggest (however pleasing the fadeout) that their relationship may not last, and even if it does may not be a very happy one. At the time of the film's release one reviewer said 'as for the young man… and his falling in love with an elevator girl who's had an affair with his boss in his own apartment, well, young American males of today may be that stupid, but I doubt it…' *Harrison's Reports*, which previewed films for theatre owners, judged *The Apartment* to be 'a top box office romantic comedy', but in discussing Kubelik and Baxter concluded somewhat dubiously that 'the two will apparently be together…'[39]

The film's general ambiguity, its moral confusion, are to a considerable extent a result of the superb acting of its cast, especially the leads. Jack Lemmon shines as Baxter. An attractive, multitalented, intelligent, thoughtful star, he made his movie debut in 1953. After *The Apartment* he would make a number of films over the next two decades with Wilder, who later declared himself 'a slave to Lemmon's talent'. Shirley Maclaine's impish quality gave Kubelik a necessary

Cartoonist Al Hirschfeld shows Jack Lemmon preparing a bachelor dinner for Shirley MacLaine in his apartment. A tennis racquet is used as a drain for spaghetti. It's all in Billy Wilder's "The Apartment," which will open .... at the ....
Theatre through United Artists release.

Publicity material for *The Apartment*

warmth; she expertly and engagingly played a complex role. A gifted actress, characterised as 'a pixie with moxie', she had made her first film in 1955 and had quickly become a star. She would work once more with Wilder (*Irma La Douce*) and respected his talents ('he is brilliant at every level'), but considered him 'a male chauvinist pig' – in part because of the female characters in *The Apartment*.[40]

Sheldrake originally was to have been played by Paul Douglas, a burly man and a first-rate actor, but he died of a heart attack two weeks before shooting was scheduled to begin. Fred MacMurray, who played Sheldrake, had a career stretching back to the mid-1930s; he usually played light comedy leads and did not feel comfortable departing from such roles. MacMurray had played very successfully against type in the Wilder-directed film noir classic *Double Indemnity* as a murderous, conniving insurance man. But it took two days of 'intense negotiations' for Wilder to convince MacMurray to again play a 'counterfeit nice guy'. He played Sheldrake extremely well, and Wilder subsequently called him 'our salvation'.[41]

Wilder completed his last film in 1981. Age had not seriously reduced his energy or capacity. But he had lost touch with the movie-going audience. Given the box-office track-record of his films over the preceding 15 years, Wilder simply could not find financial backing. Nor did age temper Wilder's well-known ascerbic wit. He remained as acid-tongued as ever – one biographer called Wilder 'an aging... surly cherub'. Wilder – who after the completion of *Some Like It Hot* publicly declared, 'I'm the only director who ever made two pictures with Marilyn Monroe. It behooves the Screen Directors Guild to award me a Purple Heart' – did not mellow.[42]

Wilder remained the same man who utilised his apparent desire for revenge on Monroe in writing a scene in *The Apartment* which underscored Baxter's unhappy situation. One of the philandering executives picks up a dumb blonde who looks like Monroe, speaks like Monroe, and moves like Monroe. To underscore the resemblance for anybody in the audience who might miss the reference, the executive who phones a sleepy Baxter says 'she looks like Marilyn Monroe'. An unhappy Baxter vacates the apartment and with a coat over his pajamas goes out into the cold night.[43]

As Wilder grew older, attitudes towards him and his work overcame the failure of his final productions, in large part because he was, as one writer noted, among the last of 'the generation of directors who dominated Hollywood in the period that shaped American movies and consequently America's view of itself'. During the 1980s and 1990s Wilder picked up award after award, was honoured with a retrospective of his work at the Berlin Film Festival, and was given opportunities to speak at special functions. And with all these honours came a renewed appreciation of his films, including *The Apartment*, which in 1998 ranked 93 on the American Film Institute list of 'the 100 greatest American movies of all time'.[44]

That ranking indicates well how responses to *The Apartment* have varied since its initial release. These responses have covered a very interesting and disparate range. Jack Lemmon has perhaps come closest to articulating the film's impact. Years after it premiered he asserted that with this film, 'Wilder grew a rose in a garbage pail... He was throwing cold water right into our faces... He challenged our priorities... at a time when it wasn't fashionable to challenge these things.' That the film made an impact on its viewers is undeniable. The nature of the responses by various viewers, whether complex or simpleminded, whether positive or negative, highlight changes in American culture. Ultimately, *The Apartment* is a touchstone for the state of American societal values in any given era.[45]

NOTES TO CHAPTER 1

1   Marwick, *The Sixties*, op. cit., p 801.
2   Michael Elliott, *Day Before Yesterday: Remembering America's Past, Rediscovering the Present* (New York, 1996, Simon and Schuster), p 141.
3   Andrew Sarris, 'From the Kaiser to the Oscar', *The New York Times Book Review*, 22 December 1998, p 5.
4   *The Writer Speaks: Billy Wilder*, 1995, 60 minutes, distributed by MPI Video, from a series produced by The Writers Guild Foundation.
5   Maurice Zolotow, *Billy Wilder in Hollywood* (New York, 1987, Limelight Editions, originally published 1977), p 171.
6   Adrian Turner, 'The Wilder Side of Life' in *The Movies: The Illustrated History of the Cinema* (London, 1980, Orbis Publishing Limited), p 730; Agee quoted in Freeman, op. cit., p 75; David Thomson, *A Biographical Dictionary of Film*, (New York, 1994, Alfred A. Knopf), p 814.
7   Tom Vinciguerra, 'The Varsity Show', *Columbia College Today* (Fall, 1994) (http://www.cc.columbia.edu/cu/variety/article).
8   Philip French, 'Ace of Trumps', *Times Literary Supplement*, 17 February 1978, p 196.
9   *The Writer Speaks*, op. cit.
10 Turner, 'The Wilder Side of Life', op. cit., p 773; Ed. Sikov, *On Sunset Boulevard: The Life and Times of Billy Wilder* (New York, 1998, Hyperion), p 477.
11 Turner, 'The Wilder Side of Life', op. cit., p 723; Steven Seidman, *The Film Career of Billy Wilder* (Pleasantville, NY, 1977, Redgrave Publishing Company), p 36.
12 *The Writer Speaks*, op. cit.
13 *Variety*, 18 May 1960, p 25; *The Writer Speaks*, op. cit.
14 *The Apartment and The Fortune Cookie: Two Screenplays by Billy Wilder and I.A.L. Diamond* (New York, 1971, Praeger), pp 14, 19, 94 (this published version of the script varies slightly from the VHS version of the film, which, for example, raises Baxter's rent $1 from $84 to $85 a month: the published script MGM/UA Vintage Classics M206317).
15 *The Apartment*, op. cit., p 37.
16 Ibid., p 48; *The Writer Speaks*, op. cit.
17 *Harrison's Reports*, 21 May 1969, p 82; *The Apartment*, op. cit., pp 58, 198.
18 *The Apartment*, op. cit., p 102.
19 Ibid., p 103.

20 Ibid., pp 99, 106, 110.

21 *Time*, 6 June 1960, p 47; *The New York Times*, 16 June 1960, p 37.

22 Zolotow, op. cit., p 315; McCartin quoted in John Walker (ed.), *Halliwell's Film Guide*, 8th edn (London, 1991, Harper Collins), pp 49–50; Macdonald quoted in Zolotow, op. cit., p. 316; *New Republic*, June 27, 1969, p 20; Kael quoted in George P. Garrett et al. (eds), *Film Scripts Three: Charade, The Apartment, The Misfits* (New York, 1989, Irvington Publishers, originally published 1972), p 37; *Saturday Review*, 11 June 1960, p 29.

23 Neil Sinyard and Adrian Turner, *Journey Down Sunset Boulevard* (Ryde, Isle of Wight, 1979, BCW Publishing), p 159.

24 Michael Selzer, *Kike! A Documentary History of Anti-Semitism in America* (New York, 1972, Meridian, World Publishing), pp 3–4.

25 Maria Syrkin, *The State of the Jews* (Washington, DC, 1980, New Republic Books), p 270.

26 James T. Patterson, *Grand Expectations: The United States, 1945–1974* (New York, 1996, Oxford University Press), p 360; Irwin and Dobi Unger (eds), *The Times Were A Changin': The Sixties Reader* (New York, 1998, Three Rivers Press), p 197.

27 Robert Benton and David Newman, 'The New Sentimentality' in Harold Hayes (ed.), *Smiling Through the Apocalypse: Esquire's History of the Sixties* (New York, c.1970, McCall Publishing), pp 408–9, also xxiii.

28 Zolotow, op. cit., p 315; Wilder quoted in Monica Hayde, 'Wild About Wilder', *Palo Alto Weekly*, 4 February 1994 (http://www/service/.com/PAW/morgue/cover/1994_Feb_4.FILMFST4.html).

29 Robert Sklar, *Movie-Made America: A Cultural History of American Movies* (New York, 1975, Vintage), p 296; Gregory D. Black, *The Catholic Crusade Against the Movies, 1940–1975* (Cambridge, 1998, Cambridge University Press), pp 181, 214.

30 Ruth Rosen, 'The Female Generation Gap: Daughters of the Fifties and the Origins of Contemporary American Feminism' in Linda K. Kerber et al. (eds), *US History and Women's History: New Feminist Essays* (Chapel Hill and London, 1995, University of North Carolina Press), p 314.

31 Sinyard and Turner, op. cit., p 184.

32 Charles Higham and Joel Greenberg, *The Celluloid Muse: Hollywood Directors Speak* (London, 1969, Angus & Robertson), p 230; Robert Connelly, *The Motion Picture Guide: Silent Film, 1910–1936* (Chicago, 1986, Cinebooks), p 55; Sinyard and Turner, op. cit., p 148; Vidor quoted in Sikov, op. cit., p 434.

33 Neil Sinyard and Adrian Turner, with Beitragen von Heinz-Gerd Rasner et al., *Billy Wilder's Filme* (Berlin, 1980, Verlag Volker Speiss), p 45; a revised and expanded German edition ('Er ist einfach der Beste').

34 The narration presented here is slightly revised from the published text, and is transcribed from the videotape of the film. The editors of the published text chose to publish 'the screenplays as written' rather than as shot, so as not to lose 'the details of dress and decor which the authors themselves thought to be important...', p 7.

35 Paul Johnson, *A History of the American People* (London, 1997, Weidenfeld & Nicolson), p 699; Richard E. Gordon et al., *The Split-Level Trap* (New York, 1962, Dell).

36 William H. Whyte, Jr, *The Organization Man* (New York, 1956, Simon and Schuster), pp 396, 404; David Riesman et al., *The Lonely Crowd: A Study of the Changing American Character* (New Haven, 1950, Yale University Press), p 10; Mills quoted in Patterson, op. cit., p 339; Lawrence S. Wittner, *Cold War America: From Hiroshima to Watergate* (New York, 1974, Praeger), p 129.

37 Anna Rochester, *Rulers of America* (New York, 1936, International Publishers), pp 301-2; John Chamberlain, *The Enterprising Americans: A Business History of the United States* (New York, 1974, Harper & Row, new and updated edition), p 243.

38 Harold C. Livesay, *American Made: Men Who Shaped the American Economy* (Boston, 1979, Little, Brown and Company), p 290. According to David Halberstam, the media tycoon in Wilson's book, 'a superior man pledged seriously to a better world', was based on 'Roy Larson, one of the founders of Time-Life' (David Halberstam, *The Fifties* [New York, 1993, Villard Books], p 523).

39 Ellen Patrick, *Films in Review, Aug–Sept 1960* in Stanley Hochman (ed.), *American Film Directors: A Library of Film Criticism* (New York, 1974, Frederick Ungar Publishing), p 503; *Harrison's Reports*, 21 May 1960, pp 62–63.

40 *The Writer Speaks*, op. cit.; Cleveland Amory (ed.), *Celebrity Register* (New York, 1963, Harper & Row), p 395; Zolotow, op. cit., pp 344, 346.

41 *The Writer Speaks*, op. cit.; Thomson, op. cit., p 466.

42 Sikov, op. cit., p 584; Zolotow, op. cit., p 264.

43 *The Apartment*, op. cit., p 22.

44 Freeman, op. cit., p 72; (http://www.afionline.org/100movies); (the 'blue ribbon panel' which created the list also ranked *Double Indemnity* as no. 38.

45 Lemmon quoted in Joe Baltake, *The Films of Jack Lemmon* (Secaucus, NJ, 1977, The Citadel Press), p 108.

2 Defining the Parameters of 'Quality' Cinema for 'the Permissive Society'

The British Board of Film Censors and *This Sporting Life*

Anthony Aldgate

Traditionally considered by critics and cultural historians alike as the last of the ostensibly 'new wave' films in British cinema history, Lindsay Anderson's *This Sporting Life* – given its premiere on 7 February 1963 – was afforded a mixed critical reaction, poor box office reception and lack of commercial success, usually attributed to the fact that it came at the end of the line of a short-lived movement which, however individually distinguished its products, was well and truly finished. The phenomenal domestic and international acclaim that greeted Tony Richardson's eventual Oscar-winning *Tom Jones*, released four months later in June 1963, ushered in a different sort of upbeat cinema. By December of 1963 the Rank Organisation's managing director, John Davis, who had actually financed the budget for *This Sporting Life*, declared at an Annual Showmanship Luncheon that 'The public has clearly shown that it does not want the dreary kitchen sink dramas'. And the likes of *Darling*, *Alfie*, and a host of archetypal 'swinging London' films which followed from 1965 onwards soon revealed they were more in keeping with cinemagoers' tastes at the height of an ongoing 'cultural revolution'. Widespread attention was really only given to Anderson's work, moreover, when his next feature film *If...* was released concurrent to the 'events' of 1968 and, in part because its themes concerned student revolt and youthful rebellion, the film enjoyed noticeably contrasting good fortune and proved an immense transatlantic and European hit.[1]

Since Lindsay Anderson's death in 1994, however, the reputation of *This Sporting Life* has been somewhat revised by commentators in recognition not least, as Erik Hedling puts it, of his evident attempt 'to pave the way for new aesthetic forms in British cinema' by challenging, in particular, the conventions of linear narrative exposition adopted in mainstream films. Now, as a result, it is seen as the harbinger of a small but impressive body of work that stamped Anderson's idiosyncratic, indelible and maverick imprint on 'the permissive society' of the 1960s, sufficient to render him one of the few genuine examples of a native *auteur* director of the sort more often found in the French or Italian avowedly 'art house' cinemas of the period. To better understand Anderson's rich and complex creative vision, in short, his sixties films are best placed within the context of the sea changes affecting British film culture at large and European cinema generally.[2]

Yet if a deeper appreciation of context is essential to lend greater insight and more rounded judgement to Anderson's sixties career, so too it is necessary to grasp the precise context surrounding the production of *This Sporting Life* in order to pinpoint exactly his individual contribution. The film is best viewed, especially, in the light of circumstances that obtained as a result of the changing nature of the intervention brought to bear upon the film-making process by the British Board of Film Censors. Since the advent of *Room at the Top* in 1959, the BBFC's Secretary, John Trevelyan, had strenuously sought to foster relations with the new wave film-makers, in particular, so as to advance the cause of 'quality' British cinema. This he tried to do by investing the critically despised 'X' category of classification – hitherto almost confined, in the main, to 'horrific', 'exploitative' or 'sensational' films – with films on genuinely 'adult themes' and done in 'good taste'. The fact that it entailed placing greater emphasis upon films bearing 'realist' credentials and a 'literary' pedigree – albeit, essentially, drawing upon the 'angry brigade' and 'kitchen sink' dramatists or novelists such as John Osborne, Shelagh Delaney, Alan Sillitoe, John Braine, Stan Barstow, David Storey, Keith Waterhouse and Willis Hall – accorded quite neatly (if still sometimes acrimoniously) with the intentions of directors like Tony Richardson or Karel Reisz, and new-found production companies like Woodfall Films, since they were also attempting to promote much the same kind of national cinema.[3]

Close analysis of the precise context for *This Sporting Life* reveals, moreover, that it was initially mooted with the censors as early as the summer of 1961, following fast upon the success which had greeted the first new wave films *Room at the Top* (1959) and *Saturday Night and Sunday Morning* (1960), concurrent with *A Taste of Honey* (1961) coming up for release, and well before *The Loneliness of the Long Distance Runner*, *A Kind of Loving* (both 1962) or *Billy Liar* (1963) were released. It was at the outset of August 1961, and fully 18 months before its premiere, that the BFFC considered the likely problems which might arise over the film. The key moment of deliberation occurred at a time, in point of fact, when both the film censors and the film-makers were still actively defining the parameters of permissiveness to be allowed new wave cinema. Moreover, to fully contextualise *This Sporting Life* is to appreciate in essence the measure of quality that was increasingly being sought and advocated for mainstream British cinema across the board throughout the course of the 1960s.

David Storey's original novel of *This Sporting Life*, published in 1960 and winner of the Macmillan Fiction Award for that year, garnered immediate critical acclaim and was an attractive proposition in the eyes of several film companies. Though Tony Richardson and John Osborne's Woodfall Films put in a bid for the rights, Rank secured them with a higher offer and handed the project over to Julian Wintle and Leslie Parkyn of Independent Artists. When their initial discussions with Joseph Losey failed to agree on either his treatment or choice of Stanley Baker for the leading role, Wintle and Parkyn turned to Karel Reisz, then enjoying the fruits of success with *Saturday Night and Sunday Morning*, as director. Reisz was not very keen to direct 'another north-country subject', but

Richard Harris in *This Sporting Life* (1963)

he did want to learn about the production side of the industry and was happy to contemplate the task of producer. He, in turn, invited Lindsay Anderson on board as director in a move which was approved by Wintle, Parkyn and, eventually, John Davis at the Rank Organisation. Though it was Anderson's first attempt at feature film direction, Davis was reassured by the fact that Reisz would be 'keeping an eye' on progress. For their part, Anderson and Reisz shared much in common from their experiences making 'Free Cinema' documentaries during the 1950s. Furthermore, they were of the same opinion, crucially, in thinking that David Storey should be employed and allowed to adapt his own novel for the screen. 'The book was such a personal piece of work that Karel and I both felt that no one but its author could write the script', Anderson wrote later: 'What I wanted was a script that had his sanction, and an artistic authority equal to that of the book'.[4]

The first draft of Storey's screenplay was forthcoming during the opening months of 1961. In two respects, albeit relatively minor matters, he was compelled to make changes to his novel from the outset. So as to avoid needless duplication or potential audience identification with Arthur Seaton, the protagonist of *Saturday Night and Sunday Morning*, the Christian name of Storey's major character was required to be altered from Arthur to Frank Machin, and his job switched from being a lathe operator in the local engineering works to that of a miner. But the other changes introduced into the screenplay that differed from the original novel were of Storey's own doing and instigation. They were substantial, furthermore, and doubtless borne of his inexperience at writing for the cinema – it was his first filmscript, after all. Thus, Storey eschewed the complex narrative structure and the series of flashbacks – prompted by Frank's need of dental treatment after a rugby injury, his thoughts and memories under anaesthetic, and his consequent disorientation at the Weavers' Christmas Eve party – that had constituted the springboard or lift-off for the opening five chapters of his book. They were dropped in favour of a straightforward narrative exposition, distinctly linear chronological development of the plot, somewhat different thematic emphasis, and a degree of rethinking about the characterisation.

That much is evident from the storyline synopsis of Storey's screenplay when tendered for pre-production scrutiny to the British Board of Film Censors, in August 1961, which read:

> Frank is a rough, tough miner and a brilliant Rugby League player. He lodges with Mrs Hammond, a young widow on whom he has his eye (this is mutual, but she is no tramp and is a slow learner). At first, Frank prospers: Weaver, the owner of the local Rugby League team, likes him and he does well in a trial game, despite having to punch a member of the team who doesn't want him to be selected. Frank's price for signing a contract is £1000 and, rather to his surprise, he actually gets it. He buys a Jaguar and takes Margaret (Mrs Hammond) and her two children out in it. She soon becomes his mistress and he treats her with lavish generosity: there is practically nothing he won't give her, except the wedding ring on which she has set her heart.

Frank is just the sort to let all this go to his head and he does, swaggering round the local smart restaurants and becoming more than fresh with Mrs Weaver. For some reason which is not quite clear to me, though I think it is class-consciousness, he gives her a lift home and then insults her, assuring her that he would have her across the sofa in two twos if he really wanted her; this annoys her, she insults him and he punches her. This was unwise. Ill fortune now conspires with unwisdom to undo Frank: he gets a fearful smash in the face during a game and, insisting on going out to the Weavers' Christmas party that evening when he should be resting, cannot hold his drink, thrusts his way into Weaver's study and insults *him*.

Luckily the Committee managing the team are at odds and the fact that Weaver is against Frank is his passport to favour in other quarters, so he is not flung out of the team. But he is less successful in private life: Margaret proposes marriage and is turned down with a good deal of unnecessary rudeness, so she sends him packing. He goes to a lodging house to join an old man called Johnson, who has been hanging round wistfully throughout the picture: it is not quite clear why or how Frank owes this character a lot but it is established that he does; it is also alleged by Mrs Hammond from time to time that Johnson is physically attracted to Frank and looks at him as if he were a girl. Getting restless in the lodging house, Frank tries to make it up with Margaret, but she has vanished. Frank has nothing now but his work as a miner and his rugby: he goes on doggedly blundering through life, doomed to make himself miserable and anger others.[5]

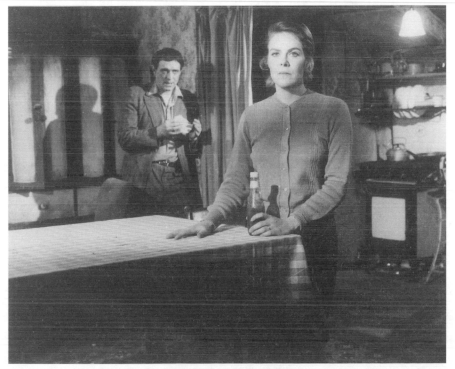

Richard Harris and Rachel Roberts in *This Sporting Life* (1963)

As the occasional interjection by way of subjective and judgmental comment clearly implies, the BBFC script-reader, Audrey Field, was not very pleased at the idea of a film being produced from David Storey's screenplay, especially in the light of what had already been achieved over *Saturday Night and Sunday Morning*. Comparisons were immediately made with the earlier film and she invariably praised the former at the expense, in contrast, of the troublesome prospect likely to be caused by proceeding with production of *This Sporting Life* – an ironic turn of events given that the same script-reader had hardly warmed to that film in the first instance either, and had considered it, in fact, 'dangerous stuff'. But then, of course, *Saturday Night and Sunday Morning* had proved an immense critical and commercial success. And, once the censorship process had instilled the requisite amount of 'social responsibility' into the various drafts of the script, it turned out to be a vital conduit for implementing the much coveted and carefully nurtured criteria of excellence that John Trevelyan espoused for his quality 'X' rating in film classification.[6]

'I would think much better of this script if we had not already had *Saturday Night and Sunday Morning*', Field maintained: 'There is some good character drawing but of a very wearisome character whom I would have found much more interesting if he had come as a lovely surprise and not after Albert Finney'. 'I wish film producers would not rush after each other like Gadarene swine', she continued, 'However, since they will, they must expect all to get the same sort of treatment from us, and this script will need to be toned down a lot if the makers of the film hope to get an "A" certificate when *Saturday Night* got an "X" and was criticised by rigid-minded people even so'. 'Admittedly, Frank is not sleeping round with other people's wives,' Field conceded, 'but he goes in for a lot of very overt passion and the language of Frank and his mates, and their bits of bawdy, are even more highly coloured than most of *Saturday Night*.'[7]

What followed thereafter, in the usual time-honoured BBFC fashion, was a meticulous and fastidious listing of those facets and features that were considered potentially controversial or contentious unless changes were to be made. And the lines of divide between what was permitted for the 'X' and 'A' categories of film classification (an 'X' certificate could only be shown to persons over sixteen years old whereas an 'A' could be shown to persons under that age, provided they were accompanied by an adult, with the 'U' film available for universal exhibition), were highlighted especially for attention. The key note of concern over *This Sporting Life* arose in regard to what Audrey Field perceptively discerned as 'a rather savage and sordid "feel"' to the script. This was one area, in particular, where she believed 'it is essential that drastic revision of details should be undertaken if they really want it to have any hope of an "A"'. But, interestingly, to Field's mind at least, she still afforded Storey's script the latitude to be considered in either of the 'X' or 'A' categories. For his part, as we shall see, John Trevelyan had an altogether different purpose in mind there.

The promise of male nudity was the first troublesome factor that captured Field's interest. Whether in the opening scenes of miners showering after work or, later, when rugby players were to be seen in showers and changing rooms, she felt that 'Care would be needed with such shots – obviously we would not want to see anything of the kind we won't have in nudist films, and we would not want a lot of full length back shots either'. The prospect of 'men peering at each other over the shower partitions', in the former case, and using phrases like 'Tha's got summat theer', '... not for thee either', or, '... who d'you think he keeps it all for?' simply would not do for the 'X' or 'A' certificates. And if certain concessions might be granted over dialogue to be employed in the rugby football showers ('I suppose the injunction to Frank and Maurice "Let's have you two fairies out o' theer" is meant harmlessly enough?'), the same could not be said of the ripostes which followed such as 'Come and join us love. Let's see what you've got', or 'I'll come in theer and show you all right'. 'For "A" or "X",' Field argued, 'I think many women find this sort of stuff offensive'. Where there was confusion over some of the 'crude' dialogue utilised in exchanges between the coach and the players – 'I am not sure what inner significance there is in "like a bloody Mary Ellen"', but it sounds non-A' – there was greater clarity about phrases that could not be condoned such as 'Don't just stand around theer as if you'd got a cig up your arse', or, 'like a pack of dogs round a bitch'.

The character of Johnson was also a major cause for concern, as Field had indicated in the summary synopsis at the outset, not least because of the obvious homosexual implications in Mrs Hammond's reference to the way he looks at Frank – 'as if you're a girl' – and her comment that 'there's something the matter with him'. 'This sort of hint is better left out of "A" films,' Field stated, and 'We do *not* want (for "A") any indications in the playing that Johnson feels anything more than hero worship'. By the same token, however, a caution was administered over the likely rendition of heterosexual love: 'For "A", we would not want Frank bearing Mrs Hammond down on the bed or lying on top of her; and even for "X" we would not want them "in spasm", as the script so prettily puts it'.

Frank Machin's relationships with both Mrs Hammond and Mrs Weaver, predictably, were the source of numerous possible problems or pitfalls. Various niggling little phrases were much in evidence, once again. Of paramount importance, moreover, was the potential for the graphic depiction of violence being done to women. Field was adamant, for instance, that 'The interview between Frank and Mrs Weaver is "X"; we would not want for "A" the line "If I'd have wanted ought from you, I'd have draped you over that sofa sooner than look at you", references to "your bloody husband", "one bloody pig", or any similarly direct sexual sparring'. But the key point made was that 'for "A" or "X" we do not want Mrs Weaver to be hit and knocked down'. And in the final scene of confrontation between Machin and Margaret Hammond it was emphasised that 'We do not want Frank to smack Mrs H's face or her to spit at him (for "A")'.

There were occasional other lesser admonishments besides, including a heartfelt plea to the effect that 'If we must have people being sick, which I do not like and I am sure most cinema audiences don't like, let us have discretion please'. But last, and by no means least, there remained the vexed question of the 'language' to be employed throughout the course of the film generally. A tentative word count on Field's part deduced that there were about 45 'bloodies' ('too many even for "A" because liable to irritate'); nine 'Christs' ('and they are never in any context where they could be regarded as a legitimate expression of agony or prayer'); and eight 'bastards' ('I think they should be asked to dispense with this word sometimes'); while the word 'tart' was 'rather freely used' ('I think a lot of women find this offensive and if they could lay off a bit I would be happier').

Though Field did not count the actual number of phrases including some variant on the word 'stuff' ('For "X", I suppose this kind of crudity may pass?', she queried), a second script-reader did just that and found there were three such permutations: 'get stuffed', 'stuff it' and 'you want stuffing'. In addition, he found another two 'bastards' and one 'bleeding'. All of which meant, somewhat inevitably, that *This Sporting Life* was deemed 'excessive'. As Karel Reisz and Woodfall Films had already discovered over *Saturday Night and Sunday Morning*, 'language' and the use of vernacular phrases by the new wave cinema were matters of considerable concern in the eyes of the BBFC and largely dictated, as readily as anything else, the certificate a film would receive. 'Quality' cinema, in short, was not expected to include too much by way of every-day, ordinary parlance, and certain words were definitely prohibited.[8]

Once the script-readers' comments were collated for John Trevelyan's consideration, of course, it was his task as BBFC Secretary to inform the film-makers of the viability of David Storey's script. His letter to Julian Wintle of Independent Artists on 10 August 1961, needless to say, showed no hesitation about the course he favoured or the action he recommended. It was obvious from the outset that, regardless of his script-readers' detailed deliberations about the various options or likely avenues open to them as between an 'A' or 'X' classification, Trevelyan was determined to see the film firmly in the 'X' category:

> We have now read the script of *This Sporting Life*. It is powerful and vivid but it does present us with some problems. First I must say that I find it difficult to consider this project for the 'A' category. It is true that the sex scenes are not as difficult as those in *Saturday Night and Sunday Morning* and that with appropriate modification they could probably be made in a way that was acceptable for the 'A' category, but this does not seem to us to be the real problem here. The development of Frank's character seems to us to be very much an adult development and, if the part is well played, Frank will be full of smouldering passion – not only sexual passion of course. There is a 'feel' of violence about this story which is sure to come out in the film.
>
> What adds to the difficulty is that Karel Reisz has a documentary approach to film making which results in his characters becoming real people and not people from a fantasy film world. This is to his credit but it will have the effect of making the film a piece of real life of a kind that is unlikely to be suitable for young children. I am bound to admit that a fair number of children will find the situation familiar, but there are at least an equal number of children to whom

that kind of pattern of behaviour and mental attitude would be a new and rather frightening experience.

The script is, of course, full of what is called 'language'. With a film in the 'X' category we could be more generous over this than we can be with a film in the 'A' category but even for an 'X' film there are limits to what we would accept and we think that this script goes beyond them. It is true that the kind of people around whom the story revolves would certainly use language of this kind but it is not even so wholly realistic since their normal speech would contain words and phrases that are still not acceptable within the conventions of stage and screen. I do feel that even for the 'X' category some modification of the language is desirable. For the 'A' category it would have to be reduced to a minimum.[9]

Although clearly not privy to the film-makers' plans about a precise breakdown of responsibilities between Anderson as director and Reisz as producer, Trevelyan already knew enough of Reisz's credentials from his work on *Saturday Night and Sunday Morning* to worry about the 'realist' import of the impending film to be made of *This Sporting Life*. Lest Wintle should fail to grasp the seriousness of his intentions to have the film fairly and squarely in the 'X' classification, moreover, Trevelyan spelled out what he was prepared to condone and what not, virtually implying that there were tangible benefits or incentives to be gained from acceding to his proposed course of action. And, interestingly, he held back from mentioning all of the script-readers' observations and cautions, doubtless saving the remainder for use at a later date should negotiations prove protracted or difficult (a tactic successfully adopted with earlier new wave films).

Thus, for all that warnings were administered on the scenes of men in showers and changing rooms ('We do not want any censorable nudity and even full length back shots should be few and discreet'), no reference was made whatsoever to the queries raised by Audrey Field regarding the likely 'hints' over Johnson's sexuality. Nor, indeed, was Trevelyan quite as explicitly censorious about the numerous examples of 'language' that had been detailed so painstakingly by both his readers. If profound reservations were expressed about certain words and lines – 'We are trying to keep the phrase "get stuffed" out of films since its meaning is only too obvious,' he noted in particular – nothing was said concerning the various 'bloodies' that liberally adorned the script or the frequent resort to blasphemous 'Christs'. Here, it seems, Trevelyan was prepared to shelter for the moment behind his overall maxim and dictat that 'even for the "X" category some modification of the language is desirable'.

The sex scenes were undoubtedly required to be 'shot with reasonable discretion', not least the initial one between Machin and Margaret Hammond. 'We would not want to see Frank moving his hands over Mrs Hammond, bearing down on her and lying on top of her,' Trevelyan asserted, 'and we would certainly not want what I imagine would be the visual described by the phrase "Their bodies are suddenly in spasm"'. Similarly the threat of violence to the two women was greeted with distinct apprehension at the prospect, albeit that a line of divide was introduced, once again, between what was definitely ruled out of

court and what would simply be deemed unwelcome depending upon circumstances surrounding the final choice of certificate. 'We would not want Frank's
violence to Mrs Weaver,' Trevelyan commented tersely in one instance, adding
that Frank's crude turn of phrase to accompany his action merited 'some modification'. Whereas, by contrast, the moment when Machin slaps his lover's face
and she retaliates warranted merely an admonishment that 'We do not like
Frank's violence to Mrs Hammond, or her spitting in his face'.

At the last, Trevelyan was no more enamoured than Field of the likelihood
of watching people suffering from a surfeit of alcohol on screen. 'Is it really necessary for us to see and hear Frank being sick?' he questioned: 'This, to put it
mildly, and appropriately, would be nauseating.' His parting shot was reserved
for further gentle reminders, in case such were still needed, that he had already
been somewhat selective in his choice of contentious matters to highlight and
that the path to accepting an 'X' certificate was paved with the prospect of getting
away with more than would otherwise be the case. Indeed, contrary to what his
script-readers had surmised for their part, Trevelyan held out scant chance – if
at all – of the film being considered for another category. 'I do not intend to give
you a list of comments on the basis of an "A" certificate at this stage,' he stated,
'because I really think that there is little point in my doing this'. The carrot of
inducement was accompanied by the stick of authority, as ever, and contained
in a thinly-veiled note of warning to the effect that 'if you want to discuss this
script with me we can go into detail then'. 'In view of this position I think it best
to keep the script in this office for the moment,' Trevelyan concluded, 'but if you
want me to return it I will send it back at once'.

The jury was still out in regard to *This Sporting Life*, then, and the case
pending. Though the matter was clear enough in Trevelyan's eyes - the script
promised a genuinely 'adult' film of precisely the sort wanted for the 'X' category.
Everything now hinged on the film-makers' response to his overtures on how to
invest it with the requisite amount of 'quality'. As Anderson and Reisz set about
contemplating the BBFC's strictures, however, they also uncovered problems of
their own in regard to Storey's script. They were, quite simply, not at all pleased
with it. 'The book proved difficult to condense without losing the subtlety and
complexity which gave it such distinction', Anderson argued, 'and I felt that the
authority I wanted was not there'. It was an opinion shared by Richard Harris,
to whom Anderson sent both Storey's novel and first draft script in an attempt to
persuade him to take on the leading male role. Harris was by this time on location
in Tahiti filming Lewis Milestone's remake of *Mutiny on the Bounty* and experiencing intractable problems with a difficult co-star, Marlon Brando. He took to the
project with considerable relief and alacrity, immediately identifying with Storey's
protagonist. A subsequent and highly productive visit by Lindsay Anderson to meet
up with Richard Harris on Tahiti ironed out some of the problems. 'We had lost what
was most unique and brilliant in the novel,' Anderson recounted, and 'We were
dangerously near, in fact, ending up with just a "filmscript"'. 'It was Richard who,
with passionate intransigence, brought us back to the book,' Anderson maintained.[10]

Once armed with the fruits of his collaborative efforts with Harris, however, Anderson returned for further discussions with David Storey. Suitably revived and prompted to revisit his own book for inspiration, Storey's second script provided much, though by no means all, of what was required by the major parties in the production. Crucially, through establishing shots of Frank playing in a rugby match intercut with his work down the mine and domestic life at Mrs Hammond's house, Storey's new screenplay began by drawing upon the flashback pattern and rup-tured chronology which had been a defining and characteristic feature of his novel from the outset. In particular, he restored the fierce tackling incident that broke Machin's teeth to its original opening place as the springboard for Frank's urgent need of a dentist and consequent lapse, under anaesthetic, into further flashbacks – quite unlike Storey's first screenplay, of course, where the incident had been forced into a strictly linear chronological development of the storyline. That said, nevertheless, his continuing use of the flashback device remained sparse and modest with, noticeably, the interjection of a single solitary sequence in Mrs Hammond's house before Frank lapses, while in the dentist's chair, into now dream-induced and memory-ridden flashbacks – one reason, doubtless, why Anderson declared himself dissatisfied still with even this latest version.[11]

In certain key respects, there again, Storey's second script revealed he was alert to other than just the guiding influences provided, principally, by Anderson and Harris, and showed he was not in the least averse to following the sort of suggestions advocated by the BBFC. Thus, for instance, he immediately dis-carded any notion of Frank striking Mrs Weaver and rewrote their scene together so as to eliminate the possible inference of 'class consciousness'. Reworking the trajectory evident in his novel, the scene reverted to a simple and straight-forward attempted seduction of Frank by Mrs Weaver, followed fast by his rejection of her advances in favour of returning to his troubled, though genuine, love for Margaret Hammond. If there were class resonances and antagonisms to be found in the book, as there were, they were not to be found in Frank's relations with women, where Storey had an altogether different purpose in mind and where 'interior drama', not social drama, was more the order of the day. Hence, far from simply vanishing (as in the initial draft of the script), Margaret dies and Frank grieves deeply over her death. On the matter of their questionable lovemaking scene, furthermore, Storey also curtailed his ambitions and settled for the modest direction, 'He folds her down to the bed, not kissing her, but with a pure physical insistence', instead of the explicit description in the earlier script. By contrast, but in keeping with his emphasis on evoking the raw power of their emotional relationship, Storey plainly intended to retain the scene where Frank slaps Margaret's face.

Johnson's characterisation remained pretty much as was fashioned for the first-draft screenplay. Albeit ostensibly at odds with the depiction of Johnson as rendered in the original novel, where he is married and lives at home with his wife, Storey clearly favoured the extra homoerotic overtones he had invested in the screen persona of Johnson. It is revealed that Johnson's wife left him ten years before and he is a long-term resident of the dilapidated lodgings where Frank takes up residence upon acrimoniously departing Mrs Hammond's house. It is Johnson to whom Frank turns when confiding his disillusion with rugby. What was formerly latent in relations between them was now brought into the foreground. And along with an occasional hint concerning Mr Weaver's sexuality – at one point in both the novel and all versions of the screenplay, for example, Weaver overtly squeezes Frank's thigh – Storey obviously felt it introduced a worthwhile and rich note into the proceedings not least in discerning just a hint of homosexuality, albeit little more than that, of course, beneath the wholly 'macho' surface features of rugby league.

Though it is difficult to determine fully what Storey intended to do to assuage the censors' fears of extensive male nudity being displayed in the proposed shower and changing-room sequences, it appears he was prepared to exercise some measure of restraint in this regard as well. The 'stage' directions to his filmscript now indicated that the players would be seen 'half-dressed', as often as not, with the sole exception of Frank who was to be viewed 'naked on the massage table' in one instance, and stoically enjoying 'the cold rinse' jokingly inflicted by the team trainer in another. Clearly, here, the likely degree of transgression or otherwise would depend entirely upon how the question of male nudity was to be visually realised in the hands of director Lindsay Anderson. But, given the force of the BBFC's strictures over this issue and the fact that his script still promised shots of players cavorting in the baths amid much merriment and 'joking below the water-line', Storey was no doubt trusting to luck that they would escape severe censure. Whatever the outcome, he obviously thought it worthwhile taking a chance just the same.

When it came to the matter of 'language', finally, Storey adopted a 'give-and-take' attitude whereby he conceded ground in some areas by reducing or dispensing with certain controversial words or phrases, while at the same time retaining and even marginally increasing his use of others. Thus, only 31 'bloodies' remained out of an original total of 46, the number of 'tarts' was reduced to seven and the 'bastards' cut by half to five, whereas the 'Christs' count stayed at nine and 'bitch' increased to two, with 'God' introduced anew, and no less than five times at that. 'Stuff', 'stuffed' and 'stuffing' were retained, though now in five variations, as was the word 'crat', which was used once and seems to have escaped the censors' attention throughout – in part, probably, because it was a strictly localised idiom but also, as likely as not, because it was impossible to fathom. In all, however, the changes proved a common enough and characteristic attempt at compromise of the sort increasingly favoured by new wave film-makers in their dealings with the BBFC. Despite the time-consuming effort involved in conjuring seemingly fussy and fastidious alterations, moreover, it usually paid dividends and certainly enhanced the desired 'realist' effect should such concessions be won for the finished film.

But *This Sporting Life* was far from fashioned into a finished film. Production had not yet started. Anderson, Harris and Reisz continued to be dissatisfied with Storey's second draft screenplay, and required another rewrite. 'It still wasn't right,' Anderson maintained, 'and the third script, which was the one we used, stuck even more closely to the book'.[12] So, indeed, it did. Storey reverted wholesale to the time-shift methods employed in his original novel with a large-scale restoration of flashback incidents which thereby inserted several domestic establishing scenes with Mrs Hammond during the opening minutes of the film alone. And he proceeded subsequently to mine the same rich flashback vein until returning to the storyline's chronological 'present' as Frank awakens from the dentist's anaesthetic and is conveyed to the Weaver's Christmas Eve party.

Only in one regard, moreover, did Storey's enthusiasm for his carefully-drawn characters appear to abate somewhat, when it is revealed that Johnson has long abandoned the lodging house where Frank is compelled to seek residence. Given that John Trevelyan had not revealed any misgivings over Johnson, so far as Storey knew at least, it is difficult to fathom what prompted his need of revision there. And though the change did nothing to lessen the homoerotic charge that informed Johnson and Frank's earlier scenes together, the results are discon-certing because the character now abruptly and mysteriously disappears from the storyline, in effect, and he is no longer around at the last to act as confidant or witness to Frank's disillusion. By contrast, on another front, it is easy to discern why Storey felt obliged to resume the task of reducing the offensive 'language' count in his screenplay. After further tinkering and elisions, if essentially modest and cosmetic, in truth, Storey must have thought his third and final version of the script had done more than enough to settle the BBFC's grave concerns on the matter. Certainly, Anderson was at long last satisfied with Storey's efforts, and he embarked upon full-scale production in the summer of 1962.[13]

In the event, the BBFC also seemed relatively placated by Storey's revisions in the domain of language and most other areas. But when the finished film was presented for scrutiny and the award of an appropriate certificate for public exhibition, their continued and long-standing reservations about the extent of male nudity on display came back forcefully into the reckoning. A measure of the importance they attached to settling this outstanding issue was evident from the fact that *This Sporting Life* was specially viewed by no less a band of high-ranking BBFC personnel than three of its leading censors, as well as its President, Lord Morrison of Lambeth, and Secretary, John Trevelyan, on Friday 11 January 1963 – barely one month before the film was destined to be given a traditional glittering West End premiere at the Odeon, Leicester Square.

There was still no doubt that the film had to be given an 'X' certificate, and it displayed, in fact, evidence of the 'quality' cinema wanted for the category. But even an 'X' would only be granted subject to the removal in two reels of 'visuals showing male genital areas'. Clearly, these were deemed too transgressive by far. Male nudity, though not wholly condemned, was condoned strictly within limits and preferably without full frontal views. A telephone call to Julian Wintle on the same day acquainted Independent Artists with the decision, and doubt-less compelled a hasty weekend rethink over the offending scenes to meet the

BBFC's dictates. Some re-editing was obviously necessary, and Wintle rang back on Monday 14 January to say they had inserted a replacement shot in one instance, made a cut in another, and that the two reels would be sent in for final BBFC vetting on Wednesday 16 January. They were seen and approved on that date, and a show print of the film was struck in time for its premiere just three weeks later, on Thursday 7 February 1963.[14]

What, then, accounted for the BBFC's attitude towards *This Sporting Life*? Although often alert to many of the subtleties evident in the role and process of screen censorship during the 1960s, one critic, Alexander Walker, concluded that the film was a beneficiary at the last of little more than simply a change of mind on Trevelyan's part. Pre-production script scrutiny of the sort traditionally forthcoming at the time from the BBFC inevitably tended, as he puts it, 'to err on the side of discretion'. 'When the finished film comes up for certification,' Walker added, 'the censor may find less cause to be censorious than the printed word offered him'. 'Remember, too,' he maintained, 'Trevelyan's reservations would almost certainly have been milder by the time the film actually appeared on the screen 18 months later. For the cinema was by then embarked on a joy-ride which progressively threw all such cautions to the winds.'[15]

Perhaps so. But perhaps, there again, Walker misses a nuance in his judgement. Another more likely reading might suggest that based on the full body of contextual evidence, for instance, Trevelyan was well pleased with the outcome over *This Sporting Life*, pretty satisfied with the results obtained and, anyway, got almost all he wanted. The film represented precisely the sort of 'quality' cinema he favoured for the 'X' category and adult cinemagoers. When the film-makers showed signs of becoming too 'permissive', the BBFC simply stepped in to ensure they stayed in line. And in the final analysis, arguably, far from just responding in makeshift and piecemeal fashion to the changed temper of the times, Trevelyan was ahead of the field in manifesting what Arthur Marwick has best described as 'measured judgement'. He was, in effect, an arch exponent of that flexible, tolerant, liberal response shown by many in positions of authority to the new cultural developments permeating British society during the course of the 1960s.

ACKNOWLEDGEMENT

My thanks go to the British Board of Film Classification for their continuing kindness and helpful support, as ever, in providing me with a copy of the file on *This Sporting Life*.

NOTES TO CHAPTER 2

1   Sir John Davis's speech to the Rank Theatre Division's Annual Showmanship Luncheon was given at the Dorchester Hotel on 12 December 1963 and is partially quoted in Robert Murphy, *Sixties British Cinema* (London, 1992), p 28. For the contemporary critical and box-office reception afforded to *If...* see Anthony Aldgate and Jeffrey Richards, *Best of British: Cinema and Society from 1930 to the Present* (London, 1999), pp 203–18. However, the slim volume by Elizabeth Sussex, *Lindsay Anderson* (London, 1969), was the only book of note on Anderson's sixties films published at the time.

2   Erik Hedling, *Lindsay Anderson: Maverick Film-Maker* (London, 1998), p 56. But see also Erik Hedling, 'Lindsay Anderson and the Development of British Art Cinema' in Robert Murphy (ed.), *The British Cinema Book* (London, 1997), pp 178–86, as well as Michael O'Pray (ed.), *The British Avant-Garde Film 1926–1995* (Luton, 1996).

3   These issues are explored at length in Anthony Aldgate, *Censorship and the Permissive Society: British Cinema and Theatre, 1955–1965* (Oxford, 1995).

4   Lindsay Anderson, 'Sport, life and art', *Films and Filming*, vol. 9, no. 5, February 1963, p 16. Further background on the film's production is recounted in Anne Francis, *Julian Wintle: A Memoir by Anne Francis* (London, 1986), pp 65–70, Tom Milne, 'This Sporting Life', *Sight and Sound*, vol. 31, no. 3, Summer 1962, pp 113–15, Alexander Walker, *Hollywood, England* (London, 1974), pp 170–7, Jonathan Hacker and David Price, *Take Ten: Contemporary Film Directors* (Oxford, 1991), pp 32–4, and Sussex, *Lindsay Anderson*, op. cit., pp 40–54. Useful and informative comparisons between Storey's novel and Anderson's film are found in Stuart Laing, *Representations of Working-Class Life 1957–1964* (Basingstoke, 1986), pp 135–8, and Marwick, *The Sixties*, op. cit., pp 140–2.

5   British Board of Film Censors file on *This Sporting Life*, reader's report, 4 August 1961.

6   The principal matters of concern over *Saturday Night and Sunday Morning* related to the promise of a successful abortion scene, occasional bits of 'violence', and the strong 'language' used throughout, all of which were eventually 'toned down' at the censors' instigation. But for precise details on the protracted negotiations conducted between the BBFC and Woodfall Films in regard to the film see Aldgate, *Censorship and the Permissive Society*, op. cit., pp 90–8.

7   BBFC file on *This Sporting Life*: reader's report, 4 August 1961. The comments that follow by Audrey Field are all taken from this report.

8   The second script-reader was Frank Crofts, whose brief additional notes and 'offensive' word counts of 7 August 1961 were appended to Audrey Field's report. The problems experienced by the new wave cinema over 'language', especially regarding the words 'bitch', 'whore' and 'bastard' in Neil Paterson's screenplay for *Room at the Top* and Alan Sillitoe's repeated attempts at using 'bogger' in his scripts for *Saturday Night and Sunday Morning* as well as *The Loneliness of the Long Distance Runner*, are considered in Aldgate, *Censorship and the Permissive Society*, op. cit., pp 44–50, 94–7, 99–104.

9   BBFC file on *This Sporting Life*: John Trevelyan to Julian Wintle, 10 August 1961. The remainder of Trevelyan's remarks also come from the same source.

10   Anderson, 'Sport, life and art', op. cit., p 16. The precise chronology of events around here is difficult to determine with absolute accuracy at the moment. Since Harris began the filming of *Mutiny on the Bounty* in Hollywood on 15 October 1961, prior to location shooting in Tahiti, and Anderson was rehearsing a stage production of Max Frisch's *The Fire Raisers* which was destined to open at the Royal Court Theatre, London, on 21 December 1961, one might surmise their meeting took place some time in late December 1961 or early January 1962. There is little to be gleaned, however, from the somewhat impressionistic and sketchy biographical account provided by Robert Hale, *Richard Harris: Actor by Accident* (London, 1990), pp 67–81, though one hopes for much better-informed detail and substance from the forthcoming collection of Anderson's correspondence being edited by Tom Sutcliffe.

11   David Storey's second screenplay for *This Sporting Life* is held at the British Film Institute Library, London (S272). Albeit undated, careful scrutiny of the internal evidence revealed during the course of the script by way of amendments, and additional comparison with both the novel and completed film, strongly suggests that it formed an obvious bridge between the first and final drafts of Storey's screenplay. The BFI Library also holds the post-production script for the film (S14134).

12   Quoted in Walker, *Hollywood, England*, op. cit., p 173, in which see also both Anderson's and Walker's comments on the debate about what the film was reputed to owe by way of influence to the then contemporary French *nouvelle vague* cinema and the films of Alain Resnais, in particular. Anderson rejected the charge that it was derivative, claiming the structure was 'explicit in the script almost from the first, because its interweaving of past and present was based on the first quarter of the book'. Whereas Walker argued that 'the boldness of the subjective editing' showed, if nothing else, 'Anderson's indebtedness to Resnais'. This question is further and extensively explored by Hedling, *Lindsay Anderson*, op. cit., pp 54–5, where he makes the important point, quite justifiably, that 'one does not need to go to France to find intertextual sources for *This Sporting Life*' and that there are enough 'possible connections between "old" and "new" British cinema' to prevent any resort to such. 'The theatrical space, as well as the flashback pattern in *This Sporting Life* can obviously be seen in relation to similar aesthetic structures in *Kind Hearts and Coronets*', Hedling counters, and 'Other relevant films would certainly be Noel Coward and David Lean's *In Which We Serve* or Lean's *Brief Encounter*, where Griersonian "realism" was combined with intricate flashback patterns, devices which recur in *This Sporting Life*, although in modified and more radical shapes'.

13   Production still did not progress smoothly, however, as all sources testify. Anderson's inexperience at working on feature films, like Storey's, must have accounted for some of the problems which ensued. But clearly Richard Harris proved 'as obstinate as Anderson', according to Anne Francis, 'in clinging to his own viewpoints'. 'Delays and interruptions were expensive, and nerve racking,' she continues. 'Finally, Lindsay began rehearsing prior to shooting, taking the artists through their scenes in continuity, and thus helping them to seal themselves into their characters. The method worked.' See Francis, *Julian Wintle*, op. cit., pp 66–7. Walker also records that Anderson 'fell back on traditional theatre methods of rehearsing them prior to shooting' to get the actors on track

again (Walker, *Hollywood, England,* op. cit., p 174). Given Anderson's evident if understandable resort to his predominantly theatrical background for inspiration and, there again, the repeated emphasis in his writings and interviews that 'From the start, the film was essentially a collaborative affair' (Anderson, 'Sport, life and art', op. cit., p 16), it is little wonder that Anderson, as with Tony Richardson, attracted critical opprobrium, then and later, for his seeming lack of genuinely auteurist credentials. Hedling does much to rectify this situation, though noticeably even the most recent and trenchant of critics on British new wave cinema, Peter Wollen, grudgingly concedes that 'A good case can be made for Lindsay Anderson as a bilious but authentic *auteur*' ('The Last New Wave: Modernism in British Films of the Thatcher Era' in Lester Friedman (ed.), *British Cinema and Thatcherism: Fires Were Started* (London, 1993), p 37). Further rebuttal of the charges usually made against British new wave cinema, generally, can be found in my chapter, 'New Waves, Old Ways and the Censors' in Aldgate and Richards, *Best of British,* op. cit., pp 184–200.

14   BBFC file on *This Sporting Life*: typewritten summary of action taken on 11 January 1963 and 14 January 1963. Arthur Marwick notes, justifiably, that 'Still the amount of male flesh on view was something of an innovation for the time – and something probably only Lindsay Anderson of film directors of the time would have particularly wished to show' (in *The Sixties,* op. cit., p 142). While Stephen Bourne elaborates at length about the changing-room scene at the beginning of the film which, he believes, 'displays a homoeroticism rarely seen in a British film', as well as the subsequent scenes of rugby players in the baths. 'For the gay spectator it is a pleasurable, and sexually exciting experience,' Bourne maintains. 'It is a vision of masculinity and male camaraderie which is overtly sexual, but it is hardly surprising that most writers who have acknowledged and praised this film classic have avoided, or missed, its overtly homoerotic content.' His reading of the characters of Johnson (played by William Hartnell) and Weaver (by Alan Badel), is also perceptive and astute: see Stephen Bourne, *Brief Encounters: Lesbians and Gays in British Cinema 1930–1971* (London, 1996), pp 175–7.

Yet Bourne's overall assessment of the film's homoerotic import – 'There is nothing being hidden here' – clearly underestimates the significance of the BBFC's impact in that regard. More of what both Anderson and Storey originally intended would undoubtedly have been made graphically explicit were it not for the interjection of the censors. But then BBFC intervention, like the critics' guarded response to homoeroticism in their review columns, was merely another sign of the times. Anderson suffered similar censorship cuts over shots of male genital areas in *If...* (1967) though, after much debate and wrangling with the BBFC, Ken Russell was finally allowed full-frontal views for the wrestling scene between Alan Bates and Oliver Reed in *Women in Love* (1969).

15   Walker, *Hollywood, England,* op. cit., pp176–7. Though favourably received at the time of release by some notable critics, the film was neither a widespread nor commercial success (for which see the microfiche of reviews held at the British Film Institute Library, London). Rachel Roberts won the 1963 British Academy Award for Best British Actress, Richard Harris was named Best Actor at the Cannes Film Festival and Lindsay Anderson received the International Critics' Prize. But *Kinematograph Weekly* perhaps best summed up its box office

potential in the following downbeat terms: 'Down-to-earth North Country romantic melodrama concerning a tough coal miner who becomes a professional rugger star, falls for a disillusioned widow, but fails to find mental comfort. Flashback presentation disconcerting but central characters clearly outlined, sex interest frank, ending touching and backgrounds kaleidoscopic' (vol. 548, no. 2887, 31 January 1963, p 11). At fully 134 minutes long, moreover, it probably proved too rigorous and daunting a proposition for many cinemagoers.

3 *The Avengers*

Television and Popular Culture During the 'High Sixties'

James Chapman

The Avengers both defines and is defined by the 1960s. It is defined by the 1960s in the sense that the original transmission of the series on British television spanned almost the whole decade, beginning in January 1961 and ending six seasons and 161 episodes later in mid-1969.[1] And it defines the 1960s through the various ways in which it illustrates, on several different levels, the processes of change that were on-going throughout the decade. On one level it exemplifies the technological changes that occurred in the television industry, moving from 'live' performance to film and from black-and-white to colour. On another level it exemplifies stylistic changes that occurred in a certain genre of popular television, the crime thriller series, from a low-key, realist mode of representation to a much more flamboyant, colourful and fantastic style strongly influenced by the pop art and fashions of the time. And, on yet another level, it provides a 'window' on the sixties by reflecting, or rather by mediating, the social changes that were taking place in Britain during the period which Arthur Marwick has termed the 'High Sixties'. Another reason for choosing *The Avengers* as a text (or, rather, a set of texts) is that it provides a highly prominent example of a 'cult' – a popular cultural form which maintains a large and devoted fan following many years later. The enduring appeal of *The Avengers* – illustrated by the fan clubs devoted to the series, by its re-runs on television and its release on video cassette, and by the big-budget cinema film based on the series released in 1998 – is a

phenomenon of some significance, suggesting that it deserves to be regarded as
one of those aspects of sixties popular culture which have, in retrospect, come
to define how the decade is remembered. Yet the popular impression of *The
Avengers* as a slick, witty and sophisticated entertainment rests principally on the
series as it developed after 1965, when it abandoned any pretence of realism or
seriousness and moved decisively in the direction of fantasy and tongue-in-
cheek humour. For this reason, although the origins of the series are to be found
in the period which saw the 'First Stirrings of a Cultural Revolution', it is as a
product of the 'High Sixties' that *The Avengers* is most celebrated. The aim of
this chapter is to discuss *The Avengers* both as text and in context by relating it
to developments in British society and culture during the 1960s. I will explore
the origins and production history of the series and discuss its contemporary
reception. Through the analysis of production discourses and narrative codes, I
will examine the ideologies underlying *The Avengers*, focusing on its construction
of 'Englishness' and its representation of women. Finally, I will conclude by
arguing that the stylistic features of *The Avengers* are such that it can be claimed
as the first genuinely postmodern television series.[2]

PRODUCTION HISTORY

The Avengers underwent various changes in production personnel and principal
cast during its long run, though the character of John Steed, played by British
actor Patrick Macnee, featured throughout the series. That the content and style
of the series changed so markedly during its run was due to a wide array of
industrial and cultural determinants. That the series proved enormously successful – it has been estimated that at the height of its popularity in the late
1960s *The Avengers* had a worldwide audience of over 30 million viewers in 70
different countries[3] – was due to the various formulae and strategies that it
adopted for responding to those determinants.

     As with any popular cultural text, *The Avengers* was the product of a parti-
cular set of conditions and circumstances. It emerged at a key moment in the
history of British broadcasting when television was expanding rapidly following
the launch of the independent television network (ITV) in 1955. The number of
combined television and radio licences issued had more than doubled in the
space of five years, rising from 4,503,766 in 1955 to 10,469,753 in 1960.[4]
Moreover, it was ITV which during these years had maintained a lead of roughly
two-to-one over the BBC in its share of audiences' viewing time. Indeed, *The
Avengers*, which was produced by the ITV company ABC (Associated British
Corporation), was seen by some senior BBC executives as symptomatic of the
low-brow and vulgar populism which they associated with the commercial
channel and which brought about competition between the networks – competition
which at this time the BBC did not relish. 'So long as a young cock can crow
from the malodorous farmyard of a series known as *The Avengers*, so long will

civilised relations be difficult,' lamented Kenneth Adam, the BBC's Controller of Television Programmes, in 1963.[5]

More specifically, *The Avengers* was originally planned as a successor to another ABC crime series, *Police Surgeon*, which had run for 13 half-hour episodes in the autumn of 1960. *Police Surgeon*, which can now be seen as a precursor of the successful medical examiner/detective genre of the 1990s such as *Dangerfield* and *Silent Witness*, had starred the twenty-nine-year-old Ian Hendry and, while the series itself had been only moderately successful, Hendry's character Dr Geoffrey Brent had attracted considerable fan mail. *The Avengers* was originally to have been a direct follow-up to *Police Surgeon*, though by November 1960 Leonard White, who had produced *Police Surgeon* and went on to be the first producer of *The Avengers*, had issued a memorandum to the effect that '[a] new name is being found for Hendry's character' and that '*The Avengers* will now have absolutely nothing to do with Police Surgeon'.[6] *The Avengers* would also differ from its predecessor in opting for the longer 50-minute episodes (an hour including commercial breaks) that many American series had been following since the late 1950s but which was still relatively rare in British television. Hendry's character in *The Avengers* became Dr David Keel, a GP whose fiancée is killed by drug dealers at the beginning of the first episode ('Hot Snow', 7 January 1961) when a package of heroin is delivered to his surgery by mistake. Keel sets out for revenge, and as he tracks down the gang

The original *Avengers*: John Steed (Patrick Macnee, left) and Dr David Keel (Ian Hendry) take to the streets of London to fight crime.

responsible he makes the acquaintance of John Steed, a shadowy secret agent figure. The leader of the drug gang escapes at the end of the first episode but is caught in the second ('Brought To Book', 14 January 1961). Having avenged his fiancée's death, Keel agrees to team up with Steed in the fight against organised crime.

At the outset, therefore, *The Avengers* was conceived within the discourse of psychological realism that informed most contemporary television drama. It set up a motivation for the hero-figure of Keel, described by Hendry as 'a most attractive character [who] combines toughness with compassion and serves as the conscience of the team'.[7] Steed, in contrast, was portrayed as a more cynical figure for whom the most obvious influence was James Bond, the tough secret agent created by Ian Fleming in a series of snobbery-with-violence thrillers that were increasing in popularity in the late 1950s and early 1960s and which would soon be adapted for the cinema. However, whereas Bond travelled to exotic foreign locations in his pursuit of international super-criminals such as Dr No and *Goldfinger*, *The Avengers* was concerned mainly with home-grown criminals whose ambitions (at least to begin with) were somewhat less grandiose. Nevertheless, *The Avengers* did have more in common with the secret agent lineage of the thriller genre than it did with the more familiar police or detective series, represented at this time on British television by *Dixon of Dock Green* and, from 1962, by *Z Cars*. This much was recognised by producer White, who explained how *The Avengers* differed from other crime series:

> Keel and Steed are essentially undercover. They are not private or public detectives and any story which follows the usual 'private eye' pattern is not right for us. They do not work with the police and usually cannot call upon more police aid than would normally be available to ordinary citizens.[8]

The nearest television equivalent to *The Avengers* when it began was *Danger Man*, starring Patrick McGoohan as secret agent John Drake, which ran between 1960 and 1966.

For a series that came to be regarded as so quintessentially English, *The Avengers* had from the beginning a production team with an international flavour. In this sense it might be seen as an example of the 'international cultural exchange' which Arthur Marwick identifies as one of the characteristic features of the 1960s. Sydney Newman, the Head of Drama at ABC who was involved in the genesis of *The Avengers*, was a Canadian who had worked with John Grierson at the National Film Board of Canada during the war and subsequently at the Canadian Broadcasting Corporation before coming to Britain in the late 1950s, where he made his mark as supervising producer of ABC's *Armchair Theatre*. Patrick Macnee had spent most of the 1950s in Hollywood, New York and Toronto as a jobbing actor on stage, radio and live television, and had recently turned his hand to producing with *The Valiant Years*, a television documentary about Winston Churchill. Brian Clemens, a long-term writer on the show, had experience of writing for American television, as did Roger Marshall, who joined the production team from the second season. 'Far from being rustic,' observes Toby Miller, '*The Avengers* was a landmark in the cultural division of labour'.[9]

Unfortunately, few episodes from the first season of *The Avengers* have survived the junking process that short-sighted economies in the television industry inflicted on much of its output from this period (the BBC's *Doctor Who*, which began in 1963, was another casualty of this process). The earliest surviving episode of *The Avengers*, 'The Frighteners' (27 May 1961), offers a tantalising glimpse into the content and style of the first season and suggests that, at least to begin with, the series was a low-key crime drama which bore little relation to the fantasy and stylistic excess that was to follow in later years. Written by Berkeley Mather, co-scenarist of the first James Bond film, *Dr No*, and directed by former juvenile actor Peter Hammond, 'The Frighteners' concerns Steed and Keel's investigation of an extortion racket run by a criminal boss known as 'The Deacon'. It is essentially a thick-ear melodrama, featuring seedy underworld locations and villains with a nice line in slang dialogue ('I'm out on ticket, see? One lumber on me present form an' I'll be eatin' porridge till it's comin' out of me flippin' ears'). Still at an early stage of the series' generic development, the episode is concerned to remind viewers that Keel and Steed are not official detectives. This is made clear in a scene where they have an injured man to deal with, the dialogue also serving as a reminder (whether intentional or not is impossible to say) of Hendry's previous television role:

> *Steed*: Doctor, we'll take him to your surgery.
> *Keel*: What for?
> *Steed*: It's quieter there.
> *Keel*: Well I'd like to keep it that way.
> *Steed*: That's precisely my point. This is a private patient – that's why I brought you along. Give the police surgeon the night off, follow me?

Thus *The Avengers* asserted its difference from the officially legitimated world of the more familiar crime and police drama, including the series that had been its own predecessor.

The Keel-Steed pairing lasted for only the first 26 episodes of *The Avengers*, until a strike over pay by the actors' union Equity brought a temporary halt to the series. Hendry had already decided to leave the show to pursue his film career (though he did return to play a different character in an episode of *The New Avengers* in 1976). Macnee's Steed was promoted from co-star to starring role from the beginning of the second season. It was intended that Steed should have a variety of different partners, but although Dr Martin King (Jon Rollason) appeared in three episodes and nightclub singer Venus Smith (Julie Stevens) in six, it was Honor Blackman's Cathy Gale, a young widow with a black belt in judo and a penchant for leather clothes, who made the most dramatic impact and who became Steed's regular partner for most of the second season and all of the third. In the first instance of the series' concern with contemporary fashions, costume designer Michael Whittaker received a screen credit for the 'Special Wardrobe for Miss Blackman'.

As with so many 'cult' series, it took some time for *The Avengers* to establish itself. It was in the autumn of 1963 that its popularity with British audiences really took off. As Christopher Booker observed in his book *The Neophiliacs*:

> A new craze took over the nation's Saturday nights, on the commercial channel
> – a black and violent thriller series, *The Avengers*, starring a bowler-hatted Old
> Etonian actor Patrick Macnee and Miss Honor Blackman as a pair of mysterious
> secret agents. The show aroused particular excitement through Miss Blackman's
> 'kinky' black leather costumes. And indeed the London-centred craze for 'kinky'
> black boots, 'kinky' black raincoats and 'kinky' black leather or plastic garments
> of all kinds raged throughout the autumn.[10]

As this quotation shows, *The Avengers* had by now become something more than just a television series: it was a phenomenon which permeated the wider realms of popular culture more generally. When Honor Blackman's wardrobe for the third season was previewed at Les Ambassadeurs Club in October 1963, it was a sign of the influence that costume design in *The Avengers* had on contemporary fashion. The pop single 'Kinky Boots' recorded by Macnee and Blackman was a rather more esoteric example of the cultural ephemera to which the series gave rise.[11]

As for the content of the series itself, for most of the Macnee-Blackman period *The Avengers* adhered to the sort of cloak-and-dagger storylines that were familiar from series like *Danger Man*, featuring such standard plot devices as the unmasking of a hired killer ('Mr Teddy Bear', 29 September 1962), armaments smuggling ('Bullseye', 20 October 1962), the murder of a diplomatic courier ('Death Dispatch', 22 December 1962) and the infiltration of an international crime syndicate ('Intercrime', 5 January 1963). During the third season, however, the first signs of a trend towards the sensational and fantastic became evident and the plots began 'leaving the ground a bit', as Honor Blackman later put it.[12] In 'November Five' (2 November 1963), for example, Steed and Cathy uncover a plot to destroy the Houses of Parliament with a nuclear warhead, while in 'The Grandeur That Was Rome' (30 November 1963) they come across a megalomaniac who plans to decimate the world's population with bubonic plague and establish a new Roman Empire. The reason for this change of direction for the series was almost certainly the influence of the first James Bond film, *Dr No*, released in October 1962. Hugely successful both in Britain and abroad, *Dr No* and its successors initiated a trend towards gimmicky spy thrillers that became one of the staple cinematic genres of the mid-1960s.[13]

By the end of the third season in 1964 *The Avengers* was on the verge of a major technological change. Hitherto the series had been recorded on videotape, which was limiting technically in that it could not be edited and so the performance had to be done 'live' (albeit not live in the sense of being broadcast simultaneously to viewers), with only a handful of exterior scenes shot on film. These technical limitations were overcome by the use of interior sets, close shots and an innovative visual style which used low-key lighting and expressionist angles to create a slightly unreal world that was markedly different from the near-documentary style of series like *Z Cars*. The 'house style' of *The Avengers* is generally attributed to designers such as Peter Dowling and Robert Fuest and to directors such as Jonathan Alwyn, Bill Bain, Peter Hammond, Don Leaver and Kim Mills. 'If we were shooting in a bank,' Brian Clemens later recalled, a director 'would just have a grille and some money and shoot through it - and that was the bank'.[14] For the fourth season, however, *The Avengers* moved onto film, which was more expensive but which allowed greater scope for location filming, exterior sequences and more elaborate sets. The reason for the change was due in large measure to the desire to sell the series in America, which duly happened when the ABC network (American Broadcasting Company) bought the US broadcast rights.

The move to film necessitated a change in the series' production base and personnel. If there was one moment at which *The Avengers* can be said to have changed decisively, then this was it. The production base of *The Avengers* moved to Elstree Studios, with Julian Wintle, a former film editor turned producer who had co-founded Independent Artists in 1958 and whose credits included *Tiger Bay* (1959) and *This Sporting Life* (1963), brought in to act as supervising producer. According to his widow, Wintle was chosen to produce the series because Howard Thomas, the Managing Director of ABC, 'had been impressed by his editing flair, post-production touches, and his reputation for turning out good films on a commercial basis'.[15] Wintle recruited a team of people who had worked in the film industry, including Albert Fennell, who had produced the horror film *The Night of the Eagle* (1963) for Wintle and who became executive producer, and composer Laurie Johnson, who wrote a new theme tune for *The Avengers*. Experienced film directors were also brought in, including Roy Ward Baker, Charles Crichton, Robert Day, Sidney Hayers, James Hill and Leslie Norman. Brian Clemens was the one member of the existing *Avengers* production team whose role was significantly enhanced when he became associate producer and script editor.

The fourth season also introduced a new heroine. With Honor Blackman having left the series to play the part of Pussy Galore in the third Bond movie, *Goldfinger* (1964) – a role which owed much to her established persona as Cathy Gale – a new partner was introduced for Steed in the form of Mrs Emma Peel, played by a young RSC actress Diana Rigg. Mrs Peel was another young widow and part-time secret agent, her name being a pun on 'M-appeal', or 'man-appeal'. It was during the Macnee-Rigg years that *The Avengers* acquired the distinctive style for which it is best remembered. The series had now become a parody of the straight thriller, creating its own quaintly unrealistic world of amiable eccentrics and diabolical criminal masterminds. Its bizarre and fantastic plots represent in extreme form one of the underlying assumptions of the thriller genre: that chaos and anarchy may erupt at any moment from beneath the 'thin protection of civilisation'.[16] *The Avengers* is informed by the notion that invasion and subversion are ever-present threats: thus a London department store conceals a giant bomb ('Death at Bargain Prices', 23 October 1965), while a

Scottish loch hides a fleet of human torpedoes ('Castle De'ath', 30 October 1965). And nothing is ever quite as it seems, with deadly threats lurking behind innocuous facades: an up-market marriage bureau is the front for a murder organisation ('The Murder Market', 13 November 1965), a luxury hotel houses a concentration camp ('Room Without A View', 8 January 1966), and a dancing school turns out to be a means of assimilating foreign agents into the country ('Quick-Quick Slow Death', 5 February 1966). With plots such as these *The Avengers* would have seemed paranoid in the extreme, were in not for the fact that Steed and Mrs Peel sailed serenely through their adventures without ever giving the impression that they were taking things at all seriously.

The sale of the series to American network television meant that from its fifth season *The Avengers* was made in colour. Ironically, as colour was not introduced to British television until the end of the 1960s, British audiences who saw '*The Avengers* in color' (*sic*) did so at first in black and white. Albert Fennell and

Mrs Emma Peel (Diana Rigg) joins Steed, now with familiar bowler, in season four of *The Avengers*

Brian Clemens were now credited as producers, with Wintle as executive producer. The content of the fifth season episodes continued the tradition of bizarre and improbable secret agent stories, with science-fiction themes becoming more prominent. Thus the plot devices featured in season five included an invisible assassin ('The See-Through Man', 4 February 1967), the cloning of scientists ('Never, Never Say Die', 18 March 1967), mind-swapping ('Who's Who?', 6 May 1967), and miniaturisation ('Mission… Highly Improbable', 18 November 1967).

For the sixth and final season there were further changes in personnel. Wintle stepped down, though he was still credited as consultant to the series, with a former film production manager Gordon L.T. Scott taking over as executive producer. Clemens and Fennell, initially out of favour with ABC, who thought the series was becoming too fantastic, were reappointed as producers when the first episodes of the new season were not thought to be up to scratch, while Terry Nation, whose writing credits included *Doctor Who* and who was later to be associate producer of the Roger Moore-Tony Curtis action adventure series *The Persuaders!*, was brought in as script editor. There was also another new female

Tara King (Linda Thorson) and secret service chief 'Mother' (Patrick Newell)
join the cast for the sixth and final season of *The Avengers*

lead, with Diana Rigg having followed Honor Blackman into 'Bondage' to play the heroine of *On Her Majesty's Secret Service* (1969). Tara King, played by Linda Thorson, a young Canadian actress fresh out of drama school, was introduced as a trainee agent who became Steed's protégé. Another regular character was created in the person of 'Mother' (Patrick Newell), Steed and Tara's wheelchair-bound chief. Although, in hindsight, the sixth season contains some of the most inventive episodes of the entire *Avengers* run, and while it did well in Britain and Europe, audience ratings for the Macnee-Thorson episodes dropped in America after being networked at the same time as *Rowan and Martin's Laugh In*, and the series was cancelled.

THE AVENGERS AND THE CRITICS

The cultural status of any text is never inherently present in the text itself, but rather is something bestowed upon it by critics and intellectuals. Questions of cultural status, therefore, are determined by critical discourses, by prevailing attitudes towards 'high' and 'popular' culture and, as often as not, by middle-brow and entirely subjective views of what constitutes 'art' and 'quality'. When it comes to assessing the products of popular culture, especially, critics and other cultural commentators have generally been disinclined to consider them worthy of serious attention. *The Avengers* is no exception.

In a critical and intellectual climate that has traditionally privileged social realism – from the films of the documentary movement in the 1930s to the cinema of the British 'new wave' at the turn of the sixties and the BBC's cele-brated drama series *The Wednesday Play* (1964–70) – it is not at all surprising that *The Avengers* was not taken very seriously by many British critics. 'The *Avengers* is easily experienced and easily forgotten; plots may offer opportunities for reaching out and making contact, sentimentally or realistically, with the out-side world, but style forbids it,' wrote Francis Hope in the *New Statesman*.[17] Such a statement exemplifies perfectly the attitude of a middle-brow critic towards popular culture: it is insubstantial, transient, privileges style over content, and is not to be taken seriously because it refuses to engage with the 'real' world.

Most critics, to be fair, realised that *The Avengers* did not set out to take itself seriously, but even so there was a tendency to disparage it as being rather too silly for its own good. This attitude became particularly evident when the series moved onto film and its plots lost all semblance of reality. Maurice Wiggin, the television critic of the *Sunday Times*, complained that even in a secret agent series, which by its nature involved far-fetched plot devices, the conventions should be played straight. For this reason, he contended, *Danger Man* was to be preferred to *The Avengers*:

> I never subscribed to the modish cult of *The Avengers*, which always seemed just that bit dafter than even escapism demands, but I was a fond and foolish follower of *Danger Man* which was straightforward dream-fodder with its own

dreamy logic. I guess the key or governing law of escapist fantasy is simply this, that having tacitly agreed to connive at the preposterous basic improbability of the whole thing, thereafter we expect a fairly rigid scrupulousness in the little things. We accept unblinkingly that the incredible hero and his occupation exist; but the six-shooter must never fire seven.[18]

Wiggin was writing following the fourth season premiere 'The Town of No Return' (2 October 1965), which indicated the direction *The Avengers* was taking. Steed and Mrs Peel investigate the disappearance of four agents in the quiet Norfolk coastal village of Little Bazely-by-the-Sea and discover a secret base beneath a derelict Second World War airfield which hides the vanguard of an invasion force. The episode is replete with absurd touches: an immaculately attired agent arrives on the beach inside a giant plastic bubble that 'walks' over water, while Steed's gladstone bag improbably contains a tea service and cake stand ('No buffet car, I'm afraid we'll have to rough it'). 'The new Avengers is self-consciously several degrees more far-fetched than the old,' Wiggin remarked, and it was that very self-consciousness that he disliked. 'It began like slow-motion kid's stuff,' he went on, 'then one began to laugh at the patently false tension mechanisms being diligently and laboriously planted all over the place, then finally one grew bored with the whole absurd farrago'.

This is not to say there were no critics who liked *The Avengers*, but they still tended to regard it as nothing more than a popular entertainment that could not really be taken seriously. '*The Avengers* is urbane and amusing. It has very good jokes,' said Philip Purser. However, he thought it inferior to *Doctor Who* because there was no seriousness beneath the surface: 'But if it's in the business of engaging the imagination as well as flattering the intelligence, if it's trying to touch the nape of the neck as well as the funny bone, I'm afraid that it's outclassed by its BBC rival produced at a fraction of the cost'.[19] Once again, there is an assumption on the part of the critic that somehow the series should take itself more seriously than it did. Francis King, while an avowed fan of the series, echoed Wiggin's criticism that there were too many plot loopholes even for a fantasy storyline:

> *The Avengers*, an endless fairy-tale for adults, has always been one of my favourite programmes, but even a fairy-tale must have its internal logic and in "The Return of the Cybernauts" (robots guided to their victims by their cardiograms) it struck me that though the decoration was as excitingly baroque as ever and though Miss Rigg had seldom looked more charming, there was a certain carelessness in the assembly of the story.[20]

Critical responses to *The Avengers*, therefore, were mostly predicated on the notion that even in a non-realist genre there should be some internal logic that makes sense in its own terms: the plot loopholes must be filled in, the bizarre mysteries should be solved in rational terms, the inexplicable must be explained. However, *The Avengers* frequently did not offer the sort of explanations that critics wanted. Indeed, it leaves unanswered many of the basic questions that inform the secret agent thriller. It is remarkably free from political ideology: the identity of enemy powers is rarely revealed (though a few Cold War references are thrown in occasionally) and it is never revealed which government department Steed actually works for (there are nothing more than occasional references to 'the ministry'). The refusal of the series to offer such explanations surely accounts in some measure for the disparaging views of many contemporary critics.

Kingsley Amis was perhaps the first commentator to realise that the plot loopholes of *The Avengers* simply did not matter and that to berate the series because it did not exhibit the conventional terms of reference for a thriller narrative was to miss the point entirely:

> Whenever anyone sets about poisoning off most of the human race or blowing up London, Steed and Cathy are sure to turn up, often it seems by the merest chance. This on-the-spotness is often a snag in the thriller series; *The Avengers* cleverly turns it into a virtue, something to enjoy. At least two highbrow critics have shown themselves too dim to see this. 'Who actually employs Mrs Gale?' they ask triumphantly, as if they'd spotted some fatal flaw. But the whole point is that the question of employment doesn't arise. These are a pair of heroic free-lancers who knock off a couple of world-wide conspiracies in the intervals of choosing their spring wardrobes. All this is, so to speak, a wink at the audience, a joke shared with them... This kind of game is impossible unless the producers have confidence in their audience, who must have the mental agility to appreciate the odd satirical nudge while still believing in the story as a thriller.[21]

Amis, therefore, suggested a different way of appreciating *The Avengers* that was not determined by conventional notions of narrative logic. Unlike Maurice Wiggin, who believed that the conventions should be played straight in order to maintain a semblance of narrative logic, Amis believed that as the conventions themselves were absurd then it was a sign of a sophisticated production strategy that *The Avengers* could afford to have fun with them.[22]

In retrospective critical assessments of *The Avengers*, moreover, it has become the orthodoxy that the series should be seen as a parody. It is a sign of the changes in the critical and intellectual climate over the last 30 years that the very qualities disparaged by contemporaries are now celebrated by the retro-aficionados and fan culture who may not even have seen the series when it was first broadcast. Consider, for example, this eulogy penned to the series as an artefact of sixties popular culture by one recent commentator:

> For many people, *The Avengers* is the 60s – a glorious, camp and technicolour excess of 'swinging' styles and attitudes. The fictional central London, its streets paved with mad scientists, the car-chases through green-belt Hertfordshire, the eccentrics whose names reflect their obsessions and the comic-strip wit are all classic elements often cited by fans and critics as reasons for *The Avengers*' longevity. It's a suggestion that the 1960s was one long party to which everybody was invited, but that only those with the correct accent and manners could attend.[23]

Although highly impressionistic and offering little in the way of critical insight, the quotation does nevertheless illustrate how the series is now celebrated for its 'camp', 'excess' and 'comic-strip wit'. The enduring appeal of *The Avengers*, therefore, arises from what are now perceived as its quintessential sixties characteristics – ironically the same characteristics that in the 1960s had been used to disparage it.

THE AVENGERS AND THE CONSTRUCTION OF 'ENGLISHNESS'

For all that *The Avengers* became a parody of the thriller genre rather than a straight secret agent series, it still embodies a particular set of ideologies and values that are rich in historical and cultural meaning. The images of class and nation presented by the series are a case in point. Obviously *The Avengers* cannot be seen as a straightforward 'reflection' of British society in the 1960s, but social realism is not the only means of providing a 'window' on the sixties. Indeed, in certain circumstances there is as much to be gleaned by looking through the window of fantasy as through the lens of documentary realism. Analysis of the production discourses and narrative ideologies of *The Avengers* reveals a complicated and at times contradictory attitude towards the social and cultural changes of the 1960s.

National identity in *The Avengers* is defined as much by what it excludes as what it includes. In the first instance, it is an explicitly English rather than British identity in that the locations are resolutely English – and southern English at that. The industrial landscapes of the Midlands and North of England are entirely invisible in the series, which remains for the most part rooted in London and the Home Counties. The version of national identity presented in *The Avengers* is also notable for its exclusion of certain social and ethnic groups. Working-class characters appear rarely, black characters hardly at all. According to Brian Clemens, this was a deliberate production strategy:

> We admitted to only one class – and that was the upper. As a fantasy, we would not show a uniformed policeman or a coloured man… Had we introduced a coloured man or a policeman, we would have had the yardstick of social reality and that would have made the whole thing quite ridiculous. Alongside a bus queue of ordinary men-in-the-street, Steed would have become a caricature.[24]

While it is not strictly speaking true that *The Avengers* never featured uniformed policemen or black characters – in 'The Frighteners', for example, one of Steed's contacts had been a West Indian bus driver, who appeared on screen immediately after a policeman had passed by – it is nevertheless true that the desire to avoid the 'yardstick of social reality' underlay the production strategy of the series from 1965 onwards.

It is evident from what it excludes, therefore, that *The Avengers* offers a very partial and distorted image of national identity. The absence of anything remotely resembling real social problems serves to distance the series even further from the yardstick of social reality. Yet as an ideological and cultural construction of Englishness, *The Avengers* nevertheless serves its own particular purpose. *The*

Avengers is set not in the real England of the 1960s but in an imagined nation where the sun always shines and where social problems do not exist. 'It was a never-never world,' said Clemens. 'It's the England of "Is there honey still for tea?" that people imagine existed even if it didn't.'[25] *The Avengers* needs to be seen in the context of an idealised and romanticised image of Englishness that has a long cultural history: it is the England of Rupert Brooke, the England of the travel writer H.V. Morton, the England of Edward Elgar and Ralph Vaughan Williams, the England of the Ealing comedies. It is also the England of warm beer, cricket on the village green and spinsters cycling to church on a Sunday famously eulogised by John Major – except that someone may have been drowned in the beer ('A Surfeit of H_2O', 20 November 1965), the village is likely to be populated by murderous yokels ('Murdersville', 11 November 1967), the bicycling spinster is really an assassin in disguise ('The Girl from Auntie', 21 January 1966) and the church is sure to be haunted by a deadly poltergeist ('Thingumajig', 2 April 1969).

This is not to say, however, that the ideologies of *The Avengers* are entirely backward-looking. One of the defining characteristics of the series is that it presents two distinct faces of England. Images of heritage and tradition are contrasted with images of modernity and technological futurism. This was again part of a deliberate production strategy intended to promote the cultural export of a particular version of Englishness. The rationale for this was explained in publicity notes issued at the start of the fourth season in 1965:

> The new *Avengers* formula is set against a tongue-in-cheek panorama of the picture-postcard Britain illustrated in tourist brochures. Every aspect of British life as it is promoted overseas, from atom-stations, bio-chemical plants and modern industry on the one hand to fox-hunting, stately homes and Olde Englishe Inne [*sic*] on the other, is used as a good-humoured counterpoint to the tough and fast-moving adventures of two dedicated Secret Agents, who hide their iron fists beneath the velvet gloves of high living and luxurious sophistication.[26]

In the terms of the official publicity discourse, therefore, *The Avengers* combined images of England past with images of England present. The stately homes and sleepy villages represent what might be termed a heritage industry construction of Englishness, whereas the atomic power plants and laboratories represent the cutting edge of scientific progress at a time when the Prime Minister, Harold Wilson, was speaking of 'the white heat of science and technology'.

Yet this modern England is still essentially a class society. *The Avengers* presents an England in which class distinctions are rigidly observed and where little is permitted in the way of social mobility. When social mobility occurs it is invariably from the top down rather than from the bottom up. Thus an upper-class character such as Bertram Fortescue Wyndthrope-Smythe can choose to work as lowly chimney sweep Bert Smith ('From Venus With Love', 14 January 1967), but the reverse is quite unthinkable. When a pair of lower-class killers take over Steed and Emma's identities in 'Who's Who?', they give themselves away through their lack of social graces. Steed is shocked by their behaviour:

'The last of my '47 – and not even chilled!' he exclaims. 'My cigars! He's been smoking my cigars – and he's bitten the ends off! What sort of a fiend are we dealing with?'

The class values of *The Avengers* are evident in the characterisation of its principal hero figure. The series' own publicity material shows that the character of John Steed was conceived as a personification of traditional values:

> In his tastes and character he embodies tradition and the qualities that people overseas have come to associate with the British way of life – gracious living, a London house full of family heirlooms and handsome antiques, a cultivated appreciation of food, wine, horseflesh and pretty women, proficiency at ancient and gentlemanly sports such as fencing, archery and polo, exquisite tailoring, a high-handed way with underlings and an endearing eccentricity which manifests itself in such preferences as driving a vintage Bentley convertible and fighting with swordstick, rolled umbrella or any handy implement rather than the more obvious weapons such as guns.[27]

Steed is clearly an upper-class figure: cultured, well-tailored and a gentleman of independent means. His elegant good manners and dandified appearance signal his old-fashioned values and moneyed status. If his dress code marks him out as a member of the establishment – his ubiquitous bowler and umbrella recall the uniform of legions of civil servants and City bankers – it is worn with a much greater sense of fashion and style than would have been common (from the fifth season Macnee's suits were designed by Pierre Cardin). Steed – whose very name is redolent of solid, trustworthy British values – was characterised in a very different manner from the more down-to-earth heroes of police series like *Z Cars*. His spiritual predecessors are figures such as Dorothy L. Sayers's Lord Peter Wimsey and Margery Allingham's Albert Campion. 'Steed's interest in clothes is a significant irrelevance that links him with the senior detectives mentioned earlier,' wrote Kingsley Amis. 'He is right at the opposite end of the scale from the wretched Inspector Barlow, who has no life outside the Force at all unless the plot requires it.'[28]

The class politics of *The Avengers* are inscribed in an episode such as 'The Living Dead' (25 February 1967). Steed and Emma are called in to investigate the appearance of a ghost in a church near the estate of the Duke of Benedict. Steed's suspicions are aroused because the estate manager, Masgard, appears to have some sort of hold over the 16th Duke. It turns out that Masgard has built an underground city beneath the estate using slave labour and where an army awaits to take over the country after an atomic bomb has been dropped. A class reversal has taken place: on the surface Masgard is ostensibly a servant, but underground the 15th Duke – presumed dead in a mining accident – is held prisoner as a slave worker. The rumours of a ghost were started when the 15th Duke temporarily escaped to the surface, his deathly pallor after five years of living underground accounting for his 'ghostly' appearance. The episode may be interpreted as an allegory of a socialist revolution: the plebeian Masgard sets out to overthrow the class system and creates his own dictatorship of the proletariat.

The discourses of tradition and modernity are constantly in tension in *The Avengers*. 'Overwhelmingly,' Steve Chibnall remarks, '*The Avengers* is concerned with the policing of progress, the management of social change in an age of transition. The ideologies of conservation and futurism are constantly contrasted in the series.'[29] This is shown through the nature of the threats to civilisation, which often come from either extreme reactionaries (ex-military types or old school aristocrats with totalitarian ambitions) or extreme technocrats (mad scientists intent upon replacing the human race with machines). The reactionary threat is exemplified by episodes such as 'Esprit de Corps' (14 March 1964) in which an army general who believes himself to be a direct descendant of the Stuarts attempts to overthrow the monarchy, and 'A Touch of Brimstone' (19 February 1966) in which a modern-day version of the Hellfire Club plots to blow up the Cabinet. The technocratic threat is exemplified by episodes such as 'The Cybernauts' (16 October 1965) in which a crippled scientist plans to take over the world with an army of killer robots, and 'The House That Jack Built' (5 March 1966) in which Emma Peel is imprisoned inside a booby-trapped house designed by a dead automation expert who is exacting his revenge on her for having been made redundant by her father. The job of Steed and his partners – indeed the underlying narrative ideology of the series as a whole – is to defend civilisation (for which read English civilisation) against its lunatic extremes.

THE AVENGERS AND THE REPRESENTATION OF WOMEN

One of the claims frequently made for *The Avengers* is that it was the first television series to provide roles for women in which they were portrayed as being equal to men. The heroines of *The Avengers* were characterised as thoroughly modern, intelligent and independent young women who were more than capable of taking care of themselves. In particular, it has been claimed that Cathy Gale represented a 'feminist' heroine – not least by members of the production team. 'She was the first really emancipated feminist, and I'm quite proud that we did it first,' said Brian Clemens.[30] Even one recent academic commentator has described *The Avengers* as 'the first network show to present a feminist female lead'.[31]

As with its representation of class and nation, however, the representation of women in *The Avengers* is mediated and highly complex. To label Cathy Gale and Emma Peel feminists is problematic in that the term itself brings with it a whole cultural and intellectual baggage that has no place in the world of *The Avengers*. *The Avengers* heroines had little in common with the radical feminism of the late 1960s which urged women to throw away their bras and other traditional accoutrements of femininity. Nor did they have any problem with the institution of marriage which some radical feminists argued was simply a bourgeois tool for the oppression of women within patriarchy – both Cathy and Emma were widows, after all. The most appropriate terms to describe *The Avengers* heroines, rather, would be independent and liberated – which do not necessarily mean the same thing as feminist.

This is not to say, however, that the type of heroine represented in *The Avengers* was not at all new. *The Avengers* heroines can be related to a number of different discourses of femininity, though drawn from film rather than television. Firstly, the characters of Cathy Gale and Emma Peel belong to the same tradition of well-bred upper-middle class girls portrayed in British films by the likes of Madeleine Carroll and Margaret Lockwood. They are sophisticated, fashionable, witty, and above all modern; they have careers of their own, they do not need men to look after them, and while they may resort to domesticity in the end this is the result of a conscious choice rather than patriarchal oppression.[32] Secondly, *The Avengers* heroines have cultural forebears in the tradition of the serial-queen melodramas of the 1910s with their intrepid and adventurous outdoor heroines portrayed by the likes of Pearl White and Ruth Roland. They are healthy, robust, physical types who experience adventures outside the domestic sphere, routinely finding themselves imperilled by the devious schemes of diabolical criminal masterminds, and, in one of the more perverse conventions of the adventure serial, frequently ending up bound and gagged.[33] And thirdly, *The Avengers* heroines might be seen as precursors of the cinematic lineage of fighting women and martial arts heroines represented, variously, by Angela Mao Ying, Tamara Dobson, Pam Grier, Cynthia Rothrock and Michelle Yeoh, a lineage which has recently broken away from its origins in low-budget exploitation films to enter the mainstream of Hollywood action movies, where its principal representatives have been Sigourney Weaver in the *Alien* films and Linda Hamilton in *Terminator 2*.[34] If *The Avengers* heroines were not necessarily the first feminists on popular television, they were surely the first female martial artists.

The dominant discourse in the representation of women in *The Avengers* is that of modernity. This is evident from the statements of both critics and producers. One critic fondly recalled the moment 'when Honor Blackman strode in, all bosom and black leather, to herald the coming of the Swinging Dolly'.[35] Blackman, however, was already in her mid-thirties when she played Cathy Gale, and for all her kinky costumes the label 'swinging dolly' seems a little inappropriate for a character who was meant to be a serious-minded and intelligent woman of the world. The series' own publicity material declared that Cathy was 'way out front of the new international fashion in women who dress and fight like men as well as enjoying the more conventional privileges of emancipation'.[36] Blackman's leather fighting costumes were originally designed as a practical measure to allow her freedom of movement during the fight sequences, but they soon became one of the most commented-upon features of the show. The leather look undoubtedly added a fetishistic dimension to her screen persona which, combined with her character's habit of throwing men around the studio floor, was likened by some commentators to the female dominatrix of sadomasochistic fantasy.[37]

It was with the arrival of the younger Diana Rigg that *The Avengers* can be said to have acquired its first genuinely 'swinging' heroine. Emma Peel, while also an intelligent career woman, had a certain girlish exuberance that Cathy Gale did not. The official publicity discourse described her in terms which emphasised both her femininity and her modernity:

> Emma is a willowy, auburn-haired beauty with a sparkling wit who leads the streamlined life of an emancipated, jet-age woman, dressed in ultra-modern, man-tailored fashions which include black leather trouser-suits and boots, and tackles her opponents with a variety of spectacular fighting techniques from judo and karate to a straight left to the jaw.[38]

For her first season Rigg continued with the black leather look of her predecessor, but when the series went into colour and it was found that the costumes did not photograph as well, Emma's clothes changed in favour of brightly-coloured catsuits (known as 'Emmapeelers') and mini-skirts. The latter, of course, was undoubtedly the fashion symbol of the 1960s, in Arthur Marwick's words 'almost a logical response to sexual liberation and the new emphasis on the natural physical attributes of youth, including neat bottoms and slim legs'.[39] In wearing the mini-skirt, Emma Peel was situated at the vanguard of

In 'Murdersville' Emma finds herself in bondage – a recurrent motif in *The Avengers*

a fashion trend that was indelibly associated with youth and modern, liberated femininity.[40]

The last of *The Avengers* heroines, Linda Thorson's Tara King, marked something of a change of direction in that she was not the same cool, confident heroine as her predecessors but a bright-eyed *ingenue* who was training as a secret agent under Steed's tutelage. Tara was a single girl, and was meant to be less sexually experienced than Cathy and Emma, whose relationship with Steed had always contained a strong degree of knowing innuendo. Tara's fashions also changed, her long elegant dresses with plunging necklines and low backs suggesting a more traditional image of femininity than the leathers and jump-suits of her predecessors.

Just as the narrative ideologies of *The Avengers* offered a mediation between tradition and modernity in their representation of class and nation, so too the series adopted a middle ground in its attitude towards women's liberation. In 'Escape in Time' (28 January 1967), for example, a villain called Thyssen offers an escape route for criminals on the run via a time machine that transports them into the past. After paying a fortune, would-be time travellers have a choice between various periods, populated by Thyssen's own ancestors. Emma, posing as a criminal, chooses the Georgian period because it was a 'refined era' with

The kinkiness of *The Avengers* is illustrated in this scene from the notorious 'A Touch of Brimstone' where Emma plays the 'Queen of Sin'; Peter Wyngarde looks on.

'intelligent women', but she ends up in the Elizabethan period where she finds herself subject to an interrogation by the sadistic witch-hunter Matthew Thyssen. The dialogue between the puritan, misogynistic Thyssen and Emma provides a commentary on the changes that have occurred between the 1560s and the 1960s:

> *Thyssen*: These strange clothes you wear – the devil's work! Designed to daze and bewitch a man's senses! To inflame him to lust!
> *Emma*: You should see me four hundred years from now.
> *Thyssen*: You're a heretic, a bawd, a witch!
> *Emma*: I can think of some names to call you too – short, up-to-date, highly descriptive names.

It turns out that the 'time machine' is really a trick done with mirrors and sets, in which the would-be time travellers, after parting with their money, are killed by Thyssen himself in period costume. As Steed and Emma return to the 'present', Emma, still in Georgian dress, discovers a woman handcuffed to a pillar (a villainess left there by Steed) and quips: 'Didn't we get the vote?' The episode is unequivocal that change has taken place for women, and for the better.

At the same time, however, *The Avengers* distances itself from the more extreme manifestations of feminism. 'How to Succeed... at Murder' (19 March 1966) exhibits what can only be termed an acute paranoia about female empowerment. A number of businessmen are murdered; the only connection between them is that they employed secretaries from the same agency. It turns out that the secretaries are murdering their male employers in order to gain career advancement and wealth, taking over the businesses concerned because they had introduced filing systems so complex that no-one else could understand them. The conspiracy is masterminded by Henrietta Throgbottom, who in the sort of bizarre twist that only *The Avengers* can pull off successfully is a ventriloquist's dummy. Emma is put through an initiation ritual:

> *Henrietta*: I understand you want to become your own boss.
> *Emma*: Yes.
> *Henrietta*: Why?
> *Emma*: Well, I...
> *Henrietta*: Because you have been subjugated to man too long? Always at his beck and call? Commanded, used, abused, always the slave, never the master. That is the function of this organisation, Mrs Peel. To take woman out of the secretary's chair and put her behind the executive desk. To bring men to heel and put women at the pinnacle of power.
> *Emma*: Twentieth-century Amazons.
> *Henrietta*: Exactly. Do you still wish to support our organisation?
> *Emma*: Yes.
> *Henrietta*: Whatever it may entail?
> *Emma*: Whatever.
> *Henrietta*: Then raise your hand and swear. Ruination to all men!
> *Emma*: Ruination to all men!

While this sounds like a paranoid case of radical feminism taken to extremes, it turns out that Henrietta's voice is actually provided by her meek, put-upon husband Henry, the real Henrietta having been dead for many years. The irony of this is not lost on Steed: 'No man will ever dominate you? You've been taking orders from a man all the time! You've been fooled by a very brilliant ventriloquist.' The episode therefore neuters female empowerment by suggesting that even the 'twentieth-century Amazons' are in fact subject to male control.

Ultimately, *The Avengers* offers a contradictory image of modern womanhood that both celebrates female empowerment and yet at the same time attempts to establish control mechanisms whereby women can be kept in their place. On the one hand, Thomas Andrae asserts that '*The Avengers* refunctioned the patriarchal discourse of the spy genre, transforming woman from an object of male desire into a subject who possessed "masculine" power and independence'.[41] To some extent this is true, in so far as *The Avengers* heroines are shown to be physically and intellectually equal to men. Not only can they fight, but Cathy has a PhD in anthropology while Emma publishes articles in scientific journals. But on the other hand, *The Avengers* heroines do still function as the fetishised objects of the male gaze that feminist theorists have argued determines the nature of gender representation in the visual media.[42] This is no more evident than in the heavily coded motifs of bondage that see Emma Peel tied to the railway tracks, trussed up in a dentist's chair, shackled in the stocks, bound to a ducking stool or heading horizontally for the buzz-saw. As Diana Rigg herself observed, there was something 'subliminally very kinky' about *The Avengers*.[43]

The kinkiness of *The Avengers* – as well as the contradictions in its representation of women – is illustrated most explicitly in the notorious 'A Touch of Brimstone' when Emma Peel appears as the 'Queen of Sin' at an orgy held by the debauched Hellfire Club. Rigg is dressed in a dominatrix costume that refers explicitly to the subculture of British pornography: high-heeled leather boots, a tight black corset and a spiked collar, not to mention a snake wrapped around her arm. But although she is visually coded as a dominatrix, the leader of the club tells his men to 'do with her as you will' and she is carried off, presumably to be used as a 'vassal of pleasure' that is the role assigned to women by the club's leader, John Cartney. Quite how she escapes this fate is never explained, for Emma is next seen in the basement fighting one man and then being whipped by Cartney before he falls to his death in the sewers. Emma is therefore made to play the roles of both dominatrix and victimised woman: *The Avengers* heroine embodies aspects of both dominant and passive femininity, a characteristic that runs throughout the series and represents its strategy for coming to terms with the rise of the women's movement.[44]

THE AVENGERS AS A POSTMODERN TEXT

Postmodernism has become such an overused term in cultural studies that there is a danger of almost any artefact of popular culture being labelled 'postmodern' by some commentator or other. This is not to say that the term has no use, but it does mean that it must be used with some care and precision. The main problem with the concept of postmodernism is that it can mean so many different things to so many different people. Postmodernism (along with its corollaries 'post-modernity' and 'the postmodern') has been used to describe, variously, an aesthetic style, a philosophical idea, a historical condition, and an approach to cultural theory which derives from all of the above. The term itself entered into the discursive language of cultural criticism in the 1960s, when it was used to describe a condition in which traditional distinctions between 'high' and 'low' culture were becoming less meaningful, while a highly theorised dimension was grafted onto the notion in the 1970s and 1980s by the work of intellectuals such as Jean-François Lyotard and Jean Baudrillard. Given the multiplicity of meanings that have become attached to postmodernism, therefore, it is incumbent upon any writer, critic or historian to be absolutely precise in their terminology.

Obviously the different ways in which postmodernism has been concep-tualised are all interrelated. In suggesting that *The Avengers* is an example of a postmodern text – and, moreover, claiming that it was the first genuinely post-modern television series – I am drawing on the notion of postmodernism as an aesthetic style. Of course, the postmodern style cannot be divorced from other aspects of what, following Lyotard, has been referred to as the 'postmodern con-dition': the style is as much a product of the condition as the condition is an influence upon the style. For Lyotard, the postmodern condition is characterised by 'the obsolescence of the metanarrative of legitimation' in which totalising and overarching systems of philosophical thought are rejected in favour of a plurality of voices which insist upon cultural diversity and difference.[45] What this implies for cultural history and cultural studies is that the traditional distinction between elite or high culture on the one hand and popular or mass culture on the other hand (what might be referred to as the metanarrative of cultural value) is called into question.

The American critic Fredric Jameson laments the breakdown of cultural distinctions which postmodernism entails:

> This is perhaps the most distressing development of all from an academic stand-point, which has traditionally held a vested interest in preserving a realm of high or elite culture against the surrounding environment of philistinism, of schlock and kitsch, of TV series and *Reader's Digest* culture, and in transmitting difficult and complex skills of reading, listening and seeing to its initiates.[46]

Writing from a Marxist perspective, Jameson's work is reminiscent of the deni-gration of mass culture by the Frankfurt School in the 1940s, and exhibits a similar distaste for the products of that culture which he sees as trivial, commercialised, and pandering to the lowest common denominator in taste.

Television is perhaps the ultimate postmodern medium. It not only collapses distinctions between high and popular culture – Shakespearean or Dickensian adaptations might sit alongside popular genres such as police series and quiz shows – but it also exhibits the triviality that commentators such as Jameson lament in postmodern culture. Television represents the 'real' world through an endless flow of images which in themselves are depthless and banal. Jim Collins writes:

> Postmodernist eclecticism might only occasionally be a preconceived design choice in individual programmes, but it is built into the technologies of media sophisticated societies. Thus television, like the postmodern subject, must be conceived as a site – an intersection of multiple, conflicting cultural messages. Only by recognizing this interdependency of bricolage and eclecticism can we come to appreciate the profound changes in the relationship of reception and production in postmodern cultures.[47]

While television itself is a postmodern medium, individual programmes may also exhibit the stylistic features that have been identified as postmodern. *The Avengers* is one of those programmes where postmodernist eclecticism is 'a preconceived design choice'.

The notion that there was such a thing as a postmodern style emerged during the 1960s, developing from the earlier work of critics such as Lawrence Alloway and the British artist Richard Hamilton, who used the term 'pop art' to describe the new, mass-produced popular culture that had emerged since the mid-1950s. 'Pop' referred to stylistic developments in media such as films, television, advertising and popular music, and its principal actors were art students, youth subcultures, and a progressive middle class of designers, technicians and media people who injected a new energy and vitality into popular culture. Pop reacted against the prevailing middle-brow assumption that culture should have some social worth or purpose. In a widely-quoted manifesto of 1957, Richard Hamilton defined pop as 'popular, transient, expendable, low cost, mass produced, young (aimed at youth), witty, sexy, gimmicky, glamorous, big business'.[48] These were precisely the sort of characteristics that critics of the time disparaged in *The Avengers*.

The characteristics of pop have since been absorbed into the notion of postmodernism as an aesthetic style. As Andreas Huyssen observes: 'Pop in the broadest sense was the context in which a notion of the postmodern first took shape'.[49] Postmodern texts in the popular arts and mass media are characterised by pastiche, by irony, by the foregrounding of style over content and, perhaps above all, by a series of intertextual references and quotations from other media and cultural forms which is generally referred to as 'bricolage'.

So what are the stylistic features of *The Avengers* that identify it as a postmodern text? In the first instance, *The Avengers* is frequently a pastiche in that it imitates other cultural forms and practices. The difference between parody and pastiche, according to Jameson, is that whereas parody has an 'ulterior motive', pastiche simply involves imitation and mimicry for its own sake, thus becoming a 'blank parody' or 'empty copy' of the original.[50] When *The Avengers* imitates other cultural forms and practices, it does so for no higher purpose than that of an in-joke. For example, the climax of 'The Grave-Diggers' (9 October 1965) has Emma tied to the tracks of a miniature railway while Steed races to the rescue – a narrative situation based on the serial melodrama. The action is presented in such a way, moreover, as to draw attention to the fact that it is pastiching the world of the silent movie serials. Thus the soundtrack is taken over by the sort of tinny piano music that so often accompanied silent films, and the action is presented through the technique of speeded-up motion, of the sort which so often resulted from silent films being shown at the wrong projection speed. These devices are not narratively motivated, but rather exist as imitation for the sake of imitation – a characteristic postmodern strategy.

Many episodes of *The Avengers* borrow from and make reference to a wide range of other cultural forms and practices. This technique of citation and quotation (often referred to as 'troping') is another characteristic of postmodernism. It is evident not only through many of the episode titles which are derived from other television series and films – a feature borrowed two decades later by the American series *Moonlighting*, which offered a distinctly postmodern take on the traditional private-eye series – but also through the content of particular episodes which borrow narrative and plot devices wholesale. 'The Winged Avenger' (18 February 1967) borrows from both the comic-book and television series of *Batman*, the 'caped crusader' of Gotham City who fought larger-than-life villains in a world as stylised and unreal as that of *The Avengers*. The episode features a comic-strip writer who dresses up as his own creation to exact his revenge on the publishers who have made him redundant, while the climax refers explicitly to the *Batman* television series as Steed hits the villain with artwork panels marked 'Pow!', 'Splat!' and 'Bam!' and the music imitates the familiar Batman theme. 'Wish You Were Here' (12 February 1969) is clearly derived from another 'cult' television series of the mid-1960s, *The Prisoner*, in which an unnamed character played by Patrick McGoohan had found himself kidnapped and imprisoned in a picturesque but threatening seaside village. This situation is replayed in 'Wish You Were Here' as Tara goes to visit her uncle in a country hotel and finds him being held there against his will, and, moreover, is herself prevented from leaving.

As well as other television series, *The Avengers* also draws on a wide range of literary sources encompassing both canonical literature and pulp fiction. 'Too Many Christmas Trees' (25 December 1965) features a publisher so enamoured of Charles Dickens that each room in his mansion is a tableau representing one of Dickens's novels; 'Silent Dust' (1 January 1966) features a gamekeeper called Mellors; and 'Legacy of Death' (20 November 1968) refers explicitly to John Huston's 1941 film of Dashiell Hammett's *The Maltese Falcon*. Some of the sources are rather more obscure: 'Mandrake' (25 January 1964), in which the graveyard of a Cornish cemetery is impregnated with arsenic to disguise a series of murders, was apparently derived from a reference in a biography of pathologist Sidney Smith.[51]

The fact that *The Avengers* borrows from so many different sources does not in itself make it a postmodern text. What is postmodern, however, is the way in which *The Avengers* is so knowing and deliberate in its use of pastiche and its troping of other texts. The in-jokes and references are there for those in the audience who recognise them and are thus made complicit in the joke. Yet the intertextuality of *The Avengers* extends beyond its borrowing from other sources. When Honor Blackman left the series, for example, it contrived to include dialogue references to her imminent move into 'Bondage' to play Pussy Galore in *Goldfinger*. Blackman's last episode, 'Lobster Quadrille' (21 March 1964), ends with Cathy announcing that she is going on holiday to the Bahamas, whereupon Steed tries to persuade her to investigate a case that has arisen out there:

> *Steed*: As you're going to be out there anyway, pussy-footing along those sun-soaked shores...
> *Cathy*: Then I might as well do a little investigating?
> *Steed*: That's the idea. What do you say?
> *Cathy*: Goodbye, Steed... That's what I say. Goodbye.
> *Steed*: Oh, but that isn't asking too much.
> *Cathy*: Yes it is. You see, I shan't be pussy-footing along those sun-soaked beaches, I'll be lying on them.
> *Steed*: Not pussy-footing? I must have been misinformed.

In 'Too Many Christmas Trees', furthermore, Steed receives a postcard from Cathy. 'Mrs Gale! How nice of her to remember me,' he remarks. 'What can she be doing at Fort Knox?' (The climax of *Goldfinger*, of course, had been based around an attempt to destroy the US gold bullion depository at Fort Knox).

Pastiche and intertextuality are the key postmodern characteristics of *The Avengers*, but there are numerous others. Most obviously, *The Avengers* is a triumph of style over content. This becomes particularly evident in the fifth and sixth seasons, where the highly stylised sets and colourful costumes draw attention to themselves and distract attention from the blatant absurdities of the plots. 'Fog' (12 March 1969), for example, is set in a stylised and unrealistic London of dark alleyways and men in billowing black cloaks that refers explicitly back to the world of the Victorian penny-dreadful. Steed and Tara investigate a series of grisly murders apparently committed by the 'Gaslight Ghoul', a notorious killer from the 1890s who it seems has started his gruesome work again. The episode exhibits a typical postmodern strategy in that it raids history for the purposes of pastiche. The obvious point of reference is the mythology of Jack the Ripper, though in this case the victims are not East End prostitutes but delegates to an International Disarmament Conference. While there are a few asides at the expense of the tourist industry that has grown up in Britain around the myth of Jack the Ripper – Steed and Tara come across the Gaslight Ghoul Club who dress up as the ghoul in cloaks and false beards – the episode is more concerned with drawing attention to the artificiality of its own setting. When the villain traps Tara using a fog machine, it amounts to a tacit acknowledgement that this neo-Victorian London is all artifice, a London that owes as much to the iconography of magazines and films as to historical actuality.

Another of the postmodern characteristics displayed in *The Avengers* is the series' evident self-awareness of its own conventions. While most genres operate around an established set of conventions, postmodern texts frequently draw attention to their conventions by either foregrounding them or breaking them. At various moments *The Avengers* does both, such as in the episode 'Game' (2 October 1968), which would seem to have been informed by the then voguish structuralist analysis of narrative by scholars such as Umberto Eco. In his analysis of Ian Fleming's James Bond novels, Eco used the metaphor of a game of chess to identify the various moves and counter-moves which determined the narrative structure of the stories. 'The reader's pleasure,' Eco argued, 'consists of finding himself immersed in a game of which he knows the pieces and the rules – and perhaps the outcome – drawing pleasure simply from the minimal variations by which the victor realises his objective'.[52] In 'Game' the conventions of the secret agent thriller become quite literally a game, the game of 'Super Secret Agent' that the villain makes Steed play in order to rescue Tara, who is imprisoned in a giant hour-glass with sand running through it. The villain explains the nature of the game to Steed thus: 'It's not particularly complex, but it calls on all the qualities required of a secret agent – courage, strategy, a certain degree of animal cunning. And of course embodied in the game is that traditional element of all spy sagas, the damsel in distress.' Steed must pass a series of obstacles and tests which are presented as moves on a board ('You encounter fiendish Japanese wrestler', 'You must disconnect time bomb') and which represent parodies of various narrative conventions of the secret agent thriller, especially the James Bond films. However, Steed finally wins the game by breaking the rules: armed with a pistol containing only one live round, and faced with six assailants at six second intervals, he shoots at the hour glass to release Tara. 'Game' therefore parodies the whole secret agent genre by reducing it to the level of a game, but ends by breaking the rules of the genre – something that would be unthinkable in a straight secret agent story.

A number of postmodern strategies are employed in 'Epic' (14 April 1967), which gives the impression of having been conceived as an extended joke for film buffs. Emma is kidnapped by a mad film-maker, Z.Z. von Schnerk, who wants her to star in his film 'The Destruction of Emma Peel'. On one level the episode works as an in-joke in that the character of von Schnerk (bald, moustachioed, Germanic) is clearly modelled on Erich von Stroheim, while his fading stars Stewart Kirby and Damita Syn are equivalents of John Barrymore and Gloria Swanson. On another level the episode revolves around a series of conventions and expectations derived from the movie world that it gleefully spoofs and disrupts. Genre becomes a redundant concept as von Schnerk embarks on the film that he intends 'will be my ultimate masterpiece – a compendium of all my films'. Emma finds herself progressing through a variety of generic scenarios, from the costume epic to the western, but then breaks free from generic regimes and is pursued around the backlot by characters as diverse as a First World War German soldier, a Napoleonic hussar and an American Indian warrior. In this respect the episode anticipates the free-for-all endings of films such as *Casino Royale* and *Blazing Saddles* in which characters and character types from different film genres are brought together for the climactic fight sequences. Conventions are turned on their heads and expectations are continually reversed: when a man in police uniform arrives at the studio, he is really an out-of-work actor looking for a job ('We'll write him into the script, then write him out again – permanently,' von Schnerk decides). The postmodern strategies of 'Epic' are evident, furthermore, not only through the way in which it draws attention to the artifice of the movie world, but through the way in which it uses devices that break down the narrative and disrupt the diegetic world of the episode. Thus, an insert card lying on the studio floor and bearing the legend 'Meanwhile back at the ranch' heralds a cut to Steed at home in his apartment, while Emma, when captured and tied up by von Schnerk, roars like the MGM lion with a halo of stars appearing around her head. The episode ends with a spoof of the visual style of German Expressionist cinema, a torture chamber set with exaggerated angled walls and a descending pendulum. Emma is heading horizontally for the circular saw while von Schnerk plays a piano accompaniment. Meanwhile, Steed arrives at the studio and picks up a copy of the filmscript that has been left lying around. Thus armed with foreknowledge of the outcome he is able to circumvent the script and rescue Emma by posing as the dead actor playing the role of John Steed.

The Avengers as postmodern text: Emma heading for the buzz
saw while Steed grapples with a mad film-maker in 'Epic'

It has become fashionable to claim that certain American television series of the 1980s and 1990s, such as *Moonlighting*, *Miami Vice*, *Thirtysomething*, *Twin Peaks* and *The X Files*, represented a new postmodern trend in popular television. In his analysis of *Twin Peaks*, for example, Jim Collins points out that the series was 'aggressively eclectic' in its use of conventions from different genres – police procedural, Gothic horror, soap opera and science-fiction – and that its mixing of these diverse elements was 'reflective of changes in television entertainment and of viewer involvement in that entertainment'.[53] However, it is my contention that the textual features identified as postmodern in these series are all to be found in *The Avengers*, especially in its fifth and sixth seasons. *The Avengers* exhibits all the characteristics of a postmodern text: pastiche, irony, the foregrounding of style over narrative and the very knowing and deliberate playing with generic conventions. Moreover, there was no comparable example of a television series before *The Avengers* which exhibited all those characteristics so thoroughly and consistently. In this respect *The Avengers* was ahead of its time, a proto-postmodern series which anticipated the direction taken by American television some two decades later. For these reasons, *The Avengers* can legitimately be claimed to be the first postmodern television series.

ACKNOWLEDGEMENTS

My thanks to Thomas Ribbits for loaning me several key early episodes of *The Avengers*. Tony Aldgate and Matthew Hilton both made helpful comments on the first draft of this chapter. Where newspaper and magazine reviews are quoted without a page reference, the source is the BFI microfiche on *The Avengers*.

NOTES TO CHAPTER 3

1   As *The Avengers* was shown on the ITV network, the transmission dates often varied from one region to another. The dates given here, and in the main body of the text, refer to the ABC broadcast (covering the Midlands and the North of England), except for the sixth and final season, which refers to the Thames Television region (London):

Season one: 7 January–30 December 1961, comprising 26 monochrome videotaped episodes broadcast weekly until the ninth episode and thereafter in alternate weeks.

Season two: 29 September 1962–23 March 1963, 26 monochrome videotaped episodes broadcast weekly.

Season three: 28 September 1963–21 March 1964, 26 monochrome videotaped episodes broadcast weekly.

Season four: 2 October 1965–26 March 1966, 26 monochrome filmed episodes broadcast weekly.

Season five: 14 January–18 November 1967, 24 colour filmed episodes broadcast weekly, though off air between 6 May and 30 September.

Season six: 25 September 1968–21 May 1969 (ABC: 19 January–14 September 1969), 33 colour filmed episodes broadcast weekly.

Some sources suggest there were seven production seasons, dividing the first colour season into two blocks of sixteen and eight episodes, but although there was a short break in filming in April 1969 production on the series did not cease during this period.

2   There are any number of celebratory, fan-oriented books on *The Avengers*, including, but not limited to: Alain Carraze and Jean-Luc Putheaud, *The Avengers Companion* (London, 1997, Titan Books); Paul Cornell, Martin Day and Keith Topping, *The Avengers Dossier* (London, 1998, Virgin Books); Dave Rogers, *The Complete Avengers: Everything You Ever Wanted To Know About The Avengers and The New Avengers* (London, 1989, Boxtree); and Dave Rogers, *The Ultimate Avengers* (London, 1995, Boxtree). Rogers's books, especially *The Ultimate Avengers*, are a goldmine of information, reproducing a range of original documentation provided for the author by production personnel such as Brian Clemens. Patrick Macnee's own memories of the series are recalled in Patrick Macnee, with Dave Rogers, *The Avengers and Me* (London, 1997, Titan Books). See also the large number of articles in 'cult' television and science-fiction magazines, including: Neil Alsop, 'Leather to Lacey', *Primetime*, 9 (Winter 1984/85), pp 16–19; Dick Fiddy, 'In Surrey Green A Plant Is Eating People?', *Primetime*, 1 (July 1981), p 13; Paul Kerr, 'Watching the Detectives', *Primetime*, 1 (July 1981), pp 2–6; John Porter, '*The Avengers*', *Starburst*, 16/6 (February 1994), pp 38–42; Michael Richardson, 'Under the Influence of *The Avengers*' (two parts), *Primetime*, 15 (Autumn 1989), pp 7–13, and 16 (Winter 1990/91), pp 28–33.

In contrast, work of a more critical and scholarly nature has been less in evidence. One recent monograph by an American academic – Toby Miller, *The Avengers* (London, 1997, British Film Institute) – tries to bridge both the academic and the fan arenas insofar as its discussions of issues such as genre and 'the postmodern' sit alongside a credits section listing, in typical anorak fashion, the various different motor vehicles driven by characters in the series. While Miller offers some useful insights into the series, they are rarely followed through in any depth and the book as a whole is intellectually shallow and too often drifts into anecdote, for example in the conclusion of his chapter on sex (pp 90–1): 'During the course of my research for this project, I spent some moments in a Charing Cross phone box, in the way that rigorous [*sic*] fieldwork often requires. As I waited for my call to go through, I picked up a card left there advertising the opportunity to "Turn your TV Fantasy into Reality" by calling a Mayfair number. This message was bracketed by images of a man and a woman. The male figure was clearly Steed-like: the bowler, carnation and suit were present, and even the slightly quizzical stoop. I went back to where I was staying to process this excellent finding with friends. True validation of my *Avengers* study was assured, along with major sales. Perhaps I could even do a deal with the people in Mayfair to send out copies of the book as part of their service. Then my hosts pointed out that "TV" stands for more than "television"... Kinky, those English.' Quite.

The best academic analysis of the series – though written very much from an ideologically oriented cultural studies perspective rather than from a cultural history perspective – is to be found in David Buxton, *From The Avengers To Miami Vice: Form and Ideology in Television Series* (Manchester, 1990, Manchester University Press), pp 96–107. Buxton sees *The Avengers* as an exemplar of what he terms 'the pop series' – a category also including *Danger Man*, *The Prisoner* and *The Man From U.N.C.L.E.* – which was different from the more dominant 'human nature series', such as *Gunsmoke*, *Bonanza*, *The Untouchables*, *The Fugitive*, *Star Trek* and *The Invaders*. The 'human-nature series', therefore, encompasses different generic forms (western, thriller, science-fiction), whereas the 'pop series' tends to take the form of the spy/secret-agent genre. Buxton's book is useful in that he considers both American and British popular television and suggests various cross-currents between them.

3   Rogers, *The Ultimate Avengers*, p 159.

4   Asa Briggs, *The History of Broadcasting in the United Kingdom*, vol. V: *Competition 1955–1974* (Oxford, 1995, Oxford University Press), Appendix A, p 1005.

5   Quoted in Briggs, p 374.

6   Quoted in Rogers, *The Ultimate Avengers*, p 16.

7   *TV Times*, 10 March 1961, p 10.

8   Quoted in Rogers, *The Ultimate Avengers*, p 23.

9   Miller, *The Avengers*, p 16.

10   Christopher Booker, *The Neophiliacs: A Study of the Revolution in English Life in the Fifties and Sixties* (London, 1969, Collins), pp 204–5.

11   'Kinky Boots' was written by Herbert Kretzmer and Benny Lee, who had also written the Peter Sellers/Sophia Loren hit 'Goodness Gracious Me' (from 1960's *The Millionairess*). The single sank without trace when released by Decca in February 1964, though it was successfully resurrected years later, reaching number four in the British charts in December 1990 – an example of the retrospective 'cult' appeal of *The Avengers*.

12   Speaking on the Channel 4 documentary *Avenging The Avengers* (Screen First Productions, 1992).

13   I have discussed the place of the James Bond movies in the film culture of the time in my book *Licence To Thrill: A Cultural History of the James Bond Films* (London, 1999, I.B.Tauris).

14   Speaking on *Avenging The Avengers*.

15   Anne Francis, *Julian Wintle: A Memoir by Anne Francis* (London, 1986, Dukeswood), p 84.

16   The notion that chaos and anarchy never lurk far beneath the surface of civilisation informs much twentieth-century thriller literature. It is evident as early as John Buchan's *The Power House* (London, 1916, William Blackwood & Sons), wherein villain Andrew Lumley asks Edward Leithen: 'Did you ever reflect, Mr Leithen, how precarious is the tenure of the civilisation we boast about?' For a discussion of the literary thriller see: Michael Denning, *Cover Stories: Narrative and Ideology in the British Spy Thriller* (London, 1987, Routledge & Kegan Paul); Bruce Merry, *Anatomy of the Spy Thriller* (Dublin, 1977, Gill and Macmillan); and Jerry Palmer, *Thrillers: Genesis and Structure of a Popular Genre* (London: Edward Arnold, 1978).

17 'Thriller Plus', *New Statesman*, 31 January 1964.

18 *Sunday Times*, 3 October 1965.

19 *Sunday Telegraph*, 15 January 1967.

20 *Financial Times*, 23 September 1967.

21 *TV Times*, 9–15 February 1964, p 7.

22 Other critics, following Amis, were to recognise this: Henry Raynor (*The Times*, 28 September 1968) considered that the series 'demonstrates the ridiculousness of several popular literary and television conventions taken seriously by other programmes'.

23 Keith Topping, 'The Medium is the Message', in Cornell, Day and Topping, *The Avengers Dossier*, p 351.

24 Quoted in Rogers, *The Ultimate Avengers*, p 132.

25 Speaking on *Avenging The Avengers*.

26 BFI microfiche on *The Avengers*: notes entitled 'A History of *The Avengers*. With a Guide to the Characters of John Steed and Emma Peel', undated.

27 Ibid.

28 Kingsley Amis, *The James Bond Dossier* (London, 1966, Pan edn), pp 13–14. The first *Avengers Annual* (London, 1967, Souvenir Press) also describes Steed in terms which place him in a generic lineage of gentleman heroes, but representing the modern 1960s equivalent: 'He's Bulldog Drummond with a beat, a hip Richard Hannay, a Wimsey who's with it'.

29 Steve Chibnall, 'Avenging the past', *New Society*, 28 March 1985, p 477. Chibnall makes some highly pertinent observations in his short but altogether useful article, though his interpretation is based essentially on episodes from the fourth season which had been repeated on Channel 4 in 1984–5 and therefore does not take account of earlier episodes. For example, his remark that '[t]here are none of the petty back-street gangsters who have haunted the London police series of the seventies and eighties' would clearly not apply to an episode such as 'The Frighteners'.

30 Speaking on *Avenging The Avengers*.

31 Thomas Andrae, 'Television's First Feminist: *The Avengers* and Female Spectatorship', *Discourse: Theoretical Studies in Media and Culture*, 18/3 (Spring 1996), p 115.

32 For an informed discussion of the star personae of Carroll, Lockwood and others see Sue Harper, *Mad, Bad and Dangerous to Know: Women and British Cinema* (forthcoming from Cassell, London). I am indebted to Dr Harper for showing me several draft chapters of her book in advance of publication.

33 For a useful account of this phenomenon of early cinema, see Ben Singer, 'Female Power in the Serial-Queen Melodrama: The Etiology of an Anomaly', *Camera Obscura: A Journal of Feminism and Film Theory*, 22 (January 1990), pp 91–129.

34 For a discussion of the 'fighting woman' in contemporary action cinema, see Yvonne Tasker, *Spectacular Bodies: Gender, Genre and the Action Cinema* (London, 1993, Routledge).

35 *The Guardian*, 16 January 1967 (Stanley Reynolds).

36 BFI microfiche 'A History of *The Avengers*', undated.

37 Francis Hope (*New Statesman*, 31 January 1964), writing after the famous episode 'Mandrake' (25 January 1964), in which Blackman had accidentally

knocked out a stunt performer, made some interesting comparisons to the James Bond films, particularly in light of the recent announcement that Blackman was leaving *The Avengers* to play Pussy Galore in *Goldfinger*: 'Last Saturday's episode of *The Avengers* reinforced my suspicions that Honor Blackman is by no means the only Flemingesque prop in the show. Of course she has those important physical prerequisites (both of them); she swathes herself in the sort of tough hide that Bondish insensitivity demands a woman should have (we're not in the age of chivalry, after all); and she can look after herself, and the viewers' sado-masochistic fantasies, to the extent of throwing the wrestler Jackie Pallo into an open grave. There are moments when either the script or her delivery of it can't quite match up to appearances, and she becomes that all-time drag, a talking dumb blonde; but on not too delicate balance she is quite fit to play opposite – or under or, thanks to Judo, over – Sean Connery's leeringly nimble Bond.'

38 BFI microfiche on *The Avengers*: '*The Avengers*: Facts about the Programme and its Stars', undated.

39 Marwick, *The Sixties*, op. cit., p 466.

40 It is evident that the production team gave much thought to keeping up with, and if possible ahead of, the latest fashion trends. On the eve of the fourth season, for example, *Kinematograph Weekly* (2 September 1965, p 14) announced: 'When production began last December, ABC Television were at first requested by American stations who were interested in the series to keep the dressing of Emma Peel as close as possible to that of Cathy Gale in the earlier "Avengers", because it was felt that the leather look was in the ascendant in America. ABC would have preferred to keep further ahead of fashion, as they had in launching Cathy Gale, but agreed to retain the leather image for the time being. However, the radical swing in world fashion this year made it obvious that changes would have to be made in Emma Peel's wardrobe.' Regarding the mini-skirt, in particular, Brian Clemens (*Avenging The Avengers*) recalled: 'I went to Paris and saw the Courrèges fashion show, where the mini-skirt was invented, really. We had to decide whether we were going to put Diana Rigg in a mini-skirt, in episodes which would not be seen for several months, by which time the mini-skirt might have failed. It was a long, hard decision, but we took it, and of course it paid off.'

41 Andrae, 'Television's First Feminist', op. cit., p 116.

42 The seminal text is still Laura Mulvey, 'Visual Pleasure and Narrative Cinema', *Screen*, 16/3 (Autumn 1975), pp 6–18.

43 Speaking on *Avenging The Avengers*.

44 The whipping scene was cut by the ITV network. Brian Clemens (*Avenging The Avengers*) said that 'I think he whipped her four times or five times, and we had to cut it down to just one whipping – just one lash of the whip'. On the day of the broadcast the *Evening Standard* (19 February 1966) featured a publicity still of Rigg in her 'Queen of Sin' attire under the headline 'What You Won't See On *The Avengers* Tonight!' The 1993 video release by Lumiere Pictures (LUM 2024) contains the full whipping scene: it is actually quite difficult to work out how many times Cartney lashes with the whip, though up to 12 cracks may be counted, albeit that on no occasion is Emma actually touched by the whip. 'A Touch of Brimstone' was not screened in the United States, though it has

become part of *Avengers* folklore that it was viewed by American network executives at private parties and conventions.

45 Jean-Francois Lyotard, *The Postmodern Condition: A Report on Knowledge* (Manchester, 1984, Manchester University Press), p xxiv. For a useful critique of the whole notion that there is such a thing as a postmodern condition, see John Clarke, 'Enter the Cybernauts: Problems in Post-modernism', *Communication*, 10 (1988), pp 383–401. The title is of course a (postmodern) reference to *The Avengers*.

46 Quoted in John Storey, *An Introductory Guide to Cultural Theory and Popular Culture* (Hemel Hempstead, 1993, Harvester Wheatsheaf), p 166.

47 Jim Collins, 'Postmodernism and television' in Robert C. Allen (ed.), *Channels of Discourse, Reassembled* (London, 1992, Routledge), p 338.

48 Richard Hamilton, *Collected Words* (London, 1982, Thames and Hudson), p 28.

49 Quoted in Storey, *An Introductory Guide*, p 158.

50 Fredric Jameson, 'Postmodernism, or the cultural logic of late capitalism', *New Left Review*, 146 (1984), p 65.

51 Rogers, *The Ultimate Avengers*, p 108.

52 Umberto Eco, 'The Narrative Structure in Fleming' in Oreste Del Buono and Umberto Eco (eds), *The Bond Affair*, trans. R.A. Downie (London, 1966, Macdonald), p 58.

53 Collins, 'Postmodernism and television', pp 345–7.

4 *Seven Days in May*

History, Prophecy and Propaganda

Michael Coyne

Ours has been a century dominated by the United States, with the 1960s the most turbulent and controversial decade in modern American history. From Kennedy to Kent State, from the Bay of Pigs to the Sea of Tranquillity, from conformity to the counterculture, and from beacon of hope to bastion of hubris, the roots of today's multicultural, post-imperial America lie deep in the 1960s. My research concerns the interplay between major artefacts of American popular culture, the era in which they were produced and the ethos they espoused. From an Americanist perspective, there is room for debate on what constitutes the key defining moment of the early 1960s. Where do the 'sixties' as a 'cultural construct' truly begin? With John F. Kennedy's election, his inauguration or his assassination? With the Years of Lightning, or with the Day of Drums?

Viewpoint dictates time-span. To many Americans, World War II truly began on 7 December 1941 with the Japanese bombing of Pearl Harbour. According to British history, the war began on 3 September 1939, two days after the German invasion of Poland. Yet, to Manchurians, the great conflict began in 1931 with the Mukden incident and the Japanese invasion of their homeland. A great many perceptions of history are founded on geography and nationality. As they used to say in Washington, it all depends on whose ox gets gored.

Just as viewpoint dictates time-span, time-span goes a long way to dictating the nature of a narrative. A historian writing in 1961 or 1962 could conclude a history of mid-twentieth century America with Kennedy's election to the Presidency – closing, if he or she wished, on a triumphant note of liberal hope. Write the same history with 22 November 1963 as the final act, and the story immediately becomes a tragedy.

My own contention is akin to the conservative Americanist interpretation which Arthur Marwick found wanting in his Introduction. 'The sixties' began with Kennedy's election, but his murder in 1963 initiated a decade of turmoil and tragedy which quite clearly has left the United States severely diminished rather than improved. It is true that the 1960s witnessed many long overdue social advances, especially in the field of civil rights. Yet the assassinations of John and Robert Kennedy and Martin Luther King, the riots which left a dozen cities in flames, the string of obscene murders from the Boston Strangler, Richard Speck and Charles Whitman to Manson and his 'family' and, above all, the interminable involvement in Vietnam – all these turned the American dream into the American nightmare. Collectively, these events sullied the nation in the 1960s and constituted a symbolic fall from grace.

From the vantage point of 1970, social commentator Alistair Cooke declared the Kennedy years a 'fool's paradise', in which JFK's Inaugural Address had itself laid the groundwork for the folly of Vietnam; that fateful vow to 'pay any price, bear any burden... to assure the survival and the success of liberty' implicitly over-committed America's military might in advance, not only in Southeast Asia but around the globe.[1]

Three days before Kennedy's Inaugural, his predecessor had delivered his own stern warning about the steady increase of the military's power and influence within American society. Dwight Eisenhower exhorted his fellow citizens to beware of 'a recurring temptation to feel that some spectacular and costly action could become the miraculous solution to all current difficulties'.[2] In emphasising the unprecedented growth of the American military establishment, Eisenhower asserted:

> Our military organization today bears little relation to that known by any of my predecessors in peacetime or indeed by the fighting men of World War II or Korea.
>
> [W]e have been compelled to create a permanent armaments industry of vast proportions. Added to this three and a half million men and women are directly engaged in the defense establishment. We annually spend on military security more than the net income of all United States corporations.
>
> This conjugation of an immense military establishment and a large arms industry is new in the American experience. The total influence – economic, political, even spiritual – is felt in every city, every State House, every office of the Federal government. We recognize the imperative need for this development. Yet we must not fail to comprehend its grave implications. Our toil, resources, and livelihood are all involved; so is the very structure of our society.
>
> In the councils of government, we must guard against the acquisition of unwarranted influence whether sought or unsought by the military-industrial complex. The potential for the disastrous rise of misplaced power exists and will persist.

We must never let the weight of this combination endanger our liberties or democratic process. We should take nothing for granted. Only an alert and knowledgeable citizenry can compel the proper meshing of the huge industrial and military machinery of defense with our peaceful methods and goals so that security and liberty may prosper together.[3]

It may seem ironic that twentieth century America's most revered military hero should end his eight years in the White House with this particular admonition. Yet here Eisenhower was following a tradition and an ideological concern as old as the republic itself. During the revolutionary era, American patriots had protested against British standing armies; Samuel Adams had pleaded '*cedant arma togae*' ('let arms yield to civic robes'); and George Washington had included in his own Farewell Address a warning to 'avoid the necessity of those overgrown military establishments which, under any form of government, are inauspicious to liberty, and which are to be regarded as particularly hostile to republican liberty'.[4] Thus, just as Washington had once been exalted as a latter-day Cincinnatus, Eisenhower's valediction reinforced his own place in America's pantheon of citizen-soldiers.

Eisenhower was not alone in his anxiety over the military-industrial complex's pervasive encroachment. In 1962, the crusading journalist Fred J. Cook's book *The Warfare State* disclosed that the American military establishment's entire payroll exceeded the total combined payrolls of the nation's automobile, steel and petroleum industries; and the book's political revelations were even more alarming.[5] The first six months of Kennedy's Administration had witnessed intense friction between White House and Pentagon, with Secretary of Defense Robert McNamara's reforms buttressing regulations which several high-ranking officers had frequently ignored, particularly in their tendency to make sabre-rattling and politically partisan speeches for public consumption.[6] In June 1961, Missouri Senator Stuart Symington, himself a former Secretary of the Air Force and one of Kennedy's rivals for the Democratic presidential nomination in 1960, had charged on the floor of the US Senate:

It has become clear that some members of the Military do not intend to give up to civilian authority any of the prerogatives of excess power they have been allowed to build up over the years at the expense of civilian control.

In fact, there now appears to be an organized effort on the part of some of the Military to attack their civilian superiors under the vicious cloak of anonymity. This not only includes the Secretary of Defense and some of his civilian assistants, but in some cases the President himself... Military men of high rank, disgruntled at their slice of the pie, are now attacking the core of the American system... in a disloyal operation.[7]

The Warfare State reported Symington's searing indictment of this military mind-set – and went further, chronicling the radical right-wing sympathies displayed by a number of named high-ranking officers, both serving and retired, and also the co-operation between several such officers and far right forums across the nation in the late 1950s and early 1960s. The most notorious officer in this regard was General Edwin A. Walker, who was to align himself with the forces of right-wing extremism in Dallas; but some of the other examples Cook turned up were no less startling, such as the retired US Marine Colonel, a winner of the Congressional Medal of Honor, who had actually advocated hanging Supreme Court Chief Justice Earl Warren.[8] Cook believed this clash between civilian and military power was genuinely one between 'traditional American principles and the kind of Prussianized military industrial concept that had produced Hitler'.[9]

Published in the United States in 1962, the first British edition of *The Warfare State* appeared in 1963, with an anti-nuclear foreword penned by Bertrand Russell, dated 21 October 1962: one day before Kennedy presented the world with evidence of missile bases in Cuba.

At the beginning of October 1962, the issue of excessive US military influence was placed before the American reading public in the format of an entertainment. Two Washington reporters fresh from a successful collaboration on the book *No High Ground* (1960), which had chronicled the history of the Hiroshima atomic bomb, now turned their talents to fiction and to a tantalising, terrifying premise: what if the American military were disaffected by presidential policy and, as a consequence, attempted to overthrow the federal government? The result was the novel *Seven Days in May*.[10]

Fletcher Knebel and Charles W. Bailey II were in Washington's Cowles news agency, and had both contributed to the book *Candidates 1960* (1959), edited by Eric Sevareid. Knebel had written a favourable profile of Kennedy, and he already had an earlier connection to the Massachusetts Senator's camp. In 1956, at the time of Kennedy's bid for the Democratic vice-presidential nomination, Knebel had penned an article titled 'Can a Catholic Become Vice-President?' for the 12 June issue of *Look* magazine. That article had been based largely on material Knebel had received from Kennedy's aide, Theodore Sorensen, submitted to the journalist with JFK's approval.[11] John Kennedy would be President when *Seven Days in May* appeared in print, and he was to become an unqualified admirer of the book.

Prefaced by an extract from Eisenhower's Farewell Address, *Seven Days in May* is set in a then-futuristic 1974 – a year which, when it finally arrived, would see its own unique crisis in the White House. In the novel, President Jordan Lyman, an Ohio Democrat, has signed a nuclear disarmament treaty with the Soviet Union, despite strong dissent from the military, led by the Chairman of the Joint Chiefs of Staff, four-star Air Force General James Mattoon Scott.

In the run-up to an All Red practice alert, Marine Colonel Martin ('Jiggs') Casey, Director of the Joint Staff, uncovers a series of irregularities: a classified dispatch from General Scott to leading area commanders, ostensibly an invitation to place a wager on the Preakness horse race; the existence of a secret military unit, its designation ECOMCON, training on an equally secret base near El Paso; and a string of minor falsehoods. Considered together, Casey's discoveries gradually lead him to the conclusion that General Scott aims to use the alert to stage a coup d'état involving California Senator Frederick Prentice, a television broadcaster, Harold MacPherson, who is closely affiliated to a number of ultra-right-wing fringe groups, and all but one of the Joint Chiefs.

Casey takes his suspicions to the President and, together, with only a handful of trusted allies, they set about thwarting the conspiracy. The very title of the novel struck a powerful Biblical chord. If God created the world in six days, then Casey and Lyman have only seven days in which to save it. Lyman sends his aide Paul Girard to Gibraltar to secure written confirmation of the coup from Vice-Admiral Barnswell, the only one of Scott's area commanders who had declined to 'place a bet'. Lyman also sends his oldest and closest political ally, Senator Raymond Clark of Georgia, down to the Texas desert in hope of finding Site Y, the base where Scott's troops are covertly training for seizure of the government and crucial communications installations. Casey is already uncomfortable in his role as informer, but now he is also forced to jeopardise his marriage by contacting an old flame who is a confidante of Scott's mistress in New York. If proof of Scott's political treachery remains elusive, then evidence of peccadillos might ultimately have to suffice.

Paul Girard acquires corroborative written testimony of the coup from Admiral Barnswell, but perishes in a plane crash on his way back to the States. Senator Clark locates Site Y, but he is held incommunicado by order of the base commander, the fascistic Colonel John R. Broderick. Clark manages to escape from the base with the help of Casey's friend, Colonel Henderson, ECOMCON's executive officer.

Girard had placed Admiral Barnswell's signed statement in a cigarette case for safekeeping. Discovered amidst the wreckage of the crash in Spain, the case falls into the hands of the US Consul-General who, learning what lies within, promptly takes it to Washington and to the President. Lyman is therefore able to confront Scott with direct evidence of the coup. He secures the General's resignation and also those of the other Joint Chiefs complicit in the plot. The disloyal Senator Prentice dies in a suicidal car crash, and American democracy survives, triumphant and intact.

Seven Days in May was popular and controversial. The book sold 2,073,434 copies and featured on the *New York Times* bestsellers list for 49 weeks in a row.[12] It was a tale well crafted and briskly told, but written in fairly average prose.

What generated excitement among contemporary reviewers was not so much the style or even the content as the concept – and the timing. *Seven Days in May* was published at the same time as another 'what if…?' political nightmare novel, *Fail-Safe* by Eugene Burdick and Harvey Wheeler.[13] *Fail-Safe* posited the nerve-wracking hypothesis of an atomic catastrophe in which a computer error sends American planes to attack Moscow. With the US President unable to recall them, he orders New York annihilated to prove good faith, and thereby sidestep a full-blown nuclear holocaust. Among the book's principal characters is the grotesquely-named Groteschele, a malevolent German-Jewish scientist advising the Pentagon. In the midst of human tragedy, Groteschele is interested only in the potential for strategic gain. Considering these two books were published in October 1962, the very month of the Cuban Missile Crisis, their dire warnings about the likelihood of overweening military solutions and nuclear calamity could hardly have been more timely.

Critics frequently reviewed *Seven Days in May* and *Fail-Safe* together. According to the hard-line Republican but Kennedy-friendly *Time* magazine, these books depicted the Pentagon as 'a den of some of the most hideous monsters this side of Cyclops cave'.[14] *Time* also noted that *Seven Days'* General Scott 'combines Eisenhower's charm with MacArthur's hauteur' – an obvious personality combination which was also directly mentioned in the novel itself.[15] The same unnamed reviewer glibly remarked, 'Knebel-Bailey save the country from the conspirators, but they might as well have let the military take over, considering that the political savvy of their top politicos is somewhere below the ward heeler level'.[16] *Time*'s reviewer adjudged *Fail-Safe* 'a far more competent gee-whiz job than *Seven Days*', but declared that these two books were simply the latest in a line of 'inside novels about big-time politics in Washington… dreaming up fantastic political skulduggery that has never occurred and never will'.[17]

Several other commentators were not so sure. In the left-wing/liberal magazine *The Nation*, Robert Hatch claimed that *Seven Days in May* and *Fail-Safe* were characteristic of

> a new type of craftsman – the prophetic entertainer. He is a writer who makes no pretence to literary art; in matters of character, narrative devices, style and psychology, he models his work on formulas developed by the large fiction magazines, by television family drama, by the commercial movies. He is out for the very largest market (and he is reaching it), but the fuel that drives his vehicle is not love or success or adventure – it is doomsday.[18]

Hatch also asserted, 'neither book allows a gap of time or place between the reader and the fiction… as immediate, in the inevitable phrase, as tomorrow's newspaper'.[19] This was a lengthy review addressing urgent liberal concerns about 'the dominant economic and moral power which the armed services already wield' and 'the secrecy to which we have become habituated since Pearl Harbor'.[20] In direct contrast with *Time*'s review of the previous week, Hatch concluded that *Seven Days in May*'s central concept was not so fantastic, after all, and certainly not at all fanciful:

> Does it appear fantastic, finally, that a television newscaster and a United States Senator might conspire to destroy the Constitution? Unhappily, the authors do not have to exert much cunning to make that supposition persuasive. I would give *Seven Days in May* a very high mark for probability… Beneath the blood-stirring excitement of their melodrama lies the clammy suspicion that just such a plot might be hatched, almost any day now, across the Potomac from the Washington Monument.[21]

This last was a fairly widespread concern among liberal journalists and other political commentators. In October 1963 White House reporters at the Western Governor's Conference held in Eugene, Oregon told Owen Dudley Edwards that

Seven Days in May was based on the actual thought-processes of leading military figures at the Pentagon and that Robert McNamara's reforms of the Defense Department were generally perceived as being in the nature of a pre-emptive strike.[22] In addition, President Kennedy himself told his friend Paul B. Fay Jr that he considered a *Seven Days*-type scenario possible if there were another Bay of Pigs-style fiasco; he had also joked that he knew a couple of generals who might wish to turn the book's fiction into a reality.[23]

On *Seven Days in May*'s publication, its scenario of a futuristic political nightmare evoked comparison with Aldous Huxley's *Brave New World* (1932), George Orwell's *1984* (1949) and Nevil Shute's *On the Beach* (1957).[24] Yet its reassuring ending avoided the downbeat, fatalistic conclusions of those earlier novels, and Hatch closed his review with a pithy warning that complacency could be just as lethal as complicity:

> The effect of reading these books is certainly to make the perils more credible. At the same time, if we are not wary, it is to make us believe that Someone Up There is watching over us and that our leaders, no matter how late the hour, can be depended upon to extricate us and themselves from the maelstrom. There is no evidence that God has ever spared man the fruits of his folly and none that a people can dare to delegate judgment to its leaders.[25]

The liberal *New Republic* deemed *Seven Days in May* important enough to run a five-page review spread under the title 'Might It Happen Here?'. One of their reviewers, Lillian de la Torre, quipped 'It is like reading 341 pages of *Time* magazine all at once', but she went on to say of the novel's characters, 'Under different names they are all on the front page of your newspaper'.[26]

The very title of Sander Vanocur's *New Republic* review, 'Drunks, Babies and the USA', invoked a warning closely akin to the one sounded by Robert Hatch in *The Nation*: Americans could not afford to nurture the rosy, cosy notion that their land was especially blessed by God and that, somehow, the forces of good would always manage to prevail in the end.[27] Vanocur wrote:

> The military will not like this book, nor will those who feed, materially and politically, off our military-industrial establishment. Yet what is it the authors are saying? They are simply dramatizing the plausibility of a military take over in this country. Why should we consider ourselves immune from this danger? The Soviet Union is not. France is not. Lesser powers in Latin America, the Middle East and the Far East are not. Why then should we consider ourselves so absolutely secure from this danger? If Communism in Cuba can produce the current demi-hysteria among politicians... then there are no limits to the psychosis which far more important frustrations will produce.
>
> This is an important book... The book is no masterpiece. It will, however, both defy and endure the efforts of those who attempt to dismiss it as superficial.[28]

Sandwiched between de la Torre and Vanocur was a dissenting review entitled 'Cooking with Dynamite' by the pro-military S.L.A. Marshall; the initials stood for Samuel Lyman Atwood so, ironically, he shared a name with *Seven Days in May*'s liberal, pro-disarmament President. Marshall had authored *Commentary*

on Infantry Operations and Weapons Usage in Korea, Winter of 1950–51 (1952),
which was published by the Department of the Army's Operations Research
Office. Clearly, *The New Republic* enlisted him to function as an apologist for the
Pentagon. He did not disappoint:

> Either there is a present-day disposition in the US military which makes this plot
> plausible, or the book is mischievous, vicious. It is so written as to blight public
> confidence in the brass, thus helping create the evil out of phantasmagoria...
>
> Knebel and Bailey don't write of betrayal by a viciously clever minority.
> Their book is a wholesale libel against the American military character. All but
> one member of the JCS collaborate in treason, and the holdout stays mum... The
> few military good guys are pictured as half mad or half-witted and generally
> befuddled characters. Only the abominable [*sic*] JCS acts self-possessed,
> military, Olympian.
>
> For the story to become credible, it must be assumed by the reader that if the
> Chairman gets a chance to blow his whistle, all bureaus and ranks would click
> heels and heil, and the spiritless millions out over America would cheer the
> coup, having tired of the President. *That would be a proper comeuppance* [italics
> added], for that worthy pays off treason with honorable retirement, full allowances
> and official silence, fearful that if the American people know the truth, all will
> be lost. In cold truth, there would be nothing to lose. The society pictured by
> Knebel and Bailey is too decadent and demoralized for salvation in any form.
>
> ... Knebel and Bailey so love their thesis that they are essayists in *Look*
> magazine warning that their novel outlines a palpable danger. When they go that
> far, knowing so little, they match in recklessness the insidious characters which
> they themselves imagine. It can't happen here, we say. Conceivably it could, if
> on all fronts we insistently substitute degradation for moral discipline.[29]

Portions of Marshall's review, I would suggest, serve as an unfortunate crystal-
lization of the military mind-set which the novel challenged and condemned. It
was precisely this attitude — that there were worse possibilities than a military
coup – which made many liberal Americans uneasy and, indeed, paved the way
for *Seven Days in May* to become a *cause célèbre* in the political discourse of
1960s America.

Certainly to proclaim the book 'a wholesale libel against the American military character' is blustering nonsense. It is worth noting that the novel took pains
to feature an exemplary loyal officer from each branch of the services: Colonel
Casey (Marines); Colonel Henderson (Army); the Navy's Admiral Palmer is the
only one of the Joint Chiefs who is not part of Scott's cabal; and General Barney
Rutkowski of the Air Force is the by-the-book NORAD commander whom
Lyman entrusts to mop up the remnants of the aborted coup.

The overall tone of the novel is unequivocally pro-establishment. After all, its
heroes are the President of the United States and a Marine Colonel. In effect, the
novel endorses America's power structures while warning us that the reins of power
could all too easily fall into the wrong hands. In short: the system works well, but
beware the invariably fallible human element. It is a classic statement of consensus ideology and a classic example of Middle America's consensus mythology.

So *Seven Days in May* was far from 'wholesale libel'. Nonetheless, there were distinct individual parallels between characters in the novel and several real-life figures. Undoubtedly, the clash between President Lyman and General Scott had its roots in the Truman-MacArthur conflict a decade earlier, in which America's most charismatic general had publicly criticised President Harry Truman's handling of the Korean War and thereby provoked his own dismissal. Knebel and Bailey portrayed Scott as a character who inspired the same awe and possessed the same magnetism as Douglas MacArthur. Yet ultimately Scott remains more a symbol than a well-rounded character in his own right. The concept of the book was a fascinating one; the book itself might have been all the more fascinating had Knebel and Bailey truly attempted to get under Scott's skin, to probe his motivation – to give him a 'deep background', as Allen Drury had given each of his major characters in another political best-seller of that era, the Pulitzer-Prize-winning *Advise and Consent* (1959). In effect, Scott remains a shadowy, almost cardboard charismatic while Lyman and Casey occupy centre stage.

The characterisation of the President is, in part, Knebel's second lionisation of Kennedy, following on from *Candidates 1960*. Yet the name itself offers clues to alternative possibilities. Lyman might very well be the other side of Truman. Most of all, Jordan Lyman sounds very like a reversal of one particular name – Lyndon Johnson, who would sit in the White House tragically soon.

Significantly, Colonel Casey, the book's military hero, is a Marine, as was JFK's own favourite among the Joint Chiefs of Staff, Commandant David M. Shoup. Yet the characterisation of another colonel in the novel would appear to have a much deeper, far sharper contemporary resonance. Colonel Broderick, the commander of ECOMCON, makes statements openly contemptuous of civilian authority. Despite speech-clearance procedures and McNamara's reforms, in 1961 the case of General Edwin Walker had proved especially embarrassing. While serving in West Germany, Walker had attempted to indoctrinate his troops by circulating ultra-rightist literature, and he had also declared that Eleanor Roosevelt and broadcaster Edward R. Murrow were left-wing dupes.[30] Walker was relieved of his command and, while pending reassignment, he resigned from the Army and retired to Dallas, where he became active in the John Birch Society and a rallying figure for the forces of rightist extremism and white supremacy. Broderick clearly serves as a thinly-veiled Walker, just as Walker himself – America's Boulanger – provided an excellent illustration of the danger inherent in giving the military its head.

On the other side of this political divide, Senator Raymond Clark of Georgia is a composite of two real-life Southern Senators: J. William Fulbright of Arkansas, whose memorandum to McNamara on the links between military officers and far right groups led to extensive hearings by the Senate Armed Services Committee; and George A. Smathers of Florida, who was John Kennedy's closest personal friend in the Senate.

Whether or not Kennedy had identified personal friend and foe in the book, he appreciated that the narrative reaffirmed his own cherished concept of civilian control over the American military establishment. In the arena of popular culture, this novel was fighting the same battle which McNamara faced within the Pentagon. *Seven Days in May* itself heightened public awareness of the need for McNamara's reforms, and also increased support for them. Image-conscious and media-conscious as John Kennedy was, with a real nuclear test ban treaty in the pipeline he was eager to see *Seven Days in May* filmed; and, at a buffet in Washington, he communicated his enthusiasm to the actor Kirk Douglas, who was about to purchase the screen rights to the book.[31]

American political melodramas were very much in vogue in early 1960s Hollywood. This was a golden age for the genre. *Advise and Consent* and *The Manchurian Candidate* were both filmed in 1962, while *Seven Days in May*, *The Best Man*, *Fail Safe* (shorn of its hyphen for the film version) and its comic twin *Dr Strangelove* were all released in 1964. Public fascination with all things Kennedyesque was in large part responsible for this resurgence. Kennedy had effectively glamorised his profession in the popular consciousness. His persona had helped revitalise the market for political films, and his politics set the tone. His progressive, pragmatic style of leadership infused the 'tough-but-liberal' ethos of the classic American political films of the early 1960s.

A case in point was Allen Drury's novel *Advise and Consent*, which depicted the vehement US Senate battle over a controversial nomination, and was filmed for Columbia with an all-star cast in 1962. In the transition from print to celluloid, director Otto Preminger and screen-writer Wendell Mayes had toned down much of author Drury's right-wing posturing. One of the finest novels ever written about the American political process, *Advise and Consent* was actually the first of a six-novel ongoing saga; intriguingly, Drury wrote these over a time-span virtually identical to Arthur Marwick's definition of 'the long sixties' (late 1957–1974).[32] Yet none of the sequels was ever filmed. Admittedly, much of the 'suspense' in these other books derived from intricacies of voting procedure, a very difficult thing to render exciting on screen. Also, Drury's novels tended to be over-wordy. Above all, they were uncommonly conservative – and this, as much as anything else, made them unfilmable as the 1960s progressed. *Advise and Consent* was not as distinctively right-wing as its five sequels; but Drury subsequently 'ghettoised' himself by going against the predominantly liberal tide of the American political melodrama in the 1960s and 1970s.

One of the most popular novels in the genre had been Richard Condon's *The Manchurian Candidate* (1959), about a US Army sergeant captured and brainwashed by the Communists during the Korean War, programmed to act as an assassin on his return to America. Condon's book was thoroughly entertaining, and the 1962 screen version was a daring, dazzling, virtuoso piece of film-making helmed by a gifted young director named John Frankenheimer. For his next project, Frankenheimer opted to remain steeped in the murky world of political paranoia. He turned to *Seven Days in May*.

Frankenheimer was a liberal Democrat who would later become a close friend of Robert Kennedy. He had read *The Warfare State* and was passionately dedicated to *Seven Days in May* and its political message.[33] Made for Paramount at a cost of $2.2 million, *Seven Days in May* starred Burt Lancaster as General Scott, co-producer Kirk Douglas as Colonel Casey, and Fredric March as President Jordan Lyman.[34] Significantly, all three stars were liberal Democrats. Even more significantly, while the film was in production, the US Senate ratified the Nuclear Test Ban Treaty on 24 September 1963; and all 18 Senators who voted against the treaty were reserve generals in either the United States Air Force or the United States Army, among them Barry Goldwater of Arizona, Margaret Chase Smith of Maine (both Air Force), and Strom Thurmond of South Carolina (Army).

Nothing could be more emblematic of 1960s American society than the film's opening scene: a demonstration which soon erupts into a riot. This riot between pro- and anti-disarmament campaigners was, in fact, filmed two days after the Test Ban Treaty was initialled in Moscow. Real protesters outside the White House found themselves shifted aside to let 'movie' picketers stage their own demonstration for the cameras.[35] America had already become accustomed to the televised spectacle of civil disturbances in the late 1950s and early 1960s, particularly in white Southern reprisals against peaceful civil rights demonstrations. As the decade wore on, the proliferation of riots increasingly became both symptom and symbol of all that was so tragically wrong in 1960s America; and the inclusion of a riot in the movie version of *Seven Days in May* was itself a sign of the times. The 1964 film begins with a riot which was not featured in the 1962 novel. There could be no more fitting illustration of urgency. In this respect, by opening with its riot sequence, *Seven Days in May* pinpointed one of the 1960s' key political phenomena, and at the same time invested its own narrative text with an extra sense of immediacy.

The fact that Frankenheimer and his crew were actually permitted to film their riot outside the White House in the first place was itself an indication of the tacit co-operation the Kennedy Administration extended to this project. Pierre Salinger, Kennedy's Press Secretary, led Frankenheimer and his assistants through the Oval Office and the presidential living quarters to help them design accurate replicas for their film sets.[36] Frankenheimer did not approach the Pentagon for assistance because, as he said in a later interview, 'we knew we wouldn't get it. But there was no active resistance to it. I'm sure the Pentagon weren't happy when they heard we were going to make it but... they didn't try to censor us.'[37]

The film had first-class credentials. Directed by Frankenheimer, produced by Edward Lewis (then chief of production for Kirk Douglas's Joel Productions), with a taut script by Rod Serling of *Twilight Zone* fame, music by Jerry Goldsmith, crisp black-and-white photography by Ellsworth Fredericks, and graced by a top-flight cast, *Seven Days in May* grossed $3.4 million at the North American box office in 1964.[38] Frankenheimer's direction, Serling's script and the quality performances of the actors elevated Scott, Casey, Lyman *et al.* above the two- (and sometimes one-) dimensional characterisations in the novel. This was a classic example of a popular book which was improved on screen because the actors truly breathed life into the characters. Serling retained much of the original dialogue, making only minor adjustments to the story.

Five of the book-to-film adjustments are worth noting here. In the book, Casey has a wife and two sons; in the film, he appears to be single. This simplifies his moral position, at least partially, when he woos Scott's ex-mistress with a view to obtaining incriminating evidence against the general. In the book, Casey woos Eleanor Holbrook, an old flame who is the confidante of Scott's mistress, Millicent Segnier; the film merges these two characters – Eleanor Holbrook (played by Ava Gardner) is Scott's former mistress. Similarly, the 'incriminating evidence' Eleanor Holbrook holds against Scott is also simplified. In the book, the Scott-Segnier affair is still ongoing, and the general's mistress has claimed $3000 as tax-deductible after spending this sum entertaining Scott; in the film, unsurprisingly, the 'incriminating evidence' is a batch of love letters from Scott, who has since discarded Eleanor cruelly and coldly. Certainly, the latter scenario would be much easier for moviegoers to relate to: it is standard soap-opera stuff. In the book, President Lyman already has Admiral Barnswell's statement in his possession when he confronts General Scott in the Oval Office and accuses him of attempting a coup; Lyman is therefore able to force Scott's resignation there and then. In the film, during the confrontation in the Oval Office Lyman does not yet have Barnswell's statement; the film's Scott does not resign gracefully at this point but instead is later outflanked. In the book, Scott's co-conspirator Senator Prentice dies in a car crash, and the implication is suicide in the face of the coup's collapse. In the film, Prentice survives. However, the film-makers actually shot a scene similar to Prentice's demise in the novel: President Lyman's voice crackles over the radio of a wrecked car – but here the crash victim is General Scott.[39] Although this footage was shot it was not used, so Burt Lancaster's General Scott survived in the final print.

Dr Johnson's famous remark about patriotism does not quite fit Scott. He is not a star-spangled charlatan but a man whose Americanism is so zealous that it has spurred him to an action which he genuinely has not recognised as the treachery it is. Yet Frankenheimer himself is clearly wary of both the trappings and the rhetoric of super-patriotism. In both *The Manchurian Candidate* and *Seven Days in May*, the threat to American democracy comes from a winner of the Congressional Medal of Honor (here we might recall the retired Marine colonel who wanted to hang Earl Warren); but *The Manchurian Candidate*'s Raymond Shaw (Laurence Harvey) is an unwitting tool of the Communists, whereas General Scott knows precisely what he is doing. Significantly, it is during Scott's stirring speech to the American Veterans' Order that Casey phones the White House to request an appointment with President Lyman. Scott's consummate performance before the wildly-cheering crowd is the factor which finally convinces Casey he has not just been nurturing an overactive imagination: the man means business.

Seven Days in May adhered closely to Hollywood's dominant ideology of consensus, just as that dominance was beginning to wane.[40] The film's message about the power of the military in American society would become increasingly relevant through the rest of the 1960s and beyond, due to the ever-spiralling involvement in Vietnam. Within only a few years, however, in the era of My Lai and Kent State, *Seven Days in May*'s plot resolution would have been considered ludicrously naïve – and box-office poison to boot. *Seven Days in May* picks out the bad apples, all the while insisting that there is nothing wrong with the barrel. By 1970, American film-makers would be focusing chiefly on the folly of war and the madness which they believed permeated military power structures in *M*A*S*H*, *Catch-22*, *Too Late the Hero* and, more ambivalently, *Patton*. By comparison, *Tora! Tora! Tora!*, a traditional-style World War II epic released the same year, looked as though it might have been filmed ten years earlier – and it flopped disastrously at the box office.

Moreover, in the age of Lyndon Johnson and Richard Nixon, fewer and fewer Americans were inclined to view their president as a beleaguered but essentially decent and honest figure; they might have conceded 'beleaguered'. This constituted a loss of faith not only in the incumbent chief executive but also in the presidency itself. By comparison, Fredric March's Jordan Lyman harked back to Franklin Roosevelt, to Truman and to Eisenhower: a fatherly president to whom you could take your troubles. Ironically, Jordan Lyman is precisely the type of president Lyndon Johnson had always wanted to be.

So although *Seven Days in May* prophesied a possible nightmare future for America, its resolution was safely conservative and consensual; and, equally, its construction of American national identity was rooted in a 1950s definition of consensus in both political and filmic terms. All the major figures in the drama were mature white males.

The only female lead, Ava Gardner's Eleanor Holbrook, is really a peripheral figure, and this world-weary beauty is much the same as the role the actress played five years earlier in Stanley Kramer's *On The Beach*. On *Seven Days in May*'s release, several critics singled her character out as a superfluous distraction in an otherwise tightly-constructed film. Certainly, this criticism has some validity. For example, John Coleman wrote in the *New Statesman* that her character 'might almost be a presence left over from *Advise and Consent*'.[41] Incidentally, this last observation was also true of Senator Raymond Clark, both portrayed in the book and played by Edmond O'Brien in the film as a cut-rate Seab Cooley (the cunning old Southern senator in Drury's novel, Charles Laughton's final screen role).[42] At times, O'Brien's delivery is so hammy that he sounds like the cartoon character Foghorn Leghorn; yet he was nominated for an Oscar as Best Supporting Actor of 1964.

Blacks were even more marginalised than women in *Seven Days in May*'s representation of America. Their minimal participation here is not surprising, given their effective exclusion from the highest echelons of power up to and beyond the early 1960s. The discerning viewer can spot a couple of blacks among the pro-Lyman demonstrators in the film's opening scene, a black woman and two children in a scene at Dulles airport, and half a dozen blacks among the journalists at President Lyman's climactic press conference. What we have here is very much a 1950s vision of 1970s America, filmed in the 1960s. While undoubtedly a liberal tract, *Seven Days in May* is still a paean to white male primacy – indeed, given Lyman's heroic status, to a white patriarchy. Thus, on the ideological spectrum, the film's Kennedyesque liberalism is much closer to Eisenhower's 'middle C' conservatism than to the anti-establishment radicalism which would gain strength in protest movements and various key film narratives later in the decade.

By the time *Seven Days in May* was released in February 1964, its greatest champion was dead. In an unfavourable review for *The New Republic*, Stanley Kauffmann wrote that the film failed 'to deal competently with this country's dangerous and growing anger with progress and the democratic process. Particularly in the light of last November, the film is impertinently frivolous.'[43] *Time* deemed the film 'more far-fetched than a campaign promise', observing, 'The movie is least successful when it tries to sound significant. Some of the dialogue in the final reels seems to have been cribbed from a prep school essay on "What Democracy Means to Me".'[44] Overall, however, critical reaction was enthusiastic and reviews were frequently laden with superlatives.

In the *New York Times*, Bosley Crowther wrote:

> a great deal about this *Seven Days in May*... is rousing and encouraging to a feeling of confidence and pride... Considerably more than melodrama and sensationalism are contained in its not too far-fetched speculations. There is, in its slick dramatic frame, a solid base of respect for democracy and the capacities of freedom-loving men.[45]

Saturday Review film critic Arthur Knight declared, '*Seven Days in May* generates all the fascination and excitement of [Frankenheimer's] earlier *Manchurian Candidate* – but to a higher purpose. For behind the melodrama, and despite Serling's frequently platitudinous dialogue, motivating both the action and its denouement is a simple, clear understanding of what democracy is all about.'[46] *Variety* termed *Seven Days in May* 'fascinating in its reflections of present-day political attitudes and its exploration of what could conceivably happen momentarily'.[47] Rather uncharacteristically for a Hollywood trade paper, this review concluded by looking beyond America's shores to the film's potential impact overseas:

> This is truly a moving picture play, with dramatic power that is certain to be felt in foreign lands. There's obviously a keen awareness of the US Presidency by peoples abroad, this awareness having been enhanced by the assassination of President John F. Kennedy, and should add to the global interest in *Seven Days in May*.
>
> Paramount has a worldwide hit.[48]

Several Congressmen also took an interest in how the movie might be received abroad. During a debate on funding for the United States Information Agency, Republican Congressman Charles Gubser of California expressed concern over a rumour he had heard: *Seven Days in May* was being distributed in India at partial federal expense. Gubser feared that screening the film 'in countries like India' would depict America's military forces 'in a bad light'.[49] Another Republican Congressman, Melvin Laird of Wisconsin, stated that he considered *Seven Days in May* a 'very fine film', but suggested that copies due for exportation should be labelled as 'fictional'; for, according to *Variety*'s report on this debate, Laird 'averred the unlabelled film has been "misleading" to overseas audiences'.[50]

Perhaps the most glowing review of all came from Robert Hatch, again writing for *The Nation*. When he reviewed Knebel and Bailey's novel in November 1962, Hatch had found their scenario uncomfortably convincing. Yet 16 months later, despite the recent shock of John Kennedy's murder in Dallas, at that time widely recognised as 'America's Hate Capital', Hatch detected a calmer and more reassuring mood throughout US society at large:

> *Seven Days in May* is a superb commercial film, opulently produced, expensively cast... sleekly timed... It also convinces me, in a way that the mocking *Dr Strangelove* never could, that the country has passed through the worst of its lunatic panic.
>
> ...After all these years of rocket rattling and the suicidal bravado of second-strike capability, it is morally invigorating to see a mass-audience picture that comes out unequivocally for negotiated arms reduction, for the ejection of the military from politics; that calls the Pentagon dangerously headstrong, and uses the names of Senator McCarthy and General Walker as terms of contempt... A very few years ago, say in the middle of Eisenhower's second term, *Seven Days* would have been a picture of unprecedented boldness; now it is no more than politically relevant and reassuring. It took the picture, though, to make me realize how much we have changed.
>
> ... Like most melodramas, it is moonshine – military juntas in our age do not flower north of the frost line; any take-over in this country would have been through the minds and votes of the people. It may well have been a close thing, but seeing the happy family groups lined up for blocks to get into *Seven Days*, I would guess that there are no Boulangers in our immediate future.[51]

In Britain, *Seven Days in May* was released in April 1964. There, too, opinion was divided. In the *Guardian*, Richard Roud dismissed the film as 'reverent and middlebrow'.[52] *Sunday Express* reviewer Thomas Wiseman quipped:

> what the film says, finally, is not that it is bad to blow up the world but that it is inexcusable to do it by undemocratic means... [I]t makes the business of government in the nuclear age seem like a gangster movie of the thirties... And as a discussion of important issues, it is about as controversial as a Richard Dimbleby summing-up.[53]

The *Daily Worker*'s critic, Nina Hibbin, posited a distinctly left-wing interpretation of Frankenheimer's film:

> it gives... a powerful and urgent warning against the megalomania of the US militarists.

There is a frightening realism about what it is saying: that American militarism would stop at nothing, including fascism, in order to maintain and build up the cold war.

What robs it of a really dynamic impact is its weak attitude to the peace treaty itself. It wants us to believe that not only top military and political personnel, but also the vast majority of the American people, would be violently opposed to total peace.

From the central character (Kirk Douglas), the officer who first suspects the plot, we get a feeling that the film itself, although in favour of 'democracy', is against peace.[54]

As in America, however, the prevailing view in Britain was that *Seven Days in May*'s blend of lavish production values and vital political message added up to first-class entertainment. Kingsley Amis began his *Observer* notice by proclaiming: 'I hereby go overboard for *Seven Days in May*'.[55] In his review for the *Financial Times*, David Robinson hailed the film as 'a sharply searching examination of the virtues and dangers of patriotism, or the sort of Little-End fanaticism that often passes for it'.[56]

The Times praised *Seven Days* as 'a superlatively efficient piece of intelligent entertainment'.[57] Isabel Quigley, reviewing for the *Spectator*, adjudged the film 'Concentrated, exciting, and humane'.[58] To Mordecai Richler, it was 'an intelligent, classy and frighteningly plausible piece of work'.[59] Alexander Walker in the *Evening Standard* and Gerald Kaufman in the *Listener* both found a number of shortcomings in the movie, but each discerned a clear connection between the character of General James M. Scott and General Douglas MacArthur.[60]

On Sunday 5 April 1964, just a few weeks after *Seven Days in May*'s release in the United States, Douglas MacArthur died aged eighty-four. Shortly before his death he had urged Lyndon Johnson to avoid a war on the Asian mainland; ironically, the General's old nemesis, Harry Truman, advocated stepping up the American military commitment to South Vietnam.[61]

Now, assuming the president in Knebel and Bailey's novel was at least partially based on John Kennedy, the prototypes for Lyman and Scott were both gone. Yet in the presidency of Lyndon B. Johnson, *Seven Days in May* continued to have the same potent, emotive contemporary resonance. During the presidential election of 1964, when Republican challenger Barry Goldwater proposed giving NATO's Supreme Commander in Europe authority over tactical (not strategic) nuclear weapons on the field of battle, this suggestion fed the same liberal anxiety about military action devoid of civilian control. Lyndon Johnson was able to depict himself as the great hope for peace, in large part on the strength of some of Goldwater's more colourful and ill-measured utterances.

Johnson was also aided by the political films released that year. 1964 was an *annus mirabilis* for the genre. Besides *Seven Days in May*, moviegoers were presented with *The Best Man*, based on Gore Vidal's sardonic 1960 play set against the backdrop of a presidential convention, *Dr Strangelove* and *Fail Safe*. Though *Strangelove* and *Fail Safe* had essentially the same plot, *Strangelove* took the nightmare of nuclear holocaust and played it for laughs, and had the added advantage of being released first – thereby obliterating *Fail Safe* at the box office. All these films were of a liberal bent, and each in its way gave sustenance to LBJ and the Democrats in a crucial election year. Political propaganda in support of liberalism is still propaganda, and the US political movies of 1964 rank among the most striking examples of Hollywood's overt participation in the American electoral process. In truth, *Seven Days in May* was as much a cinematic vote for Lyndon Johnson against Barry Goldwater in 1964 as *All the President's Men* was to be a vote for Jimmy Carter against Gerald Ford in 1976. Later, in his 1979 memoir, titled *With No Apologies*, Goldwater wrote: 'It is worth noting that the public's almost hysterical, unreasoned attitude toward nuclear war was fattened on the misrepresentations of three works of fiction': *On The Beach*, *Fail-Safe*, and *Seven Days in May*.[62]

In autumn of 1964, *Sight and Sound* carried this intriguing paragraph:

> Rio's Governor Carlos Laccerda sat in his private cinema during the April Revolution watching a series of films as he directed the defence of his palace. One of them was *Seven Days in May*, whose trailer had been shown in Rio cinemas the week before, even as the tanks started to move in. The film has yet to be shown. Yet this is an isolated instance; Brazil's present rulers, after their initial burst of spy-hunting, have not imposed any artistic censorship.[63]

Back in the United States, America's own military nightmare was just beginning – and it was to last for a decade. Ironically, one of the finest films about the Vietnam War's corrosive impact on American society was, in terms of both liberal ideology and star iconography, the companion piece to *Seven Days in May*. *Twilight's Last Gleaming* (1977), directed by Robert Aldrich (cousin of Nelson Rockefeller), again starred Burt Lancaster as a renegade Air Force General at odds with the US government. This time, however, he is a thorn in the Pentagon's side. Lancaster's General Dell captures a missile base and threatens to launch its rockets, starting World War III, unless his demands are met. Above all, he wants the President (Charles Durning) to disclose the contents of a National Security Council memorandum which will reveal that America was in Vietnam primarily to demonstrate willingness to wage a war of attrition, no matter how protracted or how terrible the cost. Shocked and sickened by the revelations contained in this memorandum, the President agrees. Yet the film's climax sees both Dell and the President gunned down by US Air Force snipers; and rows of high-ranking officers stand idly on the sidelines, watching as the President lies dying of his wounds. *Seven Days in May* had warned that the military, if unchecked, might well subvert the democratic process. *Twilight's Last Gleaming* bleakly asserted that while America had been focusing on an unwinnable war in Southeast Asia, the military had achieved this sinister aim by the back door.

When Ronald Reagan ran for the presidency in 1980 he declared that the American commitment to Vietnam had been an honourable cause and should be regarded as such. Movie critic Danny Peary astutely observed that if *Seven Days in May* had been filmed in the Reagan era, the pro-disarmament President and the loyal Marine colonel would probably have been the villians.[64] While this contingency was averted, *Seven Days in May* was the basis for a 1994 Home Box Office production titled *The Enemy Within*. Jason Robards took the Lancaster role, Sam Waterston was Fredric March's successor, and black actor Forest Whitaker played Colonel Casey (with wife and family restored). It was a needless and utterly inferior exercise, which even ludicrously featured Russian agents, in this era of *glasnost*, helping Casey to foil the dastardly plot and keep American democracy on the right track.

The Enemy Within was clearly yet another example of modern Hollywood at its most threadbare, yet another instance of the lamentable impulse to remake cinema classics as second-rate TV movies. It was a slick but essentially vacuous quasi-thriller, which in no way fed into an urgent contemporary concern as the original had. No-one is ever likely to attribute lasting significance to *The Enemy Within*. Yet both the title and the concept of *Seven Days in May* became and remain part of America's cultural consciousness – and this fact may even have cost one man the presidency.

Former General Alexander Haig's 1988 campaign nose-dived to oblivion. Why should so authoritative and imposing a figure have failed so abysmally in his quest for the greatest prize in American political life? In all probability, because of five words, said in the wrong place at the wrong time. In the American public's consciousness, Haig's long career of distinguished service was eclipsed by the memory of 30 March 1981. Then Secretary of State, in the panicky aftermath of John Warnock Hinckley's attempt on Ronald Reagan's life, Haig stepped up to the podium in the press room of the White House and, in a shaky voice, erroneously proclaimed, 'I am in control here'. Above all, Alexander Haig will always be associated with those five words; and, given his military background, the connotations were even more unfortunate. Shortly afterward, a State Department official who was friendly and sympathetic to Haig still had to admit to a *Time* correspondent, 'I thought it was *Seven Days in May*. Al didn't do it right, and it's going to hurt him'.[65]

ACKNOWLEDGEMENTS

In the course of researching and writing this article, several people have helped in a number of ways. I should particularly like to express my thanks to Owen Dudley Edwards, Professor Jeffrey Richards, Philip French and Jim Dunnigan.

NOTES TO CHAPTER 4

1　See Alistair Cooke, *America Observed: The Newspaper Years of Alistair Cooke*, selected and introduced by Ronald A. Wells (London, [1980], 1988, Penguin), p 207.

2　President Eisenhower's Farewell Address, 17 January 1961, quoted in Harrison E. Salisbury, *The Many Americas Shall Be One* (London, 1971, Secker & Warburg), p 141.

3　Ibid., pp 142–3.

4　See Richard B. Morris (ed.), *Great Presidential Decisions: State Papers That Changed the Course of History* (Greenwich, 1961, Premier/Fawcett), pp 37–8.

5　Fred J. Cook, *The Warfare State* (London, [1962], 1963, Jonathan Cape), passim.

6　Ibid., pp 4–5.

7　Quoted ibid, p 5.

8　Ibid., pp 278–83 and pp 265–6 respectively.

9　Ibid., p 7.

10　Fletcher Knebel and Charles W. Bailey II, *Seven Days in May* (New York and London, 1962, Harper & Row and Weidenfeld & Nicolson).

11　See Theodore C. Sorensen, *Kennedy* (London, [1965] 1966, Pan), pp 98–9.

12　See Nicholas Parsons, *The Book of Literary Lists* (London, 1985, Sidgwick & Jackson), p 76; and Lawrence H. Suid, *Guts & Glory: Great American War Movies* (Reading, 1978, Addison-Wesley), p 202.

13　Eugene Burdick and Harvey Wheeler, *Fail-Safe* (New York, 1962, McGraw-Hill).

14　'Potshots at the Pentagon', *Time*, 26 October 1962, p 64.

15　Ibid.; and see Knebel and Bailey, *Seven Days in May*, p 33.

16　*Time*, op. cit.

17　Ibid.

18　Robert Hatch, 'Making Tomorrow Convincing', *The Nation* (New York), 3 November 1962, p 291.

19　Ibid., p 292.

20　Ibid.

21　Ibid.

22　Interview with Owen Dudley Edwards, Reader in American History at the University of Edinburgh, 6 February 1998.

23　See Sybil Leek and Bert R. Sugar, *The Assassination Chain* (Los Angeles, 1976, Pinnacle), pp 151–2; and Sorensen, *Kennedy*, op. cit., p 670.

24　See Hatch, 'Making Tomorrow Convincing', op. cit., p 293; and Lillian de la Torre, 'Let's Hope It's an Illusion', under 'Might It Happen Here?', *The New Republic*, 1 October 1962, p 21.

25　Hatch, 'Making Tomorrow Convincing', op. cit., p 293.

26　De la Torre, 'Let's Hope It's an Illusion', op. cit., p 21.

27　Sander Vanocur, 'Drunks, babies and the USA', under 'Might it Happen Here?', op. cit., pp 23–5.

28　Ibid., pp 24–5.

29　S.L.A. Marshall, 'Cooking with Dynamite', under 'Might It Happen Here?', op. cit., pp 22–3.

30　See Arthur M. Schlesinger Jr, *A Thousand Days: John F. Kennedy in the White House* (London, 1965, André Deutsch), p 645; Sorensen, *Kennedy*, op. cit., pp 318–20; and Suid, *Guts & Glory*, op. cit., pp 202–3.

31 See Kirk Douglas, *The Ragman's Son: An Autobiography* (London, [1988] 1989, Pan), p 349.

32 Allen Drury's five sequels to *Advise and Consent* (1959) were: *A Shade of Difference* (1962); *Capable of Honor* (1966); *Preserve and Protect* (1968); *Come Nineveh, Come Tyre* (1973); and *The Promise of Joy* (1975). His novels were liberal on the issue of civil rights, but they were also fervent Cold War tracts, ultra-hawkish on foreign policy, including, implicitly, America's involvement in Vietnam.

33 John Frankenheimer, 'Seven Ways with *Seven Days in May*', *Films and Filming*, June 1964, pp 9–10; Gerald Pratley, *The Cinema of John Frankenheimer* (London and New York, 1969, A. Zwemmer and A.S. Barnes, 1969), p 113.

34 Pratley, *The Cinema of John Frankenheimer*, op. cit., and Tony Thomas, *The Films of Kirk Douglas* (Secaucus, 1972, Citadel), p 99.

35 See Suid, *Guts & Glory*, op. cit., p 203.

36 See Pratley, *The Cinema of John Frankenheimer*, op. cit., p 114; and Suid, *Guts & Glory*, op. cit., p 203.

37 Pratley, *The Cinema of John Frankenheimer*, op. cit., pp 113–14
    For extensive accounts of the production history of *Seven Days in May*, see Pratley, *The Cinema of John Frankenheimer*, op. cit., pp 103–14; Suid, *Guts & Glory*, op. cit., pp 201–5; and Douglas, *The Ragman's Son*, op. cit., pp 349–53.

38 Cobbett Steinberg, *Reel Facts: The Movie Book of Records* (Harmondsworth, 1981, Penguin), p 440.

39 See Douglas, *The Ragman's Son*, op. cit., p 353.

40 On Hollywood's creed of consensus, see Peter Biskind, *Seeing Is Believing: How Hollywood Taught Us to Stop Worrying and Love the Fifties* (London, [1983] 1984, Pluto Press), passim and Richard Maltby, *Harmless Entertainment: Hollywood and the Ideology of Consensus* (Metuchen, 1983, Scarecrow Press) passim.

41 John Coleman, 'Ides of March', *The New Statesman*, 17 April 1964. This review, like many quoted subsequently here, comes from the British Film Institute's microfiche collection; many of the reviews on the fiche omit original page numbers. In future instances, I will indicate this by the designation '(BFI)'.

42 The *Monthly Film Bulletin* of May 1964 also makes the connection between Edmond O'Brien's Ray Clark and Laughton's character in *Advise and Consent*, p 72.

43 Stanley Kauffmann, 'Seven Days, Fulsome Praise', *The New Republic*, 7 March 1964, p 35.

44 'Political Thriller', *Time*, 21 February 1964, p 63.

45 *New York Times*, 20 February 1964, p 22.

46 Arthur Knight, 'Heavy, Heavy What Hangs Over', *Saturday Review*, 14 February 1964, p 25.

47 *Variety*, 5 February 1964.

48 Ibid.

49 'Congress Thinks People Gotta Be Told *Seven Days in May* Is Fictional', *Variety*, 13 May 1964 (BFI).

50 Ibid.

51 *The Nation*, 9 March 1964, pp 251, 252.

52 Richard Round, 'New Films in London', *Guardian*, 17 April 1964, p 11.

53 Thomas Wiseman, 'Flaws maybe – but a medal goes to Mr March', *Sunday Express*, 19 April 1964 (BFI).

54 Nina Hibbin, 'A plot against the President', *Daily Worker*, 14 April 1964 (BFI).

55 Kingsley Amis, 'How it might really happen', *Observer*, 19 April 1964 (BFI).

56 *Financial Times*, 17 April 1964 (BFI).

57 'Political Thriller That Grips', *Times*, 16 April 1964, p 6.

58 Isabel Quigley, 'Count-Down Suspense', *Spectator*, 17 April 1964 (BFI).

59 Review in *Town*, June 1964 (BFI).

60 Alexander Walker, 'Top Brass in Revolt', *Evening Standard*, 16 April 1964; and *Listener*, 21 May 1964 (both BFI).

61 See William Manchester, *American Caesar: Douglas MacArthur 1880–1964* (London, [1978], 1979, Hutchinson), p 698.

62 Barry M. Goldwater, *With No Apologies: The Personal and Political Memoirs of United States Senator Barry M. Goldwater* (New York, [1979], 1980, Berkley), p 149.

63 Guy Playfair, 'In the Picture: Festivals and a Revolution', *Sight and Sound*, Autumn 1964, p 169.

64 Danny Peary, *Guide for the Film Fanatic* (London, 1987, Simon & Schuster), p 377.

65 See George J. Church, 'Business as Usual – Almost', *Time*, 13 April 1981, p 15.

5 'Nothing Like Any Previous Musical, British or American'

The Beatles' Film, *A Hard Day's Night*

Rowana Agajanian

If one were asked to make a list of the most striking features of the sixties it is certain that the Beatles would appear somewhere on it. Such is the power of their music, their image and their association with the sixties that they have become icons of that decade. Their music and phenomenal success have been, and continue to be, the subject of historical documentation and deliberation, but their film work has been surprisingly neglected.[1]

As a group the Beatles made four films, five if one includes the cartoon, *Yellow Submarine* (1968).[2] The first, *A Hard Day's Night* (1964), is a musical comedy with a storyline based on a fictional 'day in the life' of the group as they prepare to give a performance. The second film, *Help!* (1965), more of a comedy with music, is a colour fantasy adventure with an exotic storyline and a number of lavish settings. In an experimental film aimed for television broadcast, *Magical Mystery Tour* (1968) offered the audience a bizarre and often surreal coach adventure with the Beatles and friends through the British countryside. Surrealism was also the basis for *Yellow Submarine*, with its highly imaginative story full of colourful animated characters. However, the Beatles provided only the music and a brief appearance in the flesh towards the end of the film, for even the voices of their cartoon figures were dubbed by actors. And finally, *Let It Be* (1970) brought the Beatles full circle to offering an authentic documentary insight into their work and lives as opposed to the fictional 'window' provided by *A Hard Day's Night*.

The reasons for choosing their first film as a key text of the sixties are numerous and complex. Firstly, the circumstances in which the film was designed and created reflect important developments in both the film and record industries. Secondly, the film makes use of two generic conventions, the musical and the documentary, not usually associated with one another but, nevertheless, loaded with specific codes of meaning. Thirdly, beneath the light-hearted narrative which follows the Beatles' lives as pop stars and the phenomenon of 'Beatlemania', lie more serious issues concerning pop stardom, youth, class and regional divisions. Finally, placed in its context, the film reveals a pertinent relationship between Britain and the United States, one of economic and cultural exchange.

The film appears towards the beginning of the period 1964–6 frequently labelled 'the British invasion' when British pop music, fashion, film, photography and art appeared to dominate both the United States and Western Europe. In April 1966, *Time* correspondent Piri Halasz published an article that not only celebrated the contemporary London scene but would prove highly influential in sixties mythology:

> In a decade dominated by youth, London has burst into bloom. It swings; it is the scene… The city is alive with birds (girls) and beatles, buzzing with mini-cars and telly stars, pulsing with half a dozen separate veins of excitement. The guards now change at Buckingham Palace to a Lennon and McCartney tune, and Prince Charles is firmly in the long-hair set. In Harold Wilson, Downing Street sports a Yorkshire accent, a working-class attitude and tolerance toward the young that includes Pop Singer 'Screaming' Lord Sutch, who ran against him on the Teen-Age Party ticket in the last election… London is not keeping the good news to itself… London is exporting its plays, its films, its fads, its styles, its people.[3]

Firmly situated in the period Arthur Marwick defines as 'The High Sixties', Halasz's article is unproblematic in terms of the chronology of a 'long sixties'. However, one could argue that *A Hard Day's Night* belongs as much to the preceding period, to the 'First Stirrings of a Cultural Revolution', as it does to 'The High Sixties', for it reflects a combination of tradition and innovation, of rebellion and restraint. The film captures the Beatles as a national phenomenon yet signifies their imminent ascendence to international stardom. With its fantastical and exotic narrative and vibrant colour, I would argue that the Beatles second film, *Help!*, is much more of a 'High Sixties' product. However, *A Hard Day's Night* offers a richer study, particularly in view of Marwick's 16 characteristics of the social and cultural transformation during the 'long sixties'. In terms of context, *A Hard Day's Night* reflects the rise to positions of unprecedented influence of young people, not just of the Beatles but also their teenage and young-adult audience. The film represents unprecedented international exchange, both economically and culturally, drawing on the talent and traditions of a variety of countries and cultures. *A Hard Day's Night* displays artistic innovation as well as a blurring of artistic boundaries. Within the film's comic narrative the Beatles manage to reflect upheavals in class and family relationships, certainly new modes of self-presentation. That the Beatles and their audience represent a participatory and uninhibited popular culture, whose central component was rock music, is somewhat self-evident. However, the film's ambiguity on permissiveness, a new frankness, openness and honesty, provides this study with its most challenging question.

Backed by United Artists (UA) and the production chief for its European division, George M. Ornstein, produced by Walter Shenson and directed by Richard Lester, *A Hard Day's Night* depended for its creation on American finance and expertise. This is not to detract from the fact that the film uses and is about British talent and British success, but rather it represents the story of the film industry in the sixties; that of Hollywood financing the 'British look' which was doing so well at the box office both in Britain and, more importantly, in America. As film critic Alexander Walker argues, 'to talk of the "British" cinema in these years is to ignore the reality of what underpinned the industry – namely, American finance or the dollar economy of what, for convenience sake, we may call "Hollywood"'.[4]

When UA's European division opened its London offices in 1961 it was a modest set-up, economically staffed with the aim of producing four or five low-budget (under £200,000) films a year. UA was a New-York-based company. Not owning permanent studios in Hollywood saved the company huge sums in maintenance costs but also made them more willing to invest in projects abroad, especially in Britain where production teams were cheaper. Before making *A Hard Day's Night*, UA financed two British-based films that were successful at the box-office, particularly in America: these were *Dr No* (1962), the first in the James Bond series, and *Tom Jones* (1963).[5] From the eighteenth-century novel by Henry Fielding, directed by Tony Richardson and starring Albert Finney and Susannah York, *Tom Jones* was very much a British film using British production staff, yet national film financing companies turned it down. Instead, UA provided 100 percent financing for *Tom Jones*, as they did with other film projects, the profit being divided generally 75/25 percent in UA's favour.[6] *Tom Jones* grossed UA a fortune of $30–40 million and obviously encouraged them to invest further in British projects.

The idea of doing a musical with the Beatles began in the music department of UA. Ornstein had only recently decided to include the music department in production meetings, recognising that records were an important source of revenue. However, the Beatles were not the obvious choice for a British musical, since the two foremost indigenous stars were Cliff Richard and Tommy Steele, both having scored sizeable hits with teenage audiences. In 1957 Steele had appeared in a biopic, *The Tommy Steele Story*, swiftly followed by *The Duke Wore Jeans* (1958) and the comedy *Tommy the Toreador* (1959). Richard, on the other hand, had hits with *Expresso Bongo* (1959), *The Young Ones* (1961), and *Summer Holiday* (1962). But problems lay in the basic narrative. As film historian Robert Murphy pointed out, 'these musicals, aimed directly at the teenage market, tended to be inanely conformist and their main virtue lay in the professionalism with which once threatening teenage idols are transformed into lovable young men only too happy to be integrated into adult society'.[7]

It was the success of the Beatles' first LP, *Please, Please Me*, that brought them to UA's attention. Released in March 1963, the album took less than six weeks to reach number one in the British charts with sales in excess of 150,000. In fact the only LP with higher sales was Elvis Presley's *Blue Hawaii*, an album Presley had promoted with a musical film of the same name in 1961.

As early as 1956 Presley was promoting record sales with feature-length films. *Love Me Tender* (1956) was Presley's debut film, and he went on to make over 30 films in his career. Released in May 1964, *Viva Las Vegas* provided him with his biggest box-office hit, grossing $5.5 million in the USA alone.[8] However, few of his films won critical acclaim. Indeed, the Presley musicals were poor pop vehicles, all resembling each other, all about having fun, falling in love, boy makes good, with Presley using the same screen persona with a different name in a different setting. In contrast, the Beatles would always 'play' themselves irrespective of the fictional or documentary narratives employed by their films. And despite the obvious rewards of increasing sales through the medium, they made a conscious decision not to end up making films for the larger part of their pop careers, but to focus on making records that would one day overtake Presley's sales.

British pop music had been dominated by America since the invasion of rock 'n' roll in the mid 1950s. Even in 1961, of the 24 number-one hits, 15 were American. But in 1963 British pop music exploded with the 'Merseybeat' sound of groups such as Gerry and the Pacemakers, the Searchers, Billy J. Kramer and the Dakotas, and of course the Beatles. Exporting music back to the United States, however, was not as simple. Glaswegian Lonnie Donegan had managed to sell his folksy, skiffle sound both at home and across the Atlantic, but it still had limited appeal. Even the Beatles' first two singles made no impact on the American charts. *I Want to Hold Your Hand* was their first single to break into the American charts early in 1964. Indeed, 1964 saw the Beatles with three number-one hit singles and two LPs in the top 10 of the British charts, and five top singles and 12 records in the top 100 of the American charts.

In *One For The Money*, Dave Harker's analysis of the sales figures reveals the period 1955–60 to be the economic take-off point for the recording industry, particularly in America.[9] Pointing to the introduction of new technology and the commercial popularisation of the LP, he argues that the most important factor in the boom of record sales was the realisation of the new, and highly lucrative, 'teenage market'.[10] *A Hard Day's Night* was originally intended as an exploitation movie to cash in on this market, and for that reason UA insisted on the Beatles producing original material for the film. On taking delivery, UA immediately used this as a selling feature, stating clearly on the film's promotional poster that *A Hard Day's Night* contained 'six exciting new songs'.

Their British and more recent American success caught the Beatles by surprise. Indeed, the main reason they had agreed to make the film during their tight touring and recording schedule was primarily to get wider exposure for their music in the USA. Yet by mid-February 1964 the Beatles had already made two crucially successful appearances on the *Ed Sullivan Show*, which in turn gave them all the visual exposure they required to gain a firm foothold in the American record market.[11] Nevertheless, filming began in earnest in March 1964, with breaks for recording the LP. After seven weeks' shooting, the film was completed in April, and in July the film premiere coincided with the release of the album.

Despite being loosely described by the trade press at the time as a 'comedy with music',[12] the film is far more sophisticated in terms of generic conventions. *A Hard Day's Night* is both a musical comedy in the traditional Hollywood sense and a piece of social realism. Although not a documentary *per se*, the film is greatly indebted to the British documentary-realist tradition, in particular the 'free cinema' documentaries of the mid-1950s and the British 'new wave' films of 1959–63, which brought to the fore northern working-class realist stories, combining them with stark black-and-white photography.

By doing a musical not only were the Beatles able to reach the teenage markets with their popular music, but they also gained access to a wider audience, using a genre that was by tradition firmly associated with family viewing. Furthermore, a musical comedy provided the Beatles with a perfect vehicle for a group that was increasingly renowned for their wit, humour and exuberance. Steering safely clear of the overtly adult themes of new wave cinema, *A Hard Day's Night* was certified 'U' for universal release. But the film-makers also steered clear of the stereotypical narratives of the musical. As the producer of *A Hard Day's Night*, Walter Shenson, recalls, 'I told them "I don't want to make a Hollywood style pop musical about four unknown Liverpool boys who smuggle the tape of their home-made compositions into the disc jockey's studio. I want to make a broad comedy based on a day in your life."'[13] Indeed, the film was originally entitled *Beatlemania*, with a view to capturing what was being heralded by the national press as a 'phenomenon', but the title was changed at the last minute. Inspired by Ringo's quaint misphrasing, Lennon wrote the title track virtually overnight, and with no room in the film to spare, Lester had to use the music over the opening credit sequence and ending.[14]

On the whole the Shenson-Lester strategy seemed to have worked. As Michael Knight from the *People* observed, the film was 'nothing like any previous musical, British or American'.[15] Similarly, Michael Thornton of the *Sunday Express* remarked:

> Walter Shenson's 85-minute production is not, I am relieved to say, the usual kind of British pop musical in which a series of hit songs are linked loosely by an incredible plot and unspeakable dialogue... In a diamond-bright script full of laconic, incisive wit, Alun Owen captures, better than anyone else to date, the strange, elusive idiom of the Merseybeat.[16]

However, Owen was not Lester's first choice, as an approach had been made to London East-End writer Johnny Speight (the creator of *Till Death Us Do Part*). However, due to previous commitments, Speight turned down the work and so the job of writing the screenplay fell to acclaimed Liverpudlian writer Owen. As Thornton reveals, Owen's understanding of the Beatles' regional roots enabled him to provide the group with more appropriate dialogue – so appropriate that many failed to notice that it was Owen rather than the Beatles who came up with trend words such as 'grotty' (an abreviation for grotesque).[17] Moreover, as Alexander Walker pointed out at the time, 'getting Owen to write for the Beatles was the first important move to take the Beatles seriously. To turn pop into art.'[18]

Although *A Hard Day's Night* has been recognised as one of the first artistic pop musicals, it is as much a traditional musical steeped in Hollywood as it is modern in its style and design. Moreover, *A Hard Day's Night* is a back-stage musical. The self-reflective nature of the show-biz musical is a formula perfected by Hollywood through which we gain admittance to both the public and private lives of the stars. Indeed, the backstage narrative device is extremely useful to the Beatles in their attempt to become more familiar to their audience. At one of the rehearsals featured in the film, Lennon uses the old musical cliché 'Hey, kids, I've got an idea. Why don't we do the show right here?' His ironic tone seems to mock the traditions of the genre. Yet while *A Hard Day's Night* appears cynical about show business, it entertains by using that very same process.

In terms of genre, *A Hard Day's Night* remains faithful to the traditions of the backstage musical. It is about 'putting on a show', one where the Beatles provide top billing among a group of variety acts, including (Lionel Blair) dancers, operetta singers, even a (Derek Nimmo) magic act. On the whole the Beatles'

'Putting on a show': the old musical meets the new pop musical in *A Hard Day's Night*

musical numbers are 'performed', in the traditional manner, on stage. Still, there are some important exceptions. For example, some artistic licence is used with their first number in the train carriage, as the game of cards is miraculously substituted for instruments and back again to cards. In an interview with Roy Carr, Lester revealed that although his brief was to make a factual movie he felt it necessary to inject some bursts of surrealism to make the songs interesting.[19] The most visually striking musical number is 'Can't Buy Me Love', which provides Lester and the Beatles with the best opportunity to improvise and show off their comic skills as they escape from the rigours of rehearsal to fool around in a nearby playing field. In this nonsensical scene mimicking the Goons (characters in the surrealist cult radio show of that name), Lester uses unusual camera angles and fast and slow photography to capture the energy and dynamism of the four. The same number would later be used for the 'Keystone Kops'-type chase. Not content with simply staging the six new songs, *A Hard Day's Night* cleverly incorporates Beatles music as background material. For example, the twist-club episode uses three Beatles' numbers for dance music. Lester also uses an instrumental version of 'This Boy' to accompany Ringo's lonely wanderings. Yet Lester significantly updates the look of the musical to give it a contemporary feel in other ways too. During rehearsals the group are placed in some innovative stage settings, one with a background of blown-up photographic images of beetles and bugs, seemingly playing on the group's name; however, the artwork is also indicative of developments in the contemporary British art and design scene. What enforces the film's modernity is that the show is to be televised live and we (the cinema audience) see that process clearly both through the camera viewfinder and on the control-room monitors. The references to the new power of television can hardly be missed; nor, indeed, those to the recent appearance of the Beatles on televised variety shows in both Britain and the United States, which contributed greatly to the group's meteoric rise.[20]

However, *A Hard Day's Night* is distinctive precisely because it employs two genres, oppositional by nature and on a cultural level. Associated with Hollywood, the musical tends towards fiction and fantasy whereas the documentary, associated with British traditions in film-making, tends towards fact and realism. *A Hard Day's Night* cleverly interweaves the 'day-in-the-life' theme with a fictional plot, most visible in the machinations of the grandfather figure, 'Mixing John McCartney', played by Wilfrid Brambell.

The story depicts an average 36 hours in the life of the group as they tour from one city to the next. The story begins with the Beatles being chased by adoring fans onto a train. The train is bound for London where the Beatles are to perform in a show that will be broadcast live. Although there are no specific names offered for the locations one assumes the city in question is London, highlighted not by its historic landmarks but rather by the feature of the river and the night-life. On the train they are met by their Liverpudlian manager, 'Norm', and his assistant, 'Shake'. This comic duo is somewhat reminiscent of Laurel and Hardy in their opposed temperaments, statures and intelligence, and they provide the film with a more traditional form of comedy, as opposed to the Beatles' fast action and witty retorts. The other main comic character is the troublesome grandfather John McCartney, whom Paul is looking after, and is therefore accompanying the Beatles on this particular engagement. Owen uses the escapades of the grandfather to move the action along, for example to visit the gambling club and to cause a rift between the Beatles, enough to make Ringo desert the group – temporarily of course. But before this takes place, between the musical rehearsals and final performance, the Beatles encounter a variety of people with whom they interact and thereby 'reveal' themselves either as a group or as individuals.

Owen spent a great deal of time with the Beatles in order to write a convincing screenplay that captured not just their lifestyle but their personalities. He cleverly individualised the Beatles by giving each a separate role or scene in the film. John is involved in a case of mistaken identity. George's key scene is to debunk the fashion stylists in a trend-setting agency. Through Ringo we take a look at the 'real' world outside and, with the exception of the truant schoolboy, it is depicted as a hostile place. And though Paul has no individual scene as such he has the dubious honour of having to be responsible for an elderly, mischievous relative.

Yet Owen was not the first to focus on the Beatles as individuals. Journalists such as Maureen Cleave of the *Evening Standard* and William Mann of *The Times* had been offering characterisations of the Beatles in the British press for some time. Donald Zec's article in the *Daily Mirror*, entitled 'Four Frenzied Little Lord Fauntleroys', is one of the many examples where the Beatles were identified by separate photographs and 'character'-revealing quotations. George was named 'the Quiet One' and was quoted as saying: 'we're quite a normal bunch, really'. For John they chose a witty comment: 'The way people begin to look like their dogs... we're beginning to look like each other'. Ringo's quotation reveals him to be the endearing, down to earth one: 'My Dad's gone right off his nut with excitement, he's full of "yeah, yeah, wow, wow"'. Finally, Paul is depicted as the responsible one, the organiser: 'If one of us gets to be a big-head, we'd soon bring him down a bit'.[21] Owen's film characterisations of the Beatles offered no in-depth study of the Fab Four psyche, but rather more of the same.

Nevertheless, for those still unfamiliar with the four Beatles, mainly the adult section of the family audience which included the film critics, Owen's narrative strategy was extremely useful, as *Evening News* journalist Felix Barker explained:

> Like many a parent I have watched the Beatles take over the house. Their pictures cover the walls, a record player throbs to their rhythm by day and night... Writing then, as a man who until this week didn't know Ringo from Paul or George from John (and cared rather less) let me join in the high-pitched frenzied screaming of teenage enthusiasm.[22]

More important and innovative was Owen's development of the exposé-style narrative that would reveal the Beatles as prisoners of their success. Certainly, judging by the film's structure, Owen wasted little screen time in achieving this end. For as the opening credits roll, one is immediately struck by the image of three Beatles being chased by screaming fans. The opening sequence contains many visual gags created by the three (George, Ringo and John) as they try to avoid the pursuing fans whilst trying to reach the train. Even Paul has been reduced to disguising himself with a moustache and beard, and hiding behind a newspaper in order to get on board. However, the train is depicted as both a sanctuary and a prison. As it pulls out of the station, the shot from its window shows the Beatles safely within whilst bedlam reigns outside, with hundreds of fans screaming and cameras flashing blindingly. A little later, as the Beatles perform the first musical number, 'I Should've Known Better', they are pictured cage-like in the luggage compartment with girls surrounding their prison compound. And when the Beatles reach the hotel they are still prisoners of their success, having to stay in to do their 'homework', answering their fan mail. Richard Lester said, with regard to the conception of *A Hard Day's Night*:

> 'I asked John "Did you like Sweden?" And he said, "Yes, very much. It was a room and a car and a car and a room and a concert and we had cheese sandwiches sent up to the hotel room". So that feeling of claustrophobia was how we tried to think of the whole first sequence, the whole first third of the film. In closed spaces: prisoners in space, prisoners of fans, prisoners by car, train, small hotel rooms – do this, do that, sign this.'[23]

Ironically, this retort is repeated in the film, not by Lennon or any of the other three Beatles, but by the fictional character of Paul's grandfather, who complains, 'I thought I was getting a change of scenery and so far I've been in a train and a room and a car and a room and a room and a room… I'm feeling decidedly straight jacketed!' The advantage of having the grandfather figure making the complaint is that it prevents the Beatles from appearing ungrateful or resentful with regard to their success. Instead the grandfather allows us to feel sympathy for the boys, but not too much, for ultimately the film-makers instil a sense of fun into all the proceedings.

Filmed in black-and-white with a raw, spontaneous, jump-cut style almost to the point of chaos, the film aped the directness of journalism, a quality the press itself praised it for. Penelope Gilliatt of the *Observer* remarked,

> as a piece of feature journalism, this is the first film in England that has anything like the urgency and dash of an English popular daily at its best. Like a news feature, it was produced under pressure, and the head of steam behind it has produced something expressive and alive.[24]

Only when one compares the film with contemporary documentaries made of the Beatles does the contrast between the documentary style employed by Lester's film as opposed to the documentary form become apparent.

In 1964 Granada television commissioned American independent documentary film-makers Albert and David Maysles to capture on film the impact of the Beatles on their first visit to the United States in February 1964. Entitled

What's Happening! The Beatles in the USA, the Maysles brothers' documentary was never screened in its original form.[25] No doubt UA breathed a sigh of relief, for the documentary and *A Hard Day's Night* contain a number of similar components in terms of settings and experiences. For example, in the Maysles documentary there is the airport-lounge press conference, the car being mobbed by fans en route through New York City, the siege-like experience of the hotel room, the escape to the Peppermint Lounge night club, the train journey to Washington, and of course the performances accompanied by the screaming fans. But there is also a real sense of claustrophobia, imprisonment, boredom, frayed tempers and awkwardness in front of the camera, even the sleaziness of the hard sell. In the documentary, the Beatles appear to be promoting products, firstly the documentary itself, but also radio stations, drinks and cigarettes. The cameras also pick out the more garish side of Beatles merchandising. UA kept this out of the narrative of their film but did not hesitate to advertise merchandise that promoted the film, such as 'A Hard Day's Night' dresses or bed linen. More significant is the way the documentary recorded the more private side to the Beatles that the makers of *A Hard Day's Night* were anxious to keep out. For example, the documentary provides a view of the Beatles' drinking and smoking habits, even the girls being smuggled into their rooms. Despite there being a plethora of attractive young ladies around the four, *A Hard Day's Night* is careful to avoid any references to relationships, casual or otherwise. Indeed, unlike the Richard or Presley musicals, *A Hard Day's Night* goes to great lengths to avoid the usual 'love interest'. According to Walter Shenson, it was more a case of not complicating the plot. Nevertheless, maintaining the sense that the Beatles were bachelors and therefore 'available' was an important feature of the film's appeal.[26]

Owen had set out to reveal the problems of being in the public eye. He observed, 'Ever noticed how much celebrities are pushed around in public? Really pushed around? Managers guiding them, fans pulling at them, compères patting them. You get to feel so much moveable property. What it feels to be a Beatle: that's the first priority.'[27] But the humour in *A Hard Day's Night* often works against the underlying seriousness and removes the sting of each situation. Instead, the Maysles documentary proves more effective in delivering the sense of being 'pushed around', for example by the hordes of cameramen at the Central Park photoshoot. This is not to say the documentary does not capture the talent and humour of the Beatles, particularly the unrehearsed and sometimes awkward repartee at the airport press conference. When asked to sing, Lennon adamantly replies, 'No!' then moderates his response by quickly adding, 'We need money first'. In *A Hard Day's Night*, not only does Owen try to capture the Beatles' spontaneity but almost recreates the airport event with the press buffet scene. When Lennon is asked, 'How did you find America?' the well-timed response is 'Turn left at Greenland'. Indeed, *What's Happening!* makes *A Hard Day's Night* look highly constructed, even slick, and brings us full circle to face the fact that whether British or American, *A Hard Day's Night* is a musical.

Initially, UA were unsure how many prints of the film would be required, such was the escalating popularity of the group. Eventually, an unprecedented number of between 1500 and 1800 prints of the film were made: the USA accounted for 700, the UK accounted for at least 110, and the rest were distributed worldwide.[28] The film went on general release in the UK and the USA in August 1964. In the US it opened in 500 cinemas across the country, taking $1.3 million within its first week and $5.8 million by the end of the sixth week.[29] On the whole the film received a warm reception, even from the most discerning. *Sunday Times* film critic Dilys Powell commented:

> And instead of the raw excuse for Beatle-song which I had expected, here was a sharply professional piece, directed with great dash by Richard Lester, boldly photographed by Gilbert Taylor, smartly edited by John Jympson – and acted, as well as thrummed and bawled, with the most likeable aplomb by the Sacred Four.[30]

Almost everyone involved in the production received praise from one quarter or another, including the Beatles for their performance as comic actors. On the whole the group were most often likened to either the Goons or the Marx brothers. For example, the *Daily Mail* critic Cecil Wilson remarked, 'The Marx brothers exploded on to the Screen last night. Except this time they were four adenoidal young anarchists from Liverpool who call themselves the Beatles.'[31] Special praise was given to Ringo's 'chaplinesque' scene where he wanders around the city innocently getting into trouble with the locals and the police. Although the dialogue is minimal, his lonely mood is reflected by the use of an instrumental version of the Beatles' mournful number, 'This Boy'.

However, the film was not without its critics, at home and abroad. The reviewer for the *Financial Times*, for example, remained unimpressed despite the film's credentials, suggesting that 'something more could surely have been done with this quartet... The script, such as there is of it, is credited to Alun Owen, the director was Dick Lester, who always promises more than he actually accomplishes.'[32] Al Finestone of the *Hollywood Reporter* registered his dissatisfaction with the style employed:

> While imaginative and often offbeat, photography is lacking by top standards in on-the-spot location shooting and editing is not as fluent as it might be in integrating the fast-moving scenes. Sound at times doesn't help American audiences to understand the quaint dialect and slang expressions.[33]

Indeed, contrary to Shenson's belief that American audiences would be charmed by the non-American humour and accents, the *Time* film critic observed that 'sometimes the humor seems forced, the North Country slang impenetrable'.[34] John Seelye of *Film Quarterly* even went as far as to suggest 'some sequences of this film need subtitles'.[35]

French critics also found fault with the film. Rémo Forlani writing in *Cahiers du Cinéma* was scathing. Not content with denouncing *A Hard Day's Night* as a 'bad film', he ridiculed Lester:

> To justify his salary Richard Lester should have been content to film the Beatles as in the past... It is too easy to make a made-to-measure film for a singer...

Richard Lester aimed much higher – he decided to be modern – to be with it! He dispensed with colour (colour was old-fashioned – only good for Gene Kelly movies), he decided to film on the streets (cinéma-vérité is not dead!). He decided to film the Beatles with complete freedom (one dreams of Flaherty and Nanouk!), he decided to act the fool![36]

In contrast with their visit to the USA, during the early part of 1964 the Beatles had received a less rapturous reception from the French. What is surprising, however, is the source of this particular criticism, for *Cahiers du Cinéma* was the intellectual forum for the critics who became the film-makers of the French *nouvelle vague*. And while British film reviewers turned a blind eye, both the American and French reviewers were quick to point out the film's association with the *nouvelle vague*, particularly in the use of techniques such as location shooting, hand-held camera work, jump-cut editing and improvisational qualities in the narrative, filming and acting.

More recently, Bob Neaverson has examined the film in some detail and arrives at the conclusion that *A Hard Day's Night* is a 'cinematic bastard' heavily influenced by the French *nouvelle vague*. He argues, 'Lester and Owen's narrative construction and pacing is, in effect (if not intention), closer to that of the French "new wave" than to any previous British or American pop musical'.[37] Certainly, Lester admired French new wave directors, in particular the work of Alain Resnais, Jean-Luc Godard and François Truffaut. Scrutiny of Lester's film reveals many technical similarities in terms of hand-held camera work, camera swoops, freeze frames, and jump-cut editing, but in terms of its narrative construction *A Hard Day's Night* owes a great deal more to the Hollywood musical tradition and to the British documentary movement than to the French *nouvelle vague*. Lester himself believed that the most pervasive influence on his work was silent comedy, especially the work of Mack Sennett, Charlie Chaplin and particularly Buster Keaton.[38] Like the French *nouvelle vague* directors, Lester did incorporate a number of cinematic influences, but unlike them Lester did not operate as an independent film-maker with complete artistic control. Moreover, seeing Lester as the film's sole *auteur* is questionable if one takes into account Owen's contribution, along with those of photographer Gilbert Taylor and editor John Jympson, not to mention the Beatles themselves. Lester *et al.* were working to a brief supplied by Shenson and UA which required them to reach as wide an audience as possible – to 'sell' the Beatles.

While the Beatles' manager Brian Epstein has been primarily credited with packaging them for 'family consumption' and bringing them onto the world stage, Lester and Owen can be regarded as co-conspirators in this marketing coup. *A Hard Day's Night* provides us with a valuable insight into the complexities of the Beatles' image, in particular how they were able to align themselves with youth culture without alienating the adults.

Early on, in the train carriage, the Beatles are confronted with an imposing gentleman in his late fifties, smartly dressed, wearing a traditional suit with bowler hat. The UA synopsis released to the press describes this character as 'a well-established first-class ticket holder' who is 'pompously officious'. The gentleman immediately asserts his authority by closing the carriage window and turning off Ringo's transistor radio. The gentleman traveller obviously represents larger issues, such as parent-child relations, class relations, as well as representing a figure of the establishment. In stark contrast to the friendliness of the Beatles he is both impolite and austere. The Beatles try to assert that they (youth) have equal rights in a democratic society and within the carriage four out of five passengers want the window open. But he rebuts this claim with the ultimate put-down 'I fought the war for your sort'. To which Ringo cheekily responds, 'Bet you're sorry you won!' Lennon audaciously flutters his eyelashes at the gentleman and asks him to 'give us a kiss'. The gentlemen glowers contemptuously at them and returns to his paper. Realising they cannot persuade him to see their point of view, the Beatles use comedy to express the stereotypical role into which they are being forced, that of troublesome schoolboys who have had their ball confiscated. In one of the few scenes in which the bounds of realism are broken and fantasy comes into play the four appear outside the carriage while the train is moving. But it is their irreverence to this figure of authority which is both striking and refreshing, and one of the many ways the Beatles encapsulated new modes of expression and self-presentation.

Indeed it is the adults – the traveller, the manager, the director, the groundsman and the policeman – who consistently place obstacles in the way of the Beatles having fun. And, as Alexander Walker pointed out, it is Paul's fictional Irish grandfather who provides 'a novel twist to the war between adults and teenagers – for it's the old man who continually invites trouble, not the nice clean-cut set of kids'.[39] Unlike the Steele and Richard musicals, *A Hard Day's Night* gave a fresh impetus to the perceived 'war'. Not everybody was amused, however, as *Daily Mail* film critic Ann Scott-Jones revealed:

> The thing about the Beatles' film which nobody has mentioned is its total remorselessness. This is a comedy without one twinge of pity for human beings, particularly the old… *A Hard Day's Night* is brilliant, fast, funny and distinctly frightening. I had thought of the Beatles as witty, talented, charming boys, but they are also as hard as old iron.[40]

Nevertheless, the carriage scene remains poignant in the way the film-makers reflect the desire of 1960s youth for change. Such desires were cleverly seized upon by politicians like Harold Wilson, who, realising the potential voting capacity of this section of society, based his 1964 election campaign on images of a new Britain:

> This is a time for a breakthrough to an exciting and wonderful period in our history, in which all can and must take part. Our young men and women, especially, have in their hands the power to change the world. We want the youth of Britain to storm the new frontiers of knowledge, to bring back to Britain that surging adventurous self-confidence and sturdy self-respect.[41]

Certainly Philadelphian-born Richard Lester, who came to England in 1955, thought so. A student of clinical psychology, he turned to a career in television following graduation. He quickly gained a reputation for producing innovative commercials, but he came to UA's attention due to his work with the Goons, particularly the short *The Running, Jumping and Standing Still Film* (1959), and for his musical *It's Trad Dad!* (1962). Shenson and UA contracted Lester to provide the comedy sequel, *The Mouse on the Moon* (1963), and although it was not as successful as its forerunner, *The Mouse that Roared* (1959), he was ideally qualified to direct the Beatles' film. In his article, 'Keeping Up with the Beatles: Making Films for Teenagers', Robin Bean revealed a significant factor: 'Ten directors for the 'teens have an average of 65.6 years, while 80 per cent of their audience is under 35 years'.[42] Lester was only thirty-one years old when he made *A Hard Day's Night*, one of the youngest directors at the time and obviously more in tune with the tastes of young adults. From his work in commercial advertising Lester understood the importance of innovation and instant impact. Indeed it was Lester rather than photographer Gilbert Taylor who came up with innovative ideas such as using hand-held cameras in the chase sequences and employing a helicopter to shoot views of the playing-field scene. Moreover, he gave the Beatles opportunities to improvise and be themselves.

Perhaps the most interesting scenes in terms of the film's relationship with youth, and indeed Lester's own world, are the parodies of the artistic television director and the advertising agent. The television director, played by Victor Spinetti, finds it hard to cope with the unruly Beatles, and appears to be on the verge of a breakdown when Ringo disappears, jeopardising the programme's finale. He bemoans the fact that 'once you're over thirty, you're past it – it's a young man's game!' In a similar manner, the agency is ridiculed as it tries to recruit Harrison, but to their horror he upsets the scheme of things by rejecting their resident teenager icon 'Susan' as 'a drag, a well-known drag', and dismissing their new range of shirts as 'dead grotty'.

The right image, however, was essential to the wider success of the Beatles. Brian Epstein set about changing their image to incorporate a self-confident spirit that would attract the young, with the look of respectability that would satisfy the establishment. One of the most visible ways in which this was achieved was in their clothing, in particular the 'Beatle suit'. As art historian Nigel Whiteley stated, 'the aim of the Beatle Suit was to strike a balance between rebellion and respectability – rebelliousness to appeal to youth, respectability to soothe the parents – an aim that was successful'.[43] During the Cavern days, and until the time the Beatles signed a management contract with Epstein, they were still wearing rockabilly leathers, although they had done away with the corresponding hairstyles. Aware of their outfit's association with scruffiness, aggression and sexuality, Epstein persuaded the Beatles to wear the specially-designed suits that were distinctive but casual in style. As a result, not only had Epstein led them away from an antagonistic image to an acceptable one, but he had also led them away from an American image to one that would play a part in creating the Beatles' identity as British. With a surprising number of 'costume' changes and facial close-ups, *A Hard Day's Night* provided the ideal venue to show off the suits and the now familiar 'mop-top' hairstyle.

But the Beatle mop-top and the Beatle suit had one further advantage. Although each was portrayed as an individual, they appeared seemingly indistinguishable, an interchangeable community, highlighted by clever photography and promotional publicity. An example of this interchangability can be seen in the closing credits as head-shots of the four are overlaid on top of one another. Moreover, the speed of Beatle dialogue emphasised the idealistic notion that they worked as a unit. The film's narrative tends to focus humorously on the divisiveness of the grandfather character, the tensions between fictional manager Norm and Lennon, even the sensitivity and introversion of Ringo, but it avoids depicting any serious internal conflict, and certainly none of the artistic rivalry between Lennon and McCartney so often documented by Beatle biographers. Ringo's defection from the group (a result of the grandfather's meddling) and subsequent reunification is a useful narrative device to emphasise the four's special bonding.

The first-class-traveller episode also shows the film-makers engaging with the problem of class as well as highlighting regional divisions. Despite the smartness and politeness of the Beatles, the demeanour of the pompous gentleman suggests that he considers them in a class beneath him. Richard Lester commented on the Beatles' attitude to social barriers:

> The general aim of the film was to present what was apparently becoming a social phenomenon in this country. Anarchy is too strong a word, but the quality of confidence that the boys exuded... You must accept that this is a film based

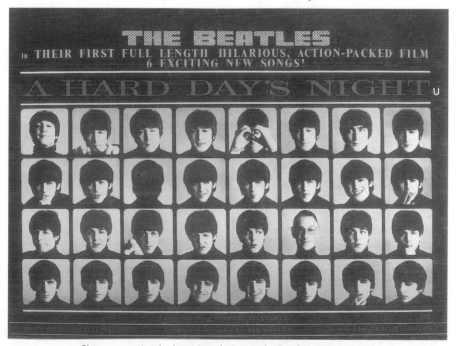

Clever promotional advertising playing on the Beatles' 'mop top' and
the sense of communality: the film poster for *A Hard Day's Night*

on a class society. It is difficult for someone coming from America, where there is a society based on money, to realise the strength... I mean a society that was still based on privilege – privilege by schooling, privilege by birth, privilege by accent, privilege by speech. They were the first people to attack this... they said if you want to do something, do it. You can do it. Forget all this talk about talent or ability or money or speech. Just do it. And this has been their great strength.[44]

Yet Lester does not rely entirely on the Beatles to mock the class system. The grandfather character provides a witty poke at the establishment as he hijacks a waiter's formal coat dress and passes himself off as one of the elite at a high-class casino. To stress the duplicity of 'the look', when the grandfather runs out of playing tokens at the gaming table he reverts to being a waiter to collect money from an unsuspecting client.

Beatle biographer Barry Miles observed, 'the British obsession with class is something that mystifies foreigners and irritates a good many Britons, but at the time the Beatles started there were very clear class divisions drawn in Britain with a variety of subtle levels and subdivisions'.[45] And, as McCartney revealed to Miles, there were subtle differences amongst the Beatles themselves:

> John lived just the other side of the golf course, literally and metaphorically. People don't realise how middle class he was. It's a very fancy neighbourhood... John was the nearest to middle class. The other three of us weren't. We were quite definitely working class... upper working class. We were in a posh area but the council bit of the posh area. John was actually in one of the almost posh houses in the posh area.[46]

Perhaps it is not surprising that the film's depiction of the British class system is simplistic, but it takes great pains in promoting the Beatles' working-class roots even though due to a combination of education, experiences and wealth they had already moved away from this position. Nevertheless, *A Hard Day's Night* makes several references to the Beatles being ordinary, working-class lads, with their scouse accents and down-to-earth language, even in the images of George with his home-made sandwiches, and Paul looking after his grandfather. Again, Owen's script echoed the depictions of the Beatles in the national press, which generally presented the group as 'the boys from next door', four ordinary lads with an extraordinary talent and winning charm. For example, Maureen Cleave's series in the *Evening Standard*, entitled '1963... The Year of The Beatles', set about listing their achievements:

> The Beatles are the first people to make rock 'n' roll respectable... They have won over the class snob, the intellectual snob, the music snob, the grown ups and the husbands... They appeal to the family; they appeal to the nation. Liverpool and the North are fiercely proud and now the rest of England has taken them over.[47]

In his analysis of the Beatles' public personas, jazz musician and art critic George Melly sets Ringo apart for special attention: 'Ringo is not the world's most inventive drummer but he is lovably plain, a bit "thick" as a public persona, and decidedly ordinary in his tastes. He acts as a bridge, reassuring proof that the Beatles bear some relation to normal people.'[48] In *A Hard Day's Night*, Owen and Lester seem to have paid special attention to the characterisation of Ringo. For example, it is Ringo who receives the most fan mail, and who is sensitive about his nose. It is Ringo who functions to reveal regional resentments, whose wanderings uncover derelict areas in London, and who shows empathy with the working-class boy playing truant from school. The narrative places him at the receiving end of all sorts of prejudices, in particular from the police, who even refer to him as a 'savage'. Within the film it is Ringo who 'acts as a bridge', maintaining an emotional link with the audience that the other three do not inspire.

Yet the Beatles as depicted in the film, like the Steele and Richard characters before them, pose no real threat to the status quo, for although they appear to be set against institutions as represented by the officious traveller, the press and the police, they do not form any real resistance or challenge. When Paul recites the slogan '"Up the Workers"... and all that stuff', it is not delivered with any conviction. If one reads the film in terms of a protest, one becomes increasingly aware of the film's complete reliance on comedy to achieve this end. The police are depicted as incompetent, particularly as their scenes mimic those of the Keystone Kops' silent comedy films. The press receive the same treatment, insofar as humour saves them from appearing parasites or vultures, feeding off the Beatles' fame and food, literally at the press conference buffet. Similarly, the Spinetti character is depicted as a comic paranoid, sick and ineffectual person. The carriage confrontation is the only one where the Beatles come anywhere close to 'revolt'.

The film also demonstrates how the Beatles were able to encapsulate qualities of both sexual innocence and sexual experience. In this respect it would appear that Epstein and the Beatles had learned a great deal from Elvis Presley's career. When Presley first appeared on national network television, on the *Ed Sullivan Show*, Sullivan insisted that Presley should be filmed only from the waist up because of the suggestiveness of his hip movements. Whereas Melly views the taming of Presley and rock 'n' roll as turning 'revolt into style', Harker regards the way in which Presley was commercialised and marketed as a process of 'encapsulation and accommodation'. However, with the Beatles one questions whether there was any attempt at 'revolt' in the first place. For instance, Harker pointed out, 'these happy little rockers accepted the uniforms, submitted to stylised version of long hair, made sweeter music and became an even bigger commercial success. They became in short, thoroughly respectable.'[49]

Throughout the film, the Beatles do indeed appear thoroughly respectable; there is nothing overtly offensive or revolutionary about their behaviour. Seemingly difficult to control and organise, the Beatles appear mischievously playful rather than menacing. Yet on closer scrutiny one is surprised at the number of sexual innuendoes in the film, apart from the advances of the screaming pubescent girls. Two scenes in which the Beatles refer to their own sexuality take place on the train journey. The first occurs when George spies two very attractive girls:

George: Eh! look at the talent.
John: Let's give 'em a pull.

Their first attempt, however, is thwarted by the grandfather figure, who pretends the Beatles are convicts being escorted by himself, but later the boys meet the girls again. This time they play out the prisoner charade and John asks jokingly, 'I bet you can't guess what I was in for?' as he leers maniacally at one of the young girls. As one expects, the girls know all too well who they are; their reaction is the obvious squeal of excitement. More unexpected is the scene where Ringo is invited by a glamorous young woman into her carriage compartment:

George: Going in then?
Ringo: No, she'll only reject me in the end and I'll be frustrated.
George: You never know, you may be lucky this time.
Ringo: No, I know the psychological pattern and it plays havoc with me drum skins.

Again, the lapse into subtle comedy saves the Beatles from appearing promiscuous and offensive, thus preserving their clean-cut, somewhat virginal image. Epstein was careful not to allow references to the Beatles' girls, or any unwholesome habits like drinking, smoking or drugs, lest it damage that image. Even when John suggestively sniffs a coke bottle it is done as a joke and ignored by the rest, being treated as just one of the many incidents of the Beatles' fooling around. Still, it is surprising that this small excerpt did not hit the cutting-room floor, especially when, as Victor Spinetti revealed, many of the Beatles' ad-libs were removed.[50]

Music historian Wilfred Mellers analyses the Beatles' music in terms of innocence and experience, and his analysis of the title track on *A Hard Day's Night* (LP) is particularly valuable here. Mellers argues that whereas the early songs were concerned with adolescence, growing up and puberty, 'A Hard Day's Night' signifies a change. Although the song is about love, it is more down-to-earth and realistic, as can be seen in the language, 'working like a dog'. Mellers points to 'the division between innocence (the ecstasy of being "held tight") and experience (things, making money, the tedium of work…)'.[51] Similarly, he draws our attention to the sexual innuendo in the reading and vocal delivery of 'things' and 'feel alright'. For Mellers, 'If I Fell' is also an adult love song incorporating an experience of another relationship, one that has gone painfully wrong. Balancing these more mature numbers are those like 'Love Me Do' and 'I'm Happy to Dance With You', that repeat the old Beatles formula, which Mellers describes as the 'edenic song'. The edenic song, Mellers argues, incorporates qualities of the 'primitive', 'childlike', 'innocence', but is also 'timeless', 'present-affirming', and through which the Beatles appear 'new born'. According to Mellers, the edenic songs were quintessential to the Beatles' early image and success.

If *A Hard Day's Night* relied heavily on the use of comedy in defusing sensitive areas such as youth power, class conflict and permissiveness, it also relied on the familiar form of the musical to make 'safe' the Beatles for both British and American consumption. Along with their music and image, the Beatles were for a short period able to appear both radical and respectable. After the release of *A Hard Day's Night* the Beatles would increasingly be 'seen' as political figures even though there is little evidence to substantiate this image. However, in September 1964 they did refuse to play at the Gater Bowl, Jacksonville, Florida, until they received assurances that the audiences would not be colour-segregated. Other factors may have contributed to this image, such as Lennon's comments on religion causing a minor uproar in the USA in 1966, and the Beatles' signatory support of the campaign to legalise cannabis in 1967, yet the Beatles involvement with the counter-culture was in fact minimal. Epstein had worked hard to keep the Beatles' 'nice boy' image in the media, and to a large extent had succeeded, particularly in keeping news of their experimentation with drugs out of the head-lines. With Epstein's death in July 1967, ironically as a result of his own drug problem, the Beatles increasingly followed their own paths. Lennon and his partner Yoko Ono became the ones most openly identified with the counter-culture, with their anti-Vietnam 'bed-ins' and support of the underground paper *Oz*. McCartney, on the other hand, would quietly support ventures such as the rival underground paper *International Times*.

1966 not only saw the end of the so-called 'British invasion', but also the last Beatles tour and performance at San Francisco's Candlestick Park. Despite their attempts to reach larger audiences by playing at stadium venues, they were tired of touring. One would have expected them at this stage to have more readily turned to the medium of film to promote their records, especially after the success of *A Hard Day's Night*, but their subsequent forays into the film industry were met with increasing disappointment, for fans and critics alike. In contrast, their music continued to be successful and win critical acclaim. As the musical work became more diverse and complex so did their public image. They were no longer willing or able to maintain their simple 'boys from next door' appeal. Indeed, one cannot underestimate the importance of the 'edenic' formula; one only has to look to the formation in 1966 of the Beatles' American counterparts – the Monkees – to see how lucrative the formula could prove. The development of this teen group whose output, in particular their television series, was heavily influenced by the Beatles and *A Hard Day's Night*, is another subject worthy of closer scrutiny. Whilst Cliff Richard's next project, *Wonderful Life* (1964), was too late to benefit from Lester's contribution, and Presley's musicals continued to follow their usual pattern, nevertheless *A Hard Day's Night* had set the standard for the new pop musical. Described by Andrew Sarris as 'the Citizen Kane of the jukebox musical',[52] *A Hard Day's Night* is, as George Melly commented, 'the most seminal of all pop films',[53] which no group seemed to match. Director John Boorman tried with the Dave Clarke Five to imitate Lester's innovative style in *Catch Us if You Can* (1965). In a similar manner, groups such as Herman's Hermits, Sonny and Cher, and Freddie and the Dreamers each attempted to locate a suitable vehicle to promote themselves in the hope of emulating the Beatles' film success. More recently, the British girl-band the Spice Girls produced their own comedy-musical, *Spiceworld – The Movie* (1997). Complete with documentary film-makers attempting to chart a 'day in the life' of the famous five, the film includes many updated if not exaggerated features of *A Hard Day's Night*. For instance, there is the bus journey, rehearsals, irreverent press conference, adoring fans and troubled manager trying to keep track of them, even the temporary internal discord before being re-united and dashing to the live performance which provides the film's finale. Indeed, the film can be viewed as a nineties feminist pastiche of *A Hard Day's Night*, proving that even now the Beatles' first film remains the 'blue-print' of the pop musical.

ACKNOWLEDGEMENTS

My thanks to Arthur Marwick, Anthony Aldgate and James Chapman for their advice and help in putting together this chapter.

NOTES TO CHAPTER 5

1   Alexander Walker still provides the definitive film production guide in *Hollywood, England*, op. cit. More recently, Roy Carr's colourful *Beatles at the Movies: Scenes From a Career* (London, 1996, UFO Music) is interesting and informative, although lacking in either textual or contextual analysis. Whilst Bob Neaverson's *The Beatles Movies* (London, 1997, Cassell) is more stimulating in this respect, he leaves plenty of room for further analysis and debate. There are of course a number of biographies of the Beatles. However, the only two authorised works are by Hunter Davies: *The Beatles: the Only Authorized Biography*, first published by Heinemann in 1968, and the more recent offering by Barry Miles, *Paul McCartney: Many Years From Now* (London, 1997, Secker & Warburg). Of the many other texts available, two were particularly helpful for the purposes of this study. Firstly, Mark Lewisohn's *The Complete Beatles Chronicle* (London, 1992, Pyramid Books) is excellent for factual information. Lewisohn is one of the few Beatle historians to include details of their numerous television appearances and draw attention to the documentary *What's Happening!* The second is Ian MacDonald's *Revolution in the Head: the Beatles' Records and the Sixties* (London, 1994, Pimlico). MacDonald combines an intelligent overview of the Beatles' career in the first part with a detailed analysis of their music in the second, followed by a chronologcial table which not only charts the Beatles' movements and products but also provides a comparative table of political and cultural events.

2   As individuals the Beatles were involved in other film projects either as actors or film-score writers. Roy Carr's book is useful in providing details of the individual projects as well as detailing the Beatles film projects that were planned but failed to go into production.

3   Piri Halasz, 'You Can Walk Across It On the Grass', *Time*, 15 April 1966, pp 30–4.

4 Walker, *Hollywood, England*, op. cit., p 16.
5 Although *Tom Jones* can be still be classified as low-budget film costing $350,000, *Dr No* cost $950,000 to produce. *A Hard Day's Night*, in contrast, cost a mere $185,000 to make (all figures from Walker, *Hollywood, England*, op. cit.).
6 Walker reveals that UA offered Epstein and the Beatles 20 percent of the net gross and £25,000 cash (Walker, *Hollywood, England*, op. cit., p 233).
7 Robert Murphy, *Sixties British Cinema* (London, 1992, BFI), p 133.
8 Jerry Hopkins, *Elvis: A Biography* (London, 1972, Open Gate Books), p 292.
9 Dave Harker, *One For The Money: The Politics of Popular Song* (London, 1980, Hutchinson) p 84.
10 As Arthur Marwick rightly points out 'youth is about the least monolithic and least stable of categories into which society can be divided'. For a more informed view of this complex area of 'teenage markets', I recommend the relevant chapter in Marwick's book, *The Sixties*, op. cit. Sadly, there is little scholarly work on film audiences of this period, and although the Beatles fan-base can be divided roughly into the pre-teens, teenagers and young adults it would be interesting to know in more detail the make-up of their film audience. However, an interesting fact unearthed by Terry Staples in his book, *All Pals Together: The Story of Children's Cinema* (Edinburgh, 1997, Edinburgh University Press) is that both Beatles films, *A Hard Day's Night* and *Help!*, proved very popular with child audiences at the Saturday morning matinees in the UK.
11 A.C. Nielsen ratings reported on 9 February 1964 around 73 million (over 60 percent) of American television viewers, the largest television audience in the world, watched the Beatles.
12 *Daily Cinema*, 8 July 1964, p 10.
13 Shenson interviewed by Walker, 14 January 1971: Walker, *Hollywood, England*, op. cit., pp 234–5.
14 There are many versions of how Ringo inadvertantly came up with the film's title but it is generally understood that Ringo would regularly come out with malapropisms, particularly when he was worse for drink. In this case, the comment 'It's been A Hard Day's Night' was made after a particularly long recording session that went on well into the night.
15 Michael Knight, *People*, 12 July 1964.
16 Micheal Thornton, 'What a triumph this is for those Beatles', *Sunday Express*, 12 July 1964.
17 Paul McCartney interviewed by Roy Carr, revealed that the word 'grotty' was not in the Beatles vocabulary. Carr, *Beatles at the Movies*, op. cit., p 31.
18 Alexander Walker, *Evening Standard*, 'The Beatles on Trial,' 17 June 1964.
19 Lester interviewed by Roy Carr, *Beatles at the Movies*, op. cit., p 31.
20 The start of Beatlemania coincided with their televised performance at *Sunday Night at the London Palladium* on 13 October 1963. An estimated 15 million viewers watched the Beatles top the bill, while 26 million watched their televised appearance on the Royal Variety Performance on 11 November 1963.
21 Donald Zec, *Daily Mirror*, 10 September 1963.
22 Felix Barker, 'At Last – I Scream For the Beatles', *Evening News*, 9 July 1964.
23 Lester interviewed by di Franco, London 1970, in J. Philip di Franco, *The Beatles in Richard Lester's A Hard Day's Night – A Complete Pictorial Record of the Movie*, (London and New York, 1977, Chelsea House), p 5.

24 Penelope Gilliatt, *The Observer*, 12 July 1964.
25 Originally commissioned by Granada Television, who withdrew from the larger project and utilised only the New York material to make *Yeah!Yeah! Yeah! New York Meets The Beatles*, broadcast in the UK on 12 February 1964. Following this, Columbia pictures offered the Maysles brothers $1 million for *What's Happening!* but also withdrew from negotiations when a suitable release posed problems. Later, in November 1964, it was aired in the USA by CBS with the addition of a Carol Burnett commentary. Finally, in 1984, the rights were sold to Apple Corps Ltd. Re-edited in 1991 to include the Beatles' three appearances on the *Ed Sullivan Show*, the video was entitled *The Beatles: The First US Visit*. My thanks to Albert Maysles for providing the background to this documentary and also to Neil Aspinall and Zöe Howard of Apple Corps Ltd for their assistance in viewing the commercial version of this documentary.
26 Lennon was of course married, a fact ignored by both documentary and feature films, but interestingly enough it is highlighted on the *Ed Sullivan Show*.
27 Owen interviewed by Walker, 11 March 1964: Walker, *Hollywood, England*, op. cit., p 237.
28 Carr, *Beatles at the Movies: Scenes From a Career*, op. cit., p 47. Compare with 1300 prints issued for the third Bond film, *Goldfinger*: see Walker, *Hollywood, England*, op. cit., p 198
29 Ibid. Carr reveals that UA raked in over $0.5 million from special previews and premieres alone. In *Hollywood, England*, p 241, Walker estimates by 1971 the film had grossed about $11 million dollars worldwide, $6 million from the US and Canada.
30 Dilys Powell, *Sunday Times*, 12 July 1964.
31 Cecil Wilson, 'Merseybeat Marxes!', *Daily Mail*, 7 July 1964.
32 *Financial Times*, 10 July 1964.
33 Al Finestone, *Hollywood Reporter*, 21 July 1964.
34 *Time*, 4 August 1964.
35 John Seelye, *Film Quarterly*, Autumn 1964, p.54.
36 Rémo Forlani, *Cahiérs du Cinéma*, n. 160, 1964, pp 82–83.
37 Neaverson, *The Beatles Movies*, op. cit., p17.
38 J. Philip di Franco, *The Beatles in Richard Lester's A Hard Day's Night*, op. cit., p 38; further evidence of Lester's influences can be found in interviews reprinted in journals such as *Film Quarterly*, vol. 19, no. 14, Summer 1966, pp 12–16; *Film* (the journal of the Federation of Film Societies), no. 48, Spring 1967, pp 16–21; *Films and Filming*, vol. 21, no. 1, October 1974, pp 10–15.
39 Alexander Walker, *Evening Standard*, 6 July 1964.
40 Ann Scott-Jones, *Daily Mail*, 16 July 1964.
41 Harold Wilson, *Wilson Speeches* (London, 1964, Penguin) p 10.
42 Robin Bean, 'Keeping Up With The Beatles: Making Films for Teenagers', *Films and Filming*, February 1964, p 12.
43 Nigel Whiteley, *Pop Design: Modernism to Mod* (London, 1987, The Design Council), p 102.
44 Lester interviewed by di Franco, London 1970: J. Philip di Franco, *The Beatles in Richard Lester's A Hard Day's Night*, op. cit., p 5.
45 Barry Miles, *Paul McCartney: Many Years From Now*, op. cit., p 43. Miles's close friendship with the Beatles, particularly McCartney, stems back to 1965.

However, the book is mainly based on 35 taped interviews with McCartney over a period of six years between 1991 and 1996.

46 Ibid., pp 43–4.

47 Maureen Cleave, *Evening Standard*, 17 October 1963, p. 7.

48 George Melly, *Revolt into Style: the Pop Arts in Britain* (Harmondsworth, 1970, Penguin), p 69.

49 Harker, *One For the Money*, op. cit., p 84.

50 Spinetti interviewed by Neaverson, 29 April 1996: *Bob Neaverson, The Beatles Movies*, op. cit., p 16.

51 Wilfred Mellers, *Twilight of the Gods: The Beatles in Retrospect* (London, 1973, Faber & Faber), p 43.

52 Andrew Sarris, *Village Voice*, 27 August 1964.

53 Melly, *Revolt into Style*, op. cit., p 161.

6 Three Alison Lurie Novels of the Long Sixties

Arthur Marwick

Probably Alison Lurie's best-known novel (now conveniently available in a Minerva paperback, which is the edition I shall refer to throughout this chapter) is *The War Between the Tates*, published in 1974, the terminal year of my 'long sixties'. An international best-seller, *The War Between the Tates* was instantly recognised as a brilliant commentary on the tribulations of American life at the end of the 1960s. Labelling it 'the most outrageously funny book about sex yet written', fellow novelist Phillip Roth, author of *Portnoy's Complaint* (1968), wrote:

> Perhaps no brief period in American history has been so charged with literary possibilities for gifted, realistic novelists as the closing years of the Vietnam war, when settled social arrangements and repressive piety began to give way to libidinous appetites and blasphemous energies, and it even appeared for a while as though the accepted institutions of order and virtue were actually about to go under. Just this sort of moral upheaval is the subject of Alison Lurie's excellent comedy about family disorder.

According to the *New York Times Book Review*, 'Alison Lurie has raised the Way We Live Now into the Human Comedy. *The War Between the Tates* is a novel not only to read, but to reread for its cool and revealing mastery of a social epoch...' A dozen years later an article about Lurie in *Horizon* remarked that 'when future historians look back on these turbulent years', *The War Between the Tates* 'is likely to be a primary text'.[1] Actually, my original intention in proposing this

114

chapter to my colleagues had been to concentrate on a much less well-known novel, *Love and Friendship*, first published in 1962 (and now available as a Vintage paperback, which is the edition I shall be using), a remarkable expression of the changing attitudes of women during 'The First Stirrings of a Cultural Revolution, c.1958–c.1963', and one which is congruent with the ideas imbricated in two more famous books, both published a year later: *The Feminine Mystique* by Betty Friedan and *The Group* by Mary McCarthy. After working on the Alison Lurie papers at Cornell University, I realised that there were also new things I could say about *The War Between the Tates*, and indeed upon the three other novels written between 1962 and 1974: *The Nowhere City* (1965), which makes up the trio for this chapter, but also *Imaginary Friends* (1967) and *Real People* (1969), both of which have some very distinctive sixties characteristics to which I shall briefly refer. Shortly afterwards, I received a letter from Alison Lurie warning me that in *Love and Friendship* what I had 'chosen was the wrong novel', it being set, she said, in 1956–7, and written in 1957–60; she recommended that I give my attention to *The Nowhere City*, set, according to her, in 1960–1, and *The War Between the Tates*, set in 1969–70.[2]

The dates given me by the author certainly match the chronology of her life. Born in 1926, she graduated in English from posh Radcliffe College in 1946, getting married two years later to Jonathan Peale Bishop, who in 1954 got a job as an instructor in English at Amherst College. The couple and their two sons remained at Amherst until 1957, and Amherst, as Convers College, is quite definitely the setting for *Love and Friendship*. From 1957 to 1961 Jonathan Bishop had a post at the University of California at Los Angeles, and *The Nowhere City* is undoubtedly Los Angeles, without disguise. In 1961, now with her third son, the family moved to Cornell University; Lurie has been there ever since, and in 1969, the year in which most of the events of *The War Between the Tates* take place, she herself began teaching. In 1960 she published a collection of poems and plays by a recently deceased friend, V. R. Lang, together with a memoir of his life. With regard to beginning on a career as a novel-writer, Lurie has said:

> I was drawn to the English novel for obvious reasons. For a young American woman who wanted to write in the nineteen fifties, there were very few models. Hemingway and Faulkner offered me nothing. I wasn't trying to write about bull fights or incestuous Southern families. I turned naturally to writers such as Virginia Woolf and Doris Lessing, having grown up on the English Victorian novel.[3]

It is a great strength of the novels as primary sources for the historian that Lurie was actually living the lifestyles of the novels in the places described. Essentially, a novel is a primary source for when it was written and published, rather than for the historical period in which it is ostensibly set. As we all know, *A Tale of Two Cities* may be a good source for attitudes towards revolutionary mobs in Victorian society at the time when Dickens was writing it; it is in no sense a primary source for the French Revolution. Still, I did have to be clear that Lurie's basic impressions of Amherst, and of university life there, were formed in the period 1954–7, as her impressions of Los Angeles, and of the Beat community there, were formed in the period 1957–1961: with small children, she had no possibility of going back to update these impressions. Perhaps *The Nowhere City* could as readily have been published in 1963 as 1965, and so relates as much to 'First Stirrings' as to 'The High Sixties', but I am absolutely sure that, because of the way in which it handles sexual matters and matters relating to the family, *Love and Friendship* could scarcely have been published before 1962: quite definitely, I will maintain, it belongs to a category of novels – by Mary McCarthy, by Edna O'Brien, by Penelope Mortimer – which all appeared subsequently, and not to those of earlier women writers such as Virginia Woolf or Doris Lessing.

Because the precise dating of a source is absolutely critical in historical analysis, and because I myself am very finicky about the chronology of 'The Long Sixties', and the sub-periodisation of 'the First Stirrings of a Cultural Revolution', 'The High Sixties', and 'Everything Goes, and Catching Up', I must make a few more points about *Love and Friendship*, which itself contains no references to external events – Alison Lurie, indeed, has said that she prefers to avoid such references lest a novel date too quickly.[4] Unfortunately, the various rough notes and sketches for this novel in the Lurie Archives are not dated. No doubt Convers of the novel is the Amherst of the later fifties; but American campus attitudes scarcely changed till a few years into the sixties.[5] Maybe Alison Lurie was already thinking rebellious thoughts about the plight of the educated wife trapped in marriage: the point is that the expression of these thoughts comes only with the writing and publication of the novel. The fact that there are no indications of them in the preliminary notes would seem to confirm that it was only as the novel began to assume its fully written-up form that the thoughts became fully coherent. One further consideration which does tend to put the novel forwards rather than backwards in time is that *Love and Friendship* was actually Lurie's third novel, both of her two previous ones having been rejected for publication.[6]

The discontents of the college wife became a media issue in 1960, the year *Love and Friendship* was being completed; Betty Friedan's research into them ran from June 1957 to July 1962, roughly coterminuously with Lurie's full formulation of her own dissentience. 'Gradually', Friedan wrote

> I came to realise that something is very wrong with the way American women are trying to live their lives today. I sensed it first as a question mark in my own life, as a wife and a mother of three small children, half-guiltily and therefore half-heartedly... using my abilities and education in work that took me away from home...

There was a strange discrepancy between the reality of our lives as women and the image to which we were trying to conform, the image I came to call the feminine mystique.[7]

In 1960 there was a CBS television programme on 'The Trapped Housewife', together with a number of articles in the grander newspapers and magazines. *The New York Times* (28 June 1960) put the issue neatly:

Many young women – certainly not all – whose education plunged them into a world of ideas feel stifled in their homes. They finish their routine lives out of joint with their training. Like shut-ins, they feel left out. In the last year, the problem of the educated housewife has provided the meat of dozens of speeches made by troubled presidents of women's colleges who maintain, in face of complaints, that sixteen years of academic training is realistic training for wifehood and motherhood.

Looking back to the time of the writing of *Love and Friendship*, Lurie herself has commented:

I told myself that my life was rich and full. Everybody else seemed to think so. Only I knew that, right at the center, it was false and empty. I wasn't what I was pretending to be. I didn't like staying at home and taking care of little children; I was restless, impatient, ambitious.[8]

Through the main character, Emmy Stockwell Turner, the point was firmly made, though, as I have already noted, it does not appear in Lurie's preliminary notes. At the outset of the finished novel we learn:

She was twenty-seven, and still had, as on the day he married her, the look of a carefully bred and beautifully groomed animal, kept permanently at the peak of its condition for some high use which has not yet arrived and possibly never will arrive [pp 3–4].

According to the notes, the novel was to be about the way in which Convers College was supported 'by men so successful materially that they can afford to support an institution devoted to idealism', and about the essential hypocrisy of this. It was to be about how the college was run by men, and the town by women. There is a whole list of townspeople with details of their relationships,[9] who do not, in the upshot, appear in the novel. What it becomes is a novel about marriage and the contemporary educated woman, specifically Emmy Stockwell Turner and her marriage to Holman Turner 'an Instructor in the Languages and Literature Division' at Convers (p 3); all of Emmy's male relatives, however, had been educated at Convers, the family having financed many of the college buildings: 'Convers, in fact, belonged to the Stockwells' (p 5). The novel relates to the early phase of that characteristic of the sixties referred to in the Introduction (characteristic 8) as 'upheavals in… family relationships'. It relates to the beginning of the development of a new, moderate, feminist subculture, of challenges to the authority of family and husband. In touching on such matters Lurie writes in a manner characteristic of what is referred to in the Introduction (characteristic 9) as the 'new frankness, openness and indeed honesty in personal relations and modes of expression'. The novel proved to be one of those 'vehicles for presenting new values and new modes of behaviour to larger or smaller sections of the public' (in this case relatively restricted audiences in America and Britain) and served 'to legitimate new modes', particularly in regard to sexual behaviour (the seventh of the opening 'propositions' in the Introduction). Above all, the novel contained remarkably uninhibited, and also extremely funny, descriptions of sexual activity. Such descriptions were to appear in a particularly detailed, and shocking, fashion in *The Group*, Mary McCarthy's novel of 1963, and were to be become commonplace in novels by women throughout the sixties, before becoming perhaps even more explicit in the new feminist novels of the early seventies.[10] Alison Lurie comments that she felt free to write in this unhibited way because, having had two novels rejected, she was not expecting this one to be published.[11] I will add the comment that a few years earlier it would not have been published.

My case, which I shall hope to substantiate through precise references to the novel, will be that it is very much a novel of the subperiod 1958–63, 'The First Stirrings of a Cultural Revolution', being both part of it and providing evidence of some of its most distinctive features. The frankness towards sex extends also to class, and indeed Lurie can be seen as a progenitor of the trend by which American writers began to abandon the silly pretence that their society was not divided by class (it may be noted, for instance, that while the first edition of the famous *Beyond the Melting Pot* [1963] by Daniel Moynihan and John Milton Glaiser made no mention at all of class, the Preface to the second edition of 1970 is liberally bespattered with class labels).[12] Lurie came from an upper-middle-class intellectual background. Her mother had been a journalist, but (*nota bene*) gave up that job on starting a family.[13] Her father had directed a national agency which co-ordinated the work of many private charities and funds, and Lurie herself had been educated at a private school, and then at Radcliffe College, sister college to Harvard. Thus she encountered members of the real upper class and was aware of the distinctions which exist at the top of society (only Marxists confuse the middle class with the upper class). In the novel, Emmy, who has a private income of $8000 a year (p 291), is upper-class, her father an extremely wealthy second-generation industrialist, her mother a member of the American aristocracy: 'daddy's grandfather was a small-town lawyer in Ohio. Mummy's different, of course. She was an Evert... it's a sort of important New Jersey family, but most of them lost their money and died' (p 128). Emmy, we are told, had 'not so much a finishing-school accent as a finishing-school voice... Emmy could crush bores or boors at a party just by pronouncing the words "Oh, no, thanks", in a certain manner' (p 13). Holman is an aspiring first-generation university man from a lower-middle-class/working-class background.

The wayward ways of teenagers were under full discussion by 1958 in America, though the demands of students came into full prominence only in 1964. Yet, intriguingly, there are student protests (two years early, one might say) in *Love and Friendship*. The campus novel itself had been invented in the fifties (Kingsley Amis, Peter de Vries, Nabokov),[14] but Lurie played an important role in establishing it as a classic genre of the sixties. Not only was the genre characteristic of the sixties, there is also a touch of the intellectual reflexiveness (in this case about humanities teaching as training for the individual) which is one of the most lasting legacies of sixties' thought (characteristic 12). And, obviously, there is a literary self-consciousness about the very title, lifted from the misspelled one of Jane Austen's brief teenage effort, composed entirely of an exchange of letters, 'Love and Freindship'.[15] A vestige of the epistolary novel is retained in the apparently disconnected correspondence between two gay characters which runs through the book, terminating each chapter: eventually we perceive that this correspondence is supplying vital contextual information. The other literary *jeu d'esprit* is that while Austen novels end with a happy marriage, the Lurie novel begins with an unhappy one.

The very first sentence of the novel tells us that Emmy has fallen out of love with Holman. He is good-looking and athletic and at one time, after making love, she would exclaim, 'oh, how utterly scrumptious!' (p 13). She had liked questioning Holman about what was going on in his, intellectual, world. Now he simply evaded her questions: 'she felt herself quivering with a rage which she could not express because she could see no reasonable object for it' (p 20). Emmy was particularly anxious to learn about the highly original Humanities Course (Hum C) – a 'Foundation Course', it might be called in British terms – run at Convers by Professor McBane, in which students were given intriguing assignments, answering questions based on maps or photographs (pp 17–18). There actually was such a course at Amherst, and among the Alison Lurie papers is an offprint from an article in the *Harvard Educational Review*, Winter 1958, 'A Study of the Freshman Composition Course at Amherst: Action, Order and Language'.[16]

She loves her four-year-old son, Freddy, though often, inevitably, his behaviour is profoundly irritating. After the preliminary precautions have been alluded to – 'she found herself automatically taking things off the top shelf of the cupboard and making ready' – the state of affairs in bed with Holman is meticulously recorded:

> I feel nothing, absolutely nothing, Emmy thought. I don't love you. I suppose prostitutes feel like this, she said to herself, meanwhile noticing that she was automatically gripping Holman's shoulders – how horrible. She let go, and it was worse, as if she were being assaulted like cases in the newspapers. I feel absolutely nothing, nothing. And he doesn't seem to notice. Well, in a moment it will be all over, she thought, recognising the customary signal and raising her legs. But Holman, who had drunk nearly a whole bottle of wine, was lasting longer than usual. As he began to make his final effort Emmy felt a quiver of interest, but too late to enjoy it.
>
> 'More', she said between her teeth as Holman, finished, fell a dead weight on her chest.
>
> 'More?' he said. 'The lady wants more,' he exclaimed incredulously to the world, raising himself on one elbow and then dropping back with a thump.
>
> Emmy said nothing; she did not even complain that he was squashing her lungs. She was overcome with shame; she felt a new and worse sensation than that of submitting to someone she did not love, the shame of asking someone she did not love for love [pp 40–1].

Julian and Miranda Fenn form a slightly eccentric, slightly Beat campus couple. A minor sub-plot is that of the likelihood of Julian's being fired from Convers.

In the end, he gets a job at a much grander place, though ironically with the same traditional male values, Princeton. To Emmy

> the Fenns were crazy, peculiar, weird, and simply impossible, but rather nice. Still, think of having to live with either of them in that house! Emmy reflected as she took off her clothes that after all she would rather be married to Holman than to someone who constantly got into trouble with the authorities and never washed his neck [p 39].

Through Miranda Fenn, Emmy hears of Will Thomas, a musician and womaniser, then accidentally encounters him in Miranda's house, when Miranda is out:

> The man on the sofa had on a dark jacket over a black sweater, but no shirt, like a burglar. He also wore sneakers. Emmy's thought was that he looked dangerous. He stood up, turning out to be both large and tall.

There is a brief exchange of words.

> At second glance Emmy could see that if his clothes were those of a burglar, it was a burglar who shopped at Brookes Brothers [pp 60–1].

As ever irritated with Holman, Emmy tries to be fair:

> ... suppose he went around town seducing girls like Will Thomas. The picture of Will going round Convers seducing girls came vividly into her mind, as it had done several times since Miranda's revelation. She wondered whether, when he was with those girls, Will did the same things Holman always did with her. Then, with a start, she realised that here she was with her husband, in the very act, imagining another man. She went stiff all over for a moment, but Holman seemed to take no notice. He went on with what was today a rather long-winded and monotonous performance, and at last brought it to a conclusion [p 100].

Emmy goes out with Will in his sports car.

> Emmy remembered that she had decided to move away if Will ever tried to kiss her again. But fitted into the bucket seat of the car as she was, there was no place to move. She let it happen.
>
> It was a long, though gentle kiss; half-way through Emmy joined in [p 131].

Emmy has to rush home for Freddy, who 'gets terribly upset if I'm the least bit late' (p 135). They arrange to meet again (p 136).

Love and Friendship has little in the way of expletives. The language is not that of Jane Austen, but it is used in a very exact way. When Will (who has long been suffering from composer's block) is drunkenly explaining to Miranda his lack of progress with Emmy, and she worries that he is not in a fit condition to drive, his response is: "'I'll be all right. Two things I can do in any condition, driving and fucking'" (p 146). Emmy and Will are in the latter's MG (the fashion for British artefacts did not begin in the sixties but certainly became an important phenomenon then – a facet of the international cultural exchange which I identified in the Introduction as characteristic 4). Will asks her if she wants to stay.

> Emmy hesitated, looking out at the snow and dead branches, and then in at Will. I can't give him up, she thought, but of course I must. She opened her mouth to say No, and said. 'Yes.'

> This time, as they kissed, Will brought his whole weight to bear against her, so that, slowly, she slid down along the seat. The background of cold bushes and sky past his head was replaced by one of car roof. She began to breathe in gasps. Well, anyhow, we can't possibly do it now here in the car, was her last, mistaken, coherent thought [p 160].

There, apart from one the usual chapter-ending epistles, part one of the novel ends.

The first chapters of part two are dominated by Emmy's affair with Will as they travel around in Will's MG seeking suitable spots for love-making. Emmy is annoyed when Will physically forces her to duck beneath the windscreen to avoid being seen by a local policeman. 'Adultery,' he reminds her, 'is a crime in this state'. Holman becomes increasingly tormented, but suspects Julian not Will. In what is the only citation of an exact date in the entire book, and one which perhaps does indicate the author's intention that we should take her events as being set in 1956 or 1957, Will gives a piano recital, which features 'Sonata in C Major (1956) by Louis Fuchs'. Lou Fuchs, it transpires, is a composer in Southern California, with whom Will corresponds when he is working: it seems that, inspired by Emmy, he has begun composing again (pp 253–4). Emmy and Will are under the trees.

> In many ways, Emmy was strangely unshockable for a 'nice' girl. She had come to Will completely ignorant of most of the variations on love. Not only had she never heard that certain games were low and dirty, she had never heard of them at all, and so she had no opinion about them until they turned out to be rather fun [p 254].

The delightfully frank, and deliciously witty, vein continues. Holman has taken to spying on Emmy's diaphragm, and as she doesn't have a spare, Will has to resort to other means.

> 'Ahh', Emmy said as Will left her. She lay back on the steep, overgrown river-bank, full in the sun, naked among crushed green leaves and weeds. 'Oh, I am so wet.'
> 'Here.' Will passed a handful of leaves over his shoulder.
> 'Thank you. Golly. It didn't break, did it?'
> 'No. That's all you' [p 266].

Only once is there a comment more notable for anatomical explicitness than sly wit: 'I like it at the end when you get bigger and bigger and I can feel myself slowly exploding and nothing can be done about it' (p 278).

Already there have been intimations of trouble among the students. This comes in the form of an end-of-chapter letter from Alain Ingram, novelist-in-residence at Convers, to his gay lover Francis Noyes, dated 17 May, but with no year:

> Spring fever marches on here too: the latest excitement is the student campaign against the new Religion Building...
> The boys took up the cause enthusiastically – they always like to get excited about something at this time of year. Religion and sex are the favourites: they get together and have riots against compulsory chapel, or the no-girls-indoors rules.

> One evening after supper they put on a parade, about a hundred of them... They all brought their waste-baskets... and dumped the waste-baskets out into the excavation... By the time I got there next day there was nothing to be seen but a couple of workmen patiently shovelling out the debris. However, I hear... that an even bigger demonstration is planned for Memorial Day... [pp 264–5].

The same mechanism is used to convey subsequent developments, which Ingram terms 'the riots'.

> ... The south quadrangle is packed with students: two hundred? three hundred? Maybe half of them are official members of the parade... The rest are just there for the show, but they are helping by shouting and pushing [p 287].

The excavation is now considerably deeper, and the students are throwing larger and larger objects into it. Ingram, who is in the company of Holman Turner and a couple of other faculty members, moves down to the edge of the excavation:

> A few feet from me, a loud noise and confusion is going on: Turner is arguing with two students who carry torches. Then a scream: ten, twenty, fifty screams; one of the students has fallen, or been pushed by Turner, into the excavation... His torch, inevitably, falls on to the rubbish, and in a second it is alight. Instant bedlam: people shriek, push, fall down, are trampled on. I am shoved against the wall of the shack, immobilized in a crush of bodies. The student in the hole is burning, is screaming, is being drawn up and extinguished by the coats of other students [p 288].

Sirens screaming, fire engines and police cars arrive. Two students are transferred to the infirmary with cuts and bruises, and one with a broken leg and second-degree burns (pp 287–8). The severely damaged student is known as Dicki Smith, and is later described by Ingram as 'already a natural beat poet'. All three are expelled.

As the academic year, and the novel, come to a close, Kitty McBane, the wife of the professor who runs Humanities C, is upset both over the riot, and over the departure of the awkward Julian Fenn (she is not aware of his Princeton triumph), and confides in Emmy:

> '... Poor Mr. Fenn having to leave. And it wasn't for very much of anything either, was it? But all these young men are so violent nowadays. I keep reading about them in the magazines. Angry young men. But of course that is in England, isn't it?'
>
> 'I guess it started there,' Emmy said.
>
> 'But it spreads, doesn't it?' (p 316).

The student riot is not a very serious one, and is probably there more as a comic and plot device (Holman comes out of it feeling deeply guilty and chastened), than as a piece of social reporting. Lurie has said that the actual incident of the construction in traditionalist style of a Religion Building was pure invention.[17] In this period of 'First Stirrings', the different elements which were to come together in the 'youth revolt' of the 'High Sixties' were just being assembled; perhaps Lurie did have some inkling of the deeply serious Free Speech Movement which was to break out at Berkeley in the autumn of 1964. The reference to the 'angry young men' is an interesting one: serious American commentators saw this British phenomenon as part of a slowly-gathering Anglo-American youth movement.[18]

Emmy is going to go off and live with Will. In a conversation with Holman, she regards him 'almost with affection'. In one of the very few direct references in the book to the theme of its title, she reflects that:

> The trouble with her and Holman was that they had ever got married at all; as a husband he was impossible. They should have just remained friends [p 296].

There is some bickering between Will and Emmy, and he lays down a timetable for when she must definitely join him, while Holman now impresses her with his views of marriage:

> 'You're my wife, and Freddy is my son. I don't have to experiment to find out whether I still love you when you are out of town, or any childish kind of game like that. I already know that I'll always love you, worse luck' [p 310].

Holman gives his explanation of McBane's course: 'That every man is alone and responsible for making up his own moral universe' (p 311). It was, Emmy reflects, 'what her parents believed... the categorical imperative of the aristocracy'.

> Behave so that your every action could be the basis of a social law. Like women should leave their husbands? Like they should break their vows and quarrel with their families and get divorced and go off with men who betrayed their best friends and hated Freddy [p 312].

Then, at the end of this critical passage, the two crucial sentences in the book: 'but, she had a flash thought, I don't have to marry him. I belong to myself. I haven't decided yet, and nobody can make me' (p 312). Emmy is the autonomous woman. She does stick with Holman, but not because of social pressures, but because it is her independent decision.

Much of the novel is about the uninhibited pleasures of sex, uninhibitedly expressed. This was an aspect of Lurie's work which was increasingly to be featured in blurbs, playing a part in spreading the gospel of the permissive society. But there is a sense in *Love and Friendship*, too, of good sex as a dangerous drug for a woman, an idea appearing at that time in the novels of French author Christiane Rochefort, and one which was to be increasingly propagated by the new wave of feminists at the beginning of the next decade.[19]

In America, *Love and Friendship* was received with only mild praise: a rather banal and unperceptive review in the *New York Times Review of Books*, headed 'Campus Casanova',[20] declared that Emmy and Will were 'both equally bored with life', without recognising the particularities of Emmy's situation as a wife. There was a more enthusiastic reception in Britain, quite a characteristic phenomenon, when, in a time of increased cultural exchange between the two countries, cultural leadership was being assumed by Britain (very much the same thing happened with another great document of the sixties, *Catch-22*).[21]

The Nowhere City was published in 1965 – revealingly, given all my agitation over dating, Lurie, in 1998, was under the impression that it had been published earlier than that.[22] Again this novel is about marriage, and woman's relationship to it. The marriage is that between East Coast, upper-class, Katherine, and her Harvard-educated husband, Paul Cattleman, whose father, from Columbus, Ohio, was a highly cultivated, and civicly active, estate agent who also owned and managed business properties; his mother painted, and made pottery (p 14). Whereas the previous novel had focused strongly on Emmy, and then on Holman and Will, Katherine is less central, considerable attention being given to Ceci, the beat artist, who becomes Cattleman's lover, and to the marriage between Glory Green, a Hollywood starlet, and Dr Iz Einsam, a thirty-two-year-old psychiatrist, with whom Katherine eventually has an affair. If anything, the propaganda on behalf of the joys (for women in particular) of uninhibited sex is even more undiluted, though, perhaps reflecting Katherine's greater reticence as compared with the innocent enthusiasm of Emmy, the descriptions are less explicit. Nonetheless, the frankness and openness which I identify as such an important sixties characteristic, is still there in strong measure. In this book frankness moves, too, into an area which becomes an increasing preoccupation with Lurie, that of personal appearance and its influence. Again, the nuances of class are addressed more directly than had been customary in America. Cattleman is a historian who has come to California to take up a highly-paid job writing the history of the Nutting Research Corporation in Los Angeles: the reflexive element shows in his pondering the nature of the historian's task:

> he had the historian's love of primary source material, however untidy. He would mine the significant facts out of the mountain of processed wood pulp and erect them into an elegant and accurate record of the spectacular growth of a southern California corporation. He had in mind something which would both satisfy Nutting and (through a judicious use of irony and comparison) interest and entertain other historians [p 14].

Above all, the subject matter is Los Angeles, the affluence, the consumerism, the counter-cultural elements: whatever precise dates Lurie may have had in mind, southern California was where many of the developments, particularly the more material ones, rightly associated with the sixties happened first. Cattleman was immensely taken by the colour and exuberance of Los Angeles; Katherine, who suffered from sinus trouble, detested it.

The frankest male-female exchange in the book, and the one which best expresses the 'sex is good for you' message, occurs in Katherine's recollections of her first couplings with Iz:

> The hair on his body was black, curly, dense and fine, as if a design had been drawn all over him in India ink. And when she was feeling most cold, clumsy, and despairing (but she hadn't said anything, only made an ambiguous noise that might even have been a sigh of passion), 'Ah, Katherine. Don't try so hard. There's nothing at stake.' And later, lying back with the pillow folded under his head, 'I'm sorry. Next time we'll take it much more slowly.'...
>
> And the next time, taking it slowly... 'Mmm,' she murmured, shutting her eyes again. 'That was so good.' 'But you didn't come.' 'Yes I did,' she whispered

defensively. 'I mean, that's how it always is for me. I don't come very hard.'
'Don't worry,' Iz said aloud. 'You will. It's in you' [pp 191–2].

The frankest of all passages is between Glory Green and a fellow starlet Mona. Mona is commenting on a fan who has sent for a photograph of Glory:

'…it's kind of disgusting to think of that creep sitting in his room somewhere playing with your photo and pulling himself off 'cause he can't find himself a girl.'

'Aw, how do you know? Maybe he's even married. There's a lot of people can't feel physical about what they've got around at home.' Glory shrugged.

Katherine, who was present, 'had never heard women speak so bluntly, and wondered if they were doing it on purpose to embarrass her'. Mona has burst out again:

'You know that kid Lucille that was in the Johnny Espy Show with me, she was going to the doctor for these awful cramps she had every month? Well, she got talking to him about her private life and she finally let on how she and her husband just weren't getting any bang out of doing it any more. Well, so this doc told her it wasn't psychological like she was scared of; the trouble was she didn't have any muscle tone down there at all, since she had her baby.'…

Lucille's really sold on this doctor,' Mona went on… 'He taught her these crazy exercises you do in the bath tub, to strengthen your muscles. She said it took her a couple months to really get into condition, but now her and her guy are having a ball. So now she's trying to turn everyone on; she wants me to go to her doc and learn the routine. What d'you think?…'

'No, thanks,' Glory said, laughing. 'Not me. There's only one kind of exercise I ever want to do with that part of me' [p 222–3].

Lurie herself is equally blunt on the matter of looks. Cattleman reflects on the situation at Nutting, where he shares an office with Skinner:

Some of the secretaries in the Publications Department were pretty and some were competent, but not both. Apparently girls who were both pretty and competent were not sent to Publications, but were routed instead to Systems or Administration. The secretary who Paul and Skinner shared was neither pretty nor competent [p 18].

In his first sexual engagement with Ceci, Paul was thrown off balance by her lack of resistance: 'From an ugly, desperate girl he might have expected such directness, but not from Ceci O'Connor. Maybe she was a nymphomaniac' (p 49).

Apart from the main sets of couplings, there is also one between Cattleman and Glory, passed over without much detail, and more from Cattleman's point of view than Glory's (pp 242–3). It follows a gloriously funny scene in which, in a Beverley Hills house which Glory has borrowed, they are almost drowned because of a bath tap the owners have left running. Cattleman has to do a daring outside climb to turn the water off.

When Cattleman first meets her, Ceci is working as a waitress. When she offers to give him a book, Paul is very class-aware about the situation. He remembered reading in some sociological text that for the working classes the word 'book' means anything printed which is not a newspaper; every magazine is a 'book'. Maybe she would bring him a copy of *Look* or the *Post* rather than some popular love story [p 20].

In fact what she gives him is a new copy of Samuel Beckett's latest play, possibly dating the episode to 1958 (*End Game*), or 1959 (*Krapp's Last Tape*), or 1961 (*Happy Days*). In a letter of 24 April 1999, Alison Lurie informed me that it was *End Game* she had had in mind. Katherine has not dissimilar feelings in the company of Glory and Mona:

> 'Yes, that must be an awful bore,' she began, and paused. She had never thought of herself as having an accent – her speech was simply that of any educated New England person. But now, in contrast to Glory and (especially) Mona, she sounded prissy and affected. She made a conscious effort to moderate her tone... [p 218].

In *The Nowhere City*, Lurie's own feminist doubts about marriage join with counter-cultural assertions on the matter. Ceci does not want to marry Cattleman, who reflects,

> They couldn't love each other more than they did, so why get married? It was only a convention. He felt good again. What a hip place, and here he was in the thick of it [p 107].

'Hip' is the sixties word which replaced 'hep'. Later, Ceci says to him,

> 'You start fixing all these plans and rules for something, it gets wrecked. I mean like as long as you want to do this and I want to do it, it'll happen; and when one of us or both of us don't want it anymore - it'll stop' [p 205].

Iz tells Katherine,

> 'The kind of relationship you call "love" is something that's been very bad for you. It's all fucked up with ideas like duty, and morality, and giving up everything for some other person in a very grudging, painful way' [p 196].

Affluence and the diffusion of ever-more-elaborate consumer goods are basic structural characteristics of sixties society. Lurie presents Southern California as the embodiment of the big-spending society, wasteful and devoted to conspicuous consumption. Paul Cattleman enjoys deploying his professional skills in writing the history of the Nutting Corporation, but gradually comes to realise that the Corporation will never publish his book:

> Nutting's hiring him was... the expensive public manufacture of nothing; the vaguely deliberate consumption of time, energy, intelligence, knowledge, and money, with no result – no product [p 158].

Consumer 'mainstream culture' and 'counter-culture' meet in the Joy Superduper Market:

> 'This is a really great place,' Ceci said as the photoelectric doors swung open to coax them in, and they entered the maelstrom of consumption. 'It's got everything.'

> People surged up and down the aisles, buying not only food, but gin, shampoo, life-sized dolls, Capri pants, electric frying-pans, and photo-murals of Yellowstone National Park. 'All the cats come here.' Silently Paul imagined, among the men and women and children, a large number of large cats of all colours, walking on their hind legs and dressed in beatnik clothes [p 42].

While Paul is agreeably impressed by the casual disorder of the 'pad' inhabited by Ceci's friends (pp 86–7), Katherine has a less happy encounter on the beach:

> Katherine turned her head, and observed the natives with displeasure over her shoulder. There were three of them. They must be some sort of actors or beatniks, because the men had beards. One, who was large and blond, had a blond beard, tightly curled; the other, who was small and wiry, had a straggly brown one. They wore the barest pretence at bathing-suits, brightly-coloured briefs that clung indecently tight, while the girl was spilling out of her bikini in every direction. Really it was pretty disgusting, on a public beach [p 97].

It is my contention, summarised in the Introduction, that change in the sixties came about by permeation rather than a dialectical conflict between 'mainstream culture' and 'counter-culture'. Something of this is suggested in a passage where Cattleman and Ceci are together in an Espresso (important symbol of international exchange) café which 'doesn't really heat up until around midnight' (p 104).

> A diversion was created now by the entrance of a group of extremely beat-looking people: men in turtle-neck sweaters and dark glasses, girls tightly wrapped in black, high-heeled, and dangling with coloured beads. 'Who're they?' he asked eagerly.
>
> 'Never saw them before.' Ceci studied the newcomers as they took their places at a table by the door, then turned her head away. 'Tourists,' she pronounced scornfully. 'Yeah. They're all tourists. Ever since that piece came out in the paper some of them always make it down here on week-ends to see the beatniks. Maybe try to buy some pot or pick up a free lay... Look at their clothes. That's supposed to be like beatnik costume. You could tell them a block off' [p 106].

'Beatniks' had not yet been replaced by 'hippies' – there were 'part-time' as well as 'full-time' beatniks, just as later there were 'full-time' and 'part-time' hippies.[23]

The notion of 'permeation' emerges very strongly in the suggestion that there were two 'undergrounds', separate, but perhaps not entirely distinct from each other. Paul Cattleman reckoned that 'among the people one meets every day', sexually predatory like himself, subverting the conventional code in private, there was 'what he liked to call "the underground"', people 'able to recognise each other upon meeting by indefinable signs, rare in academic life: half a smile, a preference in fiction, a look of erotic aptitude and calculation' (p 8). Here Lurie has sensed something truly important: the permeation of society by new lifestyles came as much from those within established positions as from the 'full-time' underground. Ceci 'didn't believe in Paul's underground', but again Lurie seems to have sensed its true significance:

'You mean like there's a club of people who cheat on the cats and chicks they're supposed to be making it with?' she asked. But she had her own underground, cruder and sloppier than his, not discreet and careful of other people's feelings, but rebellious and noisy [p 207].

For all my talk of 'permeation' and 'measured judgement', I made clear in the Introduction (characteristic 14) the responsibility of the police for much of the violence which marked the sixties. In 'The Nowhere City':

Everybody knew that the cops in Venice hated the beats. They wanted them to move out, and were following a policy of deliberate harassment and bullying to effect this purpose... [p 114].

Indeed,

Paul had noticed before how the Los Angeles police, because of their uniforms (tight gaiters, leather wind breaker, ammunition belt, black leather gloves) resemble stormtroopers or juvenile delinquents more than they do the cops back East [p 111].

One of Ceci's friends

had been picked up for questioning because he was walking on the beach at five a.m. He had been taken to the station house, shoved down half a flight of stairs as if by accident, and released covered with bruises (pp 89–90).

Seeking (correctly in my view) to locate *The Nowhere City* within the gathering permissive revolution, Lurie's publishers compared it with what was still being represented as the prototype of the early-sixties shocker, Edward Albee's play *Who's Afraid of Virginia Woolf?* (1962). In Britain, the anonymous review in the *Times Literary Supplement* was scathing, finding the second novel much inferior to the first, to which it gave high praise. Francis Hope in the *New Statesman*, on the other hand, thought it 'no better, it is just the same; which is quite good enough to be going on with'.[24] Privately, the British author David Garnett told Lurie that *The Nowhere City* was 'infinitely better' than *Love and Friendship*.[25] With respect, however, to reception, and potential influence, the most significant development was a notice in *Newsweek*, almost a year after publication. *Newsweek*, incidentally, saw no difficulty in placing *The Nowhere City* in the era of Lyndon Johnson, calling the novel 'a retarded adolescent's dream of the Good Life in the Great Society'. In common with several other reviews, *Newsweek* said of the subject matter that 'one would have supposed [it] long dead for the purposes of fiction'. Instead, declared the final punchlines, it 'springs to scintillating life at this gifted comic novelist's deft touch. Watch her.'[26] The elder statesman of American literature, Edmund Wilson, a friend of Lurie's husband, thought the ending of *The Nowhere City* forced and unconvincing.[27] He had not understood that as Emmy had found existential autonomy, so too had Katherine, although she opts for full sexual liberation and emancipation from marriage: she decides to remain in Los Angeles while Cattleman returns to New England.

However, Wilson was full of praises for *Imaginary Friends* (1967), which he associated with his own interest in the origins of religions.[28] New religious cults are an aspect of alternative sixties subcultures which have perhaps not had the attention they deserve, though everyone knows about the influence of oriental religions.[29] Senior sociologist Professor Thomas B. McMann, and his junior assistant Roger Zimmern – there is the usual Lurie attention to the nature of, and the academic debates within, sociology – join a religious cult, the Truth Seekers, under assumed identities, in order to do a sociological study of it. It was during the sixties that, among intellectuals, the notion, developed independently by Michel Foucault, R.D. Laing and by Ken Kesey, in *One Flew Over the Cuckoo's Nest*,[30] that 'madness' is simply a label which society applies to those who do not conform, became highly fashionable. By the end of *Imaginary Friends* McMann appears to have gone mad. Roger is uncertain:

> What if McMann were just role-playing at the end of our last interview? He seemed sane enough up to that point. What if he knows very well he isn't Ro of Varna, and was only trying to scare me: maybe because I didn't want to go into the hospital and work on his new project? Or maybe just for the hell of it. That would be like him. Possibly, if I hadn't already been so nervous, expecting a raving maniac to jump out of the bushes at me at any moment, I would have stood my ground and called his bluff. If it was a bluff [p 277].

The key intellectual question which runs through *Imaginary Friends* is one central to sixties 'sociology of knowledge': that of whether, by themselves participating in their own experiment, the two sociologists immediately invalidate their results (pp 221, 275–6).

In *Real People* (1969), a female novelist, Janet Belle Smith, has earned the privilege of spending time at a luxury artists' colony. The novel is her highly reflexive (some – though not me – might say 'postmodernist') account, particularly of the novel-writing process. She and her fellow-artists go to a local 'bohemian' pub:

> Kenneth and I were all in black; Leonard had a magnificent pop-art tie borrowed from Nick D.; and Gerry outdid himself in a flowered shirt and beads. Teddy, with a bandanna knotted around his neck, looked like a fat old pirate. We drank espresso and beer, and danced to the juke box [p 40].

The artist, Kenneth, is contemptuous of contemporary artistic developments (proposition 7 and characteristic 12 in my Introduction):

> There are people now composing sonatas that consist of turning a couple of portable radios off and on, and writing novels where you're supposed to shuffle the pages at random... Half the students I get today – no, more than half this year – are infected by it. They think they can become famous artists overnight, if they can only invent some new gimmick.
>
> It's not their fault, really, they're just following the crowd. Art's become a kind of magic Bingo. A get-rich-quick scheme for a few unscrupulous dealers and critics in New York and their protégés...
>
> I had a girl in my life class this spring, instead of drawing the model, she stuck a lot of old paint rags onto her canvas and poured a can of varnish over them. 'What's that supposed to be?' I asked her. 'I feel the possibilities of the picture plane have been exhausted,' she told me [pp 35–6].

Another painter, Nick, is more advanced. Janet notes:

> His wife's middle-class parents both disapprove strongly of Nick's art, which
> they consider pornographic and un-American. When this country gets back on
> the Right track politically, people like him won't be allowed [p 148].

Janet's husband, Clark, earns a large salary working for an insurance company.
Actually he would rather give up the job and devote himself to ornithology. He
doesn't because, as Janet admits in a frank dissection of upper-middle-class life,
she could not bear the drop in living standards (pp 176–8). Janet is also frank
about how she shirks realism in her novels:

> She didn't want to depress her readers; she didn't want to make them uncom-
> fortable. She didn't want to expose her family, her friends or (above all) herself;
> she didn't want them to be laughed at, or pitied or condemned – not even when
> they were in fact ridiculous, pitiable and wrong [p 179].

Janet has already reflected that the

> only reason for writing fiction at all is to combine a number of different obser-
> vations at the point where they overlap. If you already have one perfect example
> of what you want to demonstrate, you might as well write non-fiction. Indeed,
> you should, because any changes made just to avoid similarity to persons living
> or dead, or for other extraneous reasons, are bound to be wrong...
>   Fiction is condensed reality, and that's why its flavor is more intense, like
> bouillon or frozen orange juice.
>   I know all this; I've known it for years. But all the same I've begun adding
> water, more and more lukewarm water, to every batch I made. Because I was
> afraid that the undiluted stuff would freeze and burn me, and everyone around
> me [pp 178-9].

Perhaps I should clarify what I am saying. My basic assumption is that when
specific intellectual preoccupations, or details of lifestyles and behaviour,
appear in novels of general appeal (whether comedies of manners – as with
Lurie – or high-class thrillers, or whatever) which aim to convince the readers
that they engage with social reality, that indicates that they really are represen-
tative of the period being studied.[31] Of course, for a historian, concentrating
on one text, or one set of texts, is completely artificial. My quotations are only
significant if (as I maintain) they are congruent with the vast variety of other
evidence about the sixties.

As with *Love and Friendship*, the early plans (and first typed drafts) of *The
War Between the Tates* (1974) suggest something very banal and heavy-handed.
Again an undiluted campus novel, it is to be set at Cornell University, scarcely
disguised at all as Corinth, the name which also serves for the adjacent town of
Ithaca. 'Hopkins County' is an invention, but then, to British ears, the real name,
Tompkins County, sounds even more like an invention. Collegetown, the student
quarter of Ithaca, is no invention. The action was to have taken place in 1968,
starting in March. After contemplating moving fast forward to 1970, Lurie
settled for beginning in March 1969, and running into 1970. She seems to have

wanted to pass by the Black Power and student protests which, as a matter of historical record, were actually at their height in May 1969,[32] while she did wish to feature 'Women's Lib', which was only coming fully into evidence in 1969. Also, it was over the period 1969–70 that Federal and New York State abortion law reform took place. The greatest issue in all of these years, obviously, was the Vietnam War.

Lurie's fundamental idea (and the one, I think, which made it possible for the publishers to generate the publicity which took this unquestionably brilliant novel into the bestseller lists) was to construct a parallel between the conflicts within a family and the Vietnam conflict. Initially her protagonists were to be Frank, the name intended to connote a straight-laced, decent, 'upperclass WASP political scientist', and Erica, another of Lurie's East Coast, well-educated, virgin brides. The book was to be titled *The Franco-Erican War*.[33] Frank became Brian, the focus began to shift a bit from conflict between husband and wife to conflict between parents (and particularly the wife) and children. The title became *The War Between the Tates*, which has overtones of the American Civil War, though, in the early versions, there continued to be laboured parallels with the Vietnam War. No doubt the conflict between Brian and Erica, and the teenage Jeffrey and Matilda, is a sub-metaphor for generational conflict in general, much written about in 1968 and 1969. On page 78 we read: 'Things have got to the point where there is not just a conflict of generations at the Tates, but a condition of total war'. Two pages later we get the full elaborate treatment. In the eyes of Brian, his house for two years has been 'occupied territory': 'Jeffrey and Matilda have gradually taken it over, moving in troops and supplies, depleting natural resources, and destroying the local culture'. To the children, however, 'the parallel is reversed':

Cornell University – 'Corinth University' in *The War Between the Tates*

Brian and Erica are the invaders: the large, brutal, callous Americans. They are vastly superior in material resources and military experience, which makes the war deeply unfair; and they have powerful allies like the Corinth Public School System [p 80].

By the end of the novel (p 310) when Jeffrey is sixteen and Matilda fourteen, there is a polite, but distant, peace between the children and Erica. Whether this is meant to symbolise that, as I personally believe, the notion of a conflict of generations has been overstated, I don't know.

Alison Lurie has openly stated that she writes about what she knows[34] – which is what makes her so useful to historians. Marriage, family, and relations between the sexes are central topics in three of the novels under review here. In *The War Between the Tates*, apart from the eponymous couple, we have Leonard and Danielle Zimmern (a recurrent name for the Jewish characters prominent in Lurie novels). Like Erica, Danielle 'has been described by her admirers as… beautiful', but 'where Erica is narrow', 'Danielle is broad' (p 8). Danielle we learn, is more robust, less fastidious than Erica. We have two failing or failed marriages (Danielle's is already over). Brian is pursued by the hippie, and far from stunningly attractive, student, Wendy, and finally succumbs. The contrast between Erica's attitude to him and Wendy's is put with familiar economy:

> As for Erica, Brian has always known that she cared less for him than he did for her. From the start he was the one who loved, while she allowed herself to be loved. That was her nature, he had told himself. It was not as if she preferred someone else; indeed she very evidently preferred him. Brian could accept that; he did accept it for nearly twenty years – until he met Wendy, who never judges him, withholds nothing, cares more for him than for herself [p 175].

When Brian and Erica separate, she is at first overjoyed:

> At first she had hardly believed her feelings; she kept waiting for the reaction. Instead, day after day, there was only the euphoria of freedom – joy and relief at having Brian out of the house for good – in every sense for good [p 156].

Later she becomes very lonely (p 208). Although her opinion of men has not altered, and she has no desire to become romantically involved, 'it would be nice sometimes to have a respectable, attractive escort to concerts, films, and art shows' (p 223). She has an unconsummated relationship with a wimpish acquaintance she had met in 1959, Sandy Finkelstein, who now runs the Krishna Bookshop in Corinth (see characteristic 2 in Introduction). The relationship does progress far enough for Erica, in a typical piece of Lurie frankness, to see that in comparison with Sandy's normal-sized genitals, Brian's are extremely small. The frankest passage comes when Danielle is discussing with Erica how they are managing without their husbands:

> 'And I really don't like masturbation,' Danielle confides in a lower voice. 'I tried it a few times, but I could never get much out of it. I couldn't come or anything; I just always felt nervous and silly, you know?'
> 'Mm', repeats Erica, who has had the opposite experience [p 202].

Brian has got Wendy pregnant, and he pays the vast sum required for her abortion, still illegal. He gets her pregnant again, and Erica (though not living together, the Tates are still on the same small campus) insists that he should marry Wendy (though abortions are now legal). Wendy, however, has her own ideas about marriage, congruent with a wealth of 'hippie' and (some branches of) feminist literature:

> '... I don't ever want to be married to anyone...' 'I figure it's a bum trip. I mean if you just got a relationship with a guy, that's cool; you can be really straight with him. Like Ralph says, you know either of you can split any time, so if you stick it out it's because you really dig each other. The world isn't telling you you hafta stay with that dude whether you feel like it or not; in fact it's probably making some hassles for you' [p 304].

In fact, Wendy (we are at the end of the book) has decided to forget Brian, and go with fellow-student Ralph to a commune in Northern California.

> And how did Ralph feel about her pregnancy? According to Wendy, he was tolerant, even enthusiastic. 'Ralph wants to work out a total relationship. He really digs kids. He doesn't care whose kid it is; he hasn't got your thing about possessions. He lives completely in the Now' [p 300].

Right at the beginning of the book Danielle has taken up with a campus feminist group, Women for Human Equality Now (WHEN). She is disillusioned with Leonard's philandering ways, and with men in general. To Erica's snobbish disgust, she eventually takes up with the vet who had treated her dog with great sympathy, Dr Bernard Kotelchuk. We learn how it all comes out in one of those scintillating passages for which Lurie is so justly renowned:

> 'He looks cheerful' Erica says, watching him descend into the crowd. 'Resigned, even. Has he finally given up proposing to you?'
>
> 'Not exactly.' Danielle leans on her placard [which reads 'WOMEN FIGHT FOR PEACE']. 'He asked me again just last night. I've been reading an article in *Sisterhood* about marriage contracts, so I told him I'd marry him on certain terms.' She grins. 'I said, first, I had to keep my job. I wanted separate bank accounts, and I'd pay half the housekeeping expenses and do the cooking, but I wouldn't touch any of the cleaning or laundry – he'd have to do it himself, or hire somebody. And I said I had to have three weeks' vacation by myself every year, with no questions asked afterwards.'
>
> 'And what did he say?' Erica is smiling now, almost laughing with relief and anticipation.
>
> 'He agreed to everything. He said it sounded like a good deal; after all, he's been doing all his own cooking and cleaning for two years. He said he was afraid I was going to ask for separate bedrooms.'
>
> 'So what are you going to do?'
>
> 'I guess I'll have to marry him.' Danielle shrugs, then suddenly smiles brilliantly. 'It won't be so bad. He's a real help around the house, he can fix anything. Yesterday he put up that triangular screen in the attic that Leonard could never figure out, you know?'

Erica acknowledges that she knows.

'And he's great for my ego,' Danielle continues. 'He thinks everything I do is fantastic, and everything I say is brilliant. Well, you know, I am sort of keen on him too. I guess I really love him.' Unexpectedly, she flushes and looks down [p 305].

Danielle has triumphed as an existential individual. But the reconciliation between the Tates is presented as classic conflict resolution in which individual autonomy has to be compromised:

the Tates' marital conflict and related events have caused a lot of gossip and unfavourable comment. Now things are quieter, he and Erica can close ranks and present a united front.

Most important, it is what they both want and need. The conflict has damaged them morally as well as in reputation: they have both said cruel things and made bad errors in judgement. They will each have to admit this, without accusing the other. Brian, for instance, must be generous enough not to point out that all that had happened was in a way Erica's fault, since if she hadn't insisted he leave home and marry Wendy the affair would have ended much sooner... Erica, in return, will be generous to him (pp 313–4).

Some important feminist points emerge throughout the novel; in the first attempts to secure an abortion for Wendy, Erica has sought the help of the local GP and also the local vet and is repulsed (they think she is seeking the abortion for herself):

It is true, Erica thinks: men run the world, and they run it for their own convenience. It is a man who is responsible for Wendy's present condition – for her exhaustion, her desperation, her danger. And the two women who are trying to rescue her from this condition cannot do it on their own; they must beg and plead for help from other men.

... Hateful, she thinks, hateful that women should have to appeal to their natural enemy on such a matter (and in vain) – that they should have to expose themselves to the pompous assumptions and disapproval of a country doctor like Bunch; to the self-righteous anger of such a person as Bernie Kotelchuk [p 125].

Later, musing on the future of her daughter Matilda, Erica is struck by a thought which had earlier been expressed in the novels of Christiane Rochefort,[35] and which was just becoming central in much feminist thought:

Like Erica – or Danielle, or Wendy – Matilda would grow up, fall in love, have children, and be disillusioned by some man.

And this man already existed, somewhere in the world. At that moment, wherever he was – standing in line for a Thanksgiving film matinée in some small town or big city, walking in the country, playing football in a vacant lot, or in some college stadium – he was slowly moving, walking, running towards this house, towards Matilda. It might take him a long time, but eventually he would get there, and get at her, and it would all begin over again [p 159].

But Erica does not sympathise with the feminists at Corinth: 'though they criticise men', it seemed to her that they 'are trying to become like them in all the worst ways – taking on their most unpleasant qualities' (p 194). They have 'identified the enemy correctly, but their battle plan is all wrong':

> They want to scrap the old code of good manners: they don't like to have doors and coats held for them, or seats offered on crowded trains. They reject these gestures and all that they imply. But in repulsing the traditional attentions of gentlemen, in refusing to be ladies, they are throwing away their best, perhaps their only defence against the natural selfish brutishness of men [p 195)].

Brian, however, begins to advise the feminists, particularly in their campaign against a particularly male chauvinist and reactionary professor, Dibble – shades perhaps of the Allan Bloom who later published the right-wing diatribe *The Closing of the American Mind: How Higher Education has Failed Democracy and Impoverished the Souls of Today's Students* (New York, 1987). There follows a joyous sequence in which the feminists take Dibble hostage in his own office. Brian, conscience-stricken, then attempts a farcical rescue of Dibble, being himself entrapped by the feminists and subjected to various indignities. His plight is widely reported in the media (pp 255–69). Brian had always had a grievance that, though a political scientist, he never achieved the eminence of becoming a government foreign policy adviser. 'In a horrible way, he has got his wish; the spell spoken over his cradle has come true; and after trying for forty-seven years he has become a famous man' (p 269).

The Vietnam issue looms throughout the novel; and at one point the environmental issue is coupled with it (p 78). The issue of student-friendly reform in the authoritarian Corinth system comes up once (p 142). The book culminates in a blaze of feminist and anti-war demonstrations. But one rather suspects that the sentiments of Erica are those of the author too:

> I don't care about nineteen-sixty-nine at all. I don't care about rock festivals or black power or student revolutions or going to the moon. I feel like an exhausted time traveller. All these new developments they have, maybe they're interesting or depressing or amazing, but they have nothing to do with real life (p 200).

The War Between the Tates does not give a historically valid account of the black protests and student assemblies culminating in May 1969, which did bring changes in the way Cornell was governed. In *The Nowhere City* there is only a fleeting mention of one of Ceci's beatnik friends being 'coloured' (p 91). The notion that the celebrated events of 1968–9 had 'nothing to do with real life' is far from accurate, but is worth pondering none the less.[36]

The War Between the Tates was the most complex and fully developed of Lurie's novels to date, and fully earned its international status. The treatment of the new feminism and such notions as marriage contracts is particularly valuable for historians. I have, however, sought to show that there is also rich unwitting testimony in the four earlier novels, and that, even today, *Love and Friendship* in particular has a delightful power to surprise and shock. Given that the task of pinning down the beginnings of the sixties cultural revolution is a specially difficult one, then that novel, the first to be published, may be accounted specially useful.

Recently, Erica Jong explained the famous 'cheerful sexual frankness' of *Fear of Flying* (1975) by saying that she had been determined to mount a female equivalent of *Portnoy's Complaint*;[37] actually, Alison Lurie had achieved a similar, if less rumbustious, 'cheerful sexual frankness' more than a dozen years earlier. More: a new discourse of female freedom developed throughout the sixties, arguably as significant for the advancement of women's rights as the radical feminism which emerged at the very end of the decade. One important event was the formation by men and women, representatives of measured judgement, in October 1966 of NOW, the National Organisation for Women, which declared:

> the time has come for a new movement toward free equality for all women in America, and toward a truly equal partnership of the sexes, as part of the world-wide revolution of human rights now taking place within and beyond our national frontiers.[38]

A spate of women's novels, I believe, played a critical role in the formation of the new discourse. *Love and Friendship* was one of the first of these.

ACKNOWLEDGEMENTS

I wish to express my thanks to Alison Lurie for her help and advice, for permission to quote from her novels, and from the Alison Lurie archive in the Cornell University Library Division of Manuscript Collections, Ithaca, New York, and to the Curators of that library for access to the collections.

NOTES TO CHAPTER 6

1   The first two comments are printed in the three pages of extracts from reviews which precede the first American paperback edition of Alison Lurie, *The War Between the Tates* (New York, 1975, Warner Books). The third quotation is from Jay Parini, 'The Novelist at Sixty', *Horizon*, March 1986. Of course, there were magnificent novels to come, for example *Foreign Affairs* (1984) and *Last Resort* (1998).

2   Letter to the author from Alison Lurie, 7 April 1998.

3   Quoted Parini, op. cit.

4   For the chronology, see Richard Hauer Costa, *Alison Lurie* (New York, 1992, Twayne Publishers), p xiii. Alison Lurie in conversation with the author, 1 June 1998. The notes for *Love and Friendship* are in Box 1, f.19, Alison Lurie Papers, 14-12-2572, Rare Books and Manuscripts Library, Cornell University.

5   Useful sources are Paul Goodman, *Growing Up Absurd* (New York, 1972, Alfred A. Knopf and Random House), pp 27–62, 240 and Kenneth Keniston, 'Social Change and Youth in America' in Erik H. Erikson (ed.), *Youth: Change and Challenge* (New York, London, 1963, Basic Books). See generally Arthur

Marwick, *The Sixties: Cultural Revolution in Britain, France, Italy and the United States, c.1958–c.1974* (Oxford, 1998, Oxford University Press), pp 50–4.

6   *Conversation*, 1 June 1998.
7   Betty Friedan, *The Feminine Mystique* (New York, 1963, Norton), p 18.
8   Alison Lurie, 'Noone Asked me to Write a Novel', *New York Times Book Review*, 6 June 1982, quoted by Katherine M. Rogers, 'Alison Lurie: The Uses of Adultery' in Mickey Pearlman (ed.), *American Women Writing Fiction* (Lexington, KY, 1989, University Press of Kentucky), p 118.
9   Alison Lurie Papers, op. cit.
10 See Marwick, *The Sixties*, pp 157–9. The first of the new feminist novels is Erica Jong, *Fear of Flying* (New York, 1973, Holt, Rinehart and Winston).
11 *Conversation*, 1 June, 1998.
12 Arthur Marwick, *Class: Image and Reality in Britain, France and the United States Since 1930* (London, 1990, Macmillan, 2nd edn), pp 292–3, 309.
13 Parini, op. cit. Letter to the author from Alison Lurie, 24 April 1999.
14 Kingsley Amis, *Lucky Jim* (London, 1953, Victor Gollancz); Vladimir Nabokov, *Pnin* (New York, 1957, Doubleday); Peter de Vries, *The Mackerel Plaza* (Boston, 1958, Little Brown).
15 For a reprint of 'Love and Freindship: a novel in a series of letters', Jane Austen's short novel of 1790, see Jane Austen, *Love and Friendship and Other Early Works* (London, 1978, The Women's Press). In this edition the novel amounts to 35 pages.
16 Alison Lurie papers, op. cit.
17 *Conversation*, 1 June 1998.
18 Goodman, op. cit., pp 27–62.
19 Christiane Rochefort, *Le Repos du guerrier* (Paris, 1958, Grasset) and *Les petits Enfants du siècle* (Paris, 1961, Grasset). See Arthur Marwick, 'Six Novels of the Sixties – Three French, Three Italian', *Journal of Contemporary History* vol. 28, No. 4, October 1993, pp 563–91.
20 *New York Times Review of Books*, 1 April 1962, p 41.
21 Inge Kutt, 'Joseph Heller' in Jeffrey Helterman and Richard Layman (eds), *American Novelists Since World War Two*, Gale Research Company, *Dictionary of Literary Biography*, ii (Detroit, 1978, Gale).
22 *Conversation*, 1 June 1998.
23 Marwick, *The Sixties*, op. cit., pp 480–1.
24 *Times Literary Supplement*, 4 February 1965; *New Statesman*, 5 February 1965.
25 Alison Lurie Papers, Box 2, f.29.
26 *Newsweek*, 10 January 1966, p 66.
27 Alison Lurie Papers, Box 2, f.29.
28 Ibid.
29 Oriental religion is featured as one of the elements in 'the counter-culture' in Theodore Roszak, *The Making of a Counter Culture: Reflections on the Techno-cratic Society and its Youthful Opposition* (New York, 1970, Doubleday), pp xi–xiii. For sixties religious developments see Robert S. Ellwood, *The Sixties Spiritual Awakening: American Religion Moving from Modern to Postmodern* (New Brunswick, NJ, 1994, Ruttgers University Press).
30 Michel Foucault, *Folie et déraison: histoire de folie à l'âge classique* (Paris, 1961, Plon); R.D. Laing, *The Divided Self: An Existential Study in Sanity and*

Madness (London, 1962, Tavistock Publishing); Ken Kesey, *One Flew Over the Cuckoo's Nest* (New York, 1962, Viking).

31 See Marwick, 'Six Novels of the Sixties', op. cit.

32 For a brief summary see Marwick, *The Sixties*, op. cit., p 674, using the rich 'Challenge to Governance' collection in the Rare Books and Manuscripts Library at Cornell University.

33 Alison Lurie Papers, Box 4, f.12, 37.

34 Parini, op. cit.

35 See note 19.

36 See the author's own reflections in *The Sixties*, op. cit., Chapter 12.

37 The *Independent*, 'Cheerful Sexual Frankness' is Phillip Roth's phrase, quoted on the cover of the paperback of *Fear of Flying*.

38 National Organisation of Women circular, October 1966. Copy in Free Speech Movement Collection, Box 10, f.23, Bancroft Library, University of California at Berkeley.

7 The Brilliant Career of *Sgt Pepper*

Allan F. Moore

Sgt Pepper's Lonely Hearts Club Band appeared in British record shops on 1 June 1967, and in those of the USA on the following day. It had been eagerly awaited: the Beatles' eighth original album, it arrived ten months after the acclaimed *Revolver*, an interminable delay in the 1960s. On the day of its US release, it was being broadcast by radio stations across the country. It had already been heavily trailed in the British music press and was almost everywhere immediately accepted as a cultural milestone. Critic Kenneth Tynan, for instance, went typically over the top in describing its release as 'a decisive moment in the history of western civilization'.[1] There was a rare dissenting voice: American critic Richard Goldstein's summary found it an 'album of special effects, dazzling but ultimately fraudulent'.[2] In 1967, this view was well out of line, but by 1981 the influential critic Robert Christgau expressed sadness that many had come round to Goldstein's way of thinking.[3] By the end of the decade, a notable proportion of leading musicians clearly had. In the spring of 1988, *New Musical Express* sponsored a compilation, *Sgt Pepper Knew My Father*, in aid of the charity Childline. Each track of the original album was covered by a leading band of the time (Wet Wet Wet, Sonic Youth, The Fall, The Wedding Present) and, with but two exceptions, the irony is suffocatingly thick. The rise of 'Britpop', however, and the plundering of Beatles riffs by such bands as Oasis suggests a new reevaluation: the Beatles are again cool, if somewhat re-heated. At the time of writing, *Sgt Pepper* is once more riding high in the album charts.

ADDRESSING *SGT PEPPER*

The leading current paradigm in popular music scholarship lays great emphasis on the social construction of the text, a valuable corrective to the formalist emphasis of much classical music scholarship. And yet, this insistence is frequently employed as what appears to be an excuse for refusing to acknowledge and take seriously those differences which are present within music, differences between sounds which have as much objective existence as those differences which consist only of light patterns, but which produce the gestures and motion we see on film. Since this issue is crucial to my approach and is not always understood, it is worth exploring here. We, individually and collectively, hear a sound when our eardrum vibrates at, say, 440Hz, having been set in motion by sound waves vibrating at the same speed. They, in turn, have been set in motion by an object itself vibrating at that speed. There is a fairly widely-accepted code which would call the sound 'A above middle C', and in choosing whether to use that code, or some other, we are entering into an act of interpretation. But it is an interpretation of the context of the sound rather than the sound itself: our choice of code cannot affect the speed of the vibrations, nor their interference patterns with vibrations from simultaneous and subsequent sounds. In describing this sound, we can refer to objective, verifiable properties of it. By making this described object subject to analysis, we are making an interpretation of the relationships between it and antecedent, simultaneous and consequent sounds, an activity which necessarily incorporates culturally-bound interpretation of the inherent musical functions of that sound, and which can be subject to evaluation on grounds of its economy, its communicative power, its misidentification of the irreducible facets of the object (such as its musemes), or some other culturally-validated criteria. The musical details of my analyses of the songs on the album can be found in chapter 4 of my study of the album: these lay the groundwork for my discussion in this chapter.[4] It seems to me that without a willingness to encounter details of the musical decisions which form *Sgt Pepper*, we have no hope of answering the questions which its varying reception history might pose. My approach to investigating *Sgt Pepper* is, thus, to begin from the aural text we share (and, note, not with notated transcriptions of it), and to work outwards from there towards what we can glean of the actions which went into its making, and the reception it has received.

SITUATING *SGT PEPPER*

The tradition from which *Sgt Pepper* sprang was volatile and insecurely formed in 1967. Rock 'n' roll had only entered widespread public consciousness in 1956, and by 1958 it had been fully co-opted into mainstream practices (as Elvis Presley gave way to Pat Boone, Chuck Berry to Bobby Vee). The Beatles' emergence in 1962 after an extensive apprenticeship in the clubs of Liverpool

and Hamburg was important in the resurrection of a modified (Anglicised) rock
'n' roll, but Lennon and McCartney's facility with standardised song-writing
techniques was already adequate and improving constantly, enabling them to
embark on the re-negotiation of the division of labour between composer and
performer which remains one of their more important legacies. By 1964, it was
already their range of material which set them apart both from other Liverpool
'beat' bands and from bands in other parts of the country. The style found on the
first four albums represented an easy amalgam of the range of largely black
styles they were interested in emulating (soul, Motown, pop ballad, soul ballad,
rock 'n' roll, rockabilly/country and western), but 'reorchestrated' for their own
forces, such that the rich range of horns, pianos, organs, orchestral strings and
the like (all of which function either to fill out harmonies or to play subsidiary
melodic ideas) become transposed to the rhythm guitar, with occasional employment in this context of a keyboard and lead guitar.[5] This instrumentation (lead,
rhythm and bass guitars, kit, and backing vocals and a keyboard instrument only
on occasional recordings) was ultimately derived from skiffle (an indigenous
late-1950s British style) via the Shadows, and became the bedrock of British
rock until the demise of the rhythm guitar with the birth of heavy rock (through
Jimi Hendrix, Eric Clapton and Jimmy Page). On *Sgt Pepper*, the line-up is
augmented by keyboard work from George Martin, from Lennon and from
McCartney, together with assorted additional musicians on various tracks.[6] The
style emphasised a number of elements appropriated from rock 'n' roll and, ultimately, the blues: instrumental textures, melodic structure and pentatonicism,
rhythm, vocal style (impersonal and using responsorial textures); combined with
verse-refrain form and diatonic melodies (these frequently modal, marked by
the flattened seventh), elements probably derived from Anglo-Celtic folk song
situated on Merseyside; and elements from more advanced Western harmony
(ornamental chromaticisms together with triadic parallelism, ostinati and modal
progressions) challenging any secure sense of key.[7]

By the time of *Sgt Pepper*, this stylistic fusion seemed to be falling apart.
More accurately, perhaps, it was spreading out to engulf an even wider, and frequently more precisely delineated, range of practices. Thus the individual songs
which constitute the album tend in a more expansive variety of stylistic directions.
Heavy rock is apparent on both takes of the title track (tracks 1 and 12), while
a more intimate style underpins 'With a little help from my friends' (track 2) and
'Fixing a hole' (track 5). 'Getting better' (track 4) and 'Lovely Rita' (track 10) are
a little more typical of the year's upbeat pop. 'Lucy in the sky with diamonds'
(track 3) inhabits a nascent psychedelia. 'Within you without you' (track 8) could
be construed as taking this further, in its sophisticated pastiche of classical
Indian techniques, references to which became subsequently used to connote
'spirituality' or an experiential 'otherness' by bands such as Quintessence or the
Mahavishnu Orchestra. Both 'She's leaving home' (track 6) and 'When I'm sixty-
four' (track 9) seem oriented to an older market, the first in its use of string
textures (associated with the burgeoning film-music-derived 'easy listening'

arrangements of Burt Bacharach and Henry Mancini), and the second in its evocation of swing-band articulation for a small, clarinet-dominated ensemble. Neither 'Being for the benefit of Mr Kite' (track 7) nor 'Good morning good morning' (track 11) admit easy pigeonholing: both are quirky Lennon inventions on the edge of the 'humorous song'. Finally, 'A day in the life' (track 13) appears partly an urban folk song, partly upbeat pop and partly avant garde orchestral music.

Indeed, stylistically speaking, one of the more notable features of the album (and arguably the musical face of the 'special effects' which gave rise to Goldstein's indignation) is the way that individual songs appear to transcend style and genre categories. Thus 'Sgt Pepper' is not only a hard rock number: it also makes overt reference to Edwardian brass bands, and seems to fuse these disparate references in the remarkably illusory half-tempo of its central section (that moment when 'the band' addresses the audience). 'Good morning good morning' may be rock in terms of its instrumental textures, but these are so richly overlain with incidental sounds, and the style is so effectively undermined by departing from rock's regular four-beat groove, as to make the song highly idiosyncratic. For many commentators, 'Within you without you' is the crucial song on the album. Its employment of Indian instruments, techniques and textures set it apart from what all but the most radical popular music meant in early 1967, but its use of English lyrics and a normative verse-refrain structure prevent it being mistaken for Indian music. Its pomposity and penchant for preaching, however, typify all that would become unbearable in progressive rock during the ensuing decade. In short, the aesthetic strategies employed on the album are not the result of painstaking planning, but develop in the very process of working.

BUILDING *SGT PEPPER*

By and large, the songs on the album were conceived in great speed, taking real shape in the studio rather than beforehand, and within very short spaces of time. As such, this characterises the stage the Beatles' career had reached, and can be considered normal working practice at the time. While manager Brian Epstein and producer George Martin had initially conceived a marketing strategy of four singles and two albums per year, no such plan remained in place by 1967. The protracted delay before the release of *Sgt Pepper* caused at least one journalist to proclaim that the Beatles were now finished: three months out of the public eye was the death-knell to any band.[8] This is particularly important in 1967, coinciding as it did with the disappearance from the media of concentration on 'mod' subculture and its immediate replacement by an attention to psychedelia. This *volte face* became particularly visible in the music press (chiefly *New Musical Express* and *Melody Maker*) in late spring 1967, and is symbolised in the public birth of the bands Cream and Procol Harum and the stylistic reorientation of the Herd and the Small Faces.

Studio sessions for the *Sgt Pepper* project began on 24 November 1966, with the song 'Strawberry Fields Forever'. By the end of the following January, both this and 'Penny Lane' had received their final mono mixes. Both songs used as inspiration locations from Lennon's and McCartney's early years. Insistent calls from Capitol, the band's US label, for a new release caused these two songs to be removed from consideration for the album and put out as a double-A-sided single especially for the US market. (In those days, it was considered bad practice to include on an album songs released as singles within the year.) Though absent from the released album, they are indubitably a part of the whole project. With their removal, however, went any hope Lennon and McCartney had of following through their original aim, which had been to produce an album which took their Liverpool childhoods as its theme. This is itself notable, both in the very use of a theme, and also in the degree of self-consciousness this particular theme implies. 'When I'm sixty-four' had been recorded in December 1966, 'A day in the life' was put down in January and February 1967, while February and March saw the album's remaining songs committed to tape. The early recording of 'A day in the life' thus gives the lie to those interpretations which find in it the logical culmination to the album's supposed narrative as authorial intention.[9]

Thus, for each song, although a skeleton of some sort (some lyrics, melodic phrases, some chord sequences) would be in existence prior to entry into the studio, most of the creative work took place in the studio, not only in terms of giving a song a fixed form, but also in terms of instrumentation, studio manipulation etc. At this stage of the process, the input of producer George Martin was crucial, to such an extent that the sound of the finished product, even as far as the running order, was his responsibility.[10] The particular emphasis on the album's sonic quality is one of the reasons *Sgt Pepper* made such an impact. It is surely no coincidence that the band's recent decision (late 1966) to quit touring (and, in most cases, live performance) removed concerns about what might be reproducible live. The division of labour between composer/performers and producer is made particularly clear both by biographer Hunter Davies' account of the serendipitous genesis of 'With a little help from my friends',[11] and by the stages of development through which 'Strawberry Fields Forever' passed from Lennon's demo to the finished product, as made plain on the album *Anthology 2*.[12]

Not all songs were found equally pertinent by the album's audience. Among contemporary hippies ('freaks'), 'When I'm sixty-four' was considered an overt accommodation of mainstream culture. There is sense to this: the song was written for McCartney's father, who had himself played in dance bands, and was composed in the late 1950s (this was not known at the time).[13] One American commentator even found a drug reference here, in the line 'digging the weeds'.[14] In context, of course, the 'weed' of 'doing the garden, digging the weeds' is needed for the internal rhyme with the subsequent 'will you still need me, will you still feed me'. Indeed, if one looked hard enough, drug references could be found not only in the likely places ('Lucy in the Sky with Diamonds') but also in the most innocuous ('taking tea with Rita... fixing a hole... getting high with a little help from my friends'). The need to find these references (and therefore to support the view that the album did speak for the counter-culture in at least one respect) is far more important than whether or not they were intended.

At first sight, from the economically secure position the Beatles had achieved by 1967, there is little sign of the underprivileged, or the provincial. And yet they can be found, in the characters who people the landscape. Take the meter-maid, Rita. Her song recounts a very tentative liaison – with an unglamorous role, she becomes noticeable only through McCartney's in(ter)vention – while the strange key of the song's final section, and its emphatic breathing, might suggest a slightly sordid outcome to the affair. Billy Shears provides a second example. The slightly incompetent night-club singer has no great confidence in his own abilities, ably portrayed through the song's very limited melodic range. This was very much the role the song's singer Ringo Starr was invited to play, but the subtle use of supporting voices presents him with great compassion.

'She's leaving home' and 'Good morning good morning' present opposing aspects of a relationship with mainstream society. In the former, 'leaving the note that she hoped would say more', melodically unresolved as it is, symbolises the total failure of communication between the contented, middle-class couple and their daughter who, while not perhaps craving excitement, nonetheless takes it when it is offered. In the latter, however, the fact that 'I've got nothing to say' is unequivocably 'okay. Good morning!'

Remarkably for its time, *Sgt Pepper* contains no overt love songs: there are aspects of 'Rita' or 'When I'm sixty-four' which might qualify, but they present lovers from rather unusual angles. Indeed, some of the songs explore apparently mundane topics. 'Fixing a hole', sparked, according to Turner,[15] by renovations to his Campbeltown farm-house, is treated in a very matter-of-fact way by McCartney's simple tonic-dominant bass-line which supports the chromatic harmonies symbolising the 'colourful way'. In 'Getting better', we have the realistic juxtaposition of optimism (in the refrain) and confession (in the verses). Michael Bracewell's evaluation of *The White Album* is no less pertinent here: '… a sense of Englishness which had one foot in the future and the other in the past: one half of the brain engaged with the banality of daily life in rainy old England, the other pioneering within extreme states of mind to bring back reports from the edges of consciousness'.[16]

SGT PEPPER AS CULTURAL PRODUCT

In retrospect, *Sgt Pepper* has often been seen as an early marker in the negotiation with questions of 'legitimacy' for popular music, capitalised upon by progressive rock in the following decade.[17] At the time, radical US musicians and journalists in particular saw in it a call to the nascent counter-culture. Poet Ed Sanders noted that it 'brought into popular music a broader spectrum of concern – birth, death, sex, money, politics and religion'.[18] For Jefferson Airplane's Paul Kantner, sharing a first listening with unidentified dozens in a hotel, 'it confirmed our suspicions of how mad everybody was. Something enveloped the whole world at that time and it just exploded into a renaissance.'[19] While it was certainly received that way in the UK, the hype which surrounded it was transparent to some. Recalling the craze for kaftans, moustaches and the like in mid-1967, journalist Jonathan Mcades recalled, 'It sounds now as if one is assuming a terrible superiority and attributing to oneself at that age a kind of prescience, but I just knew it was absolute shit'.[20]

The Beatles, however, preferred not to see themselves as agents of change. McCartney was surprised 'to find that people thought that we were changing the world'.[21] Harrison was dismissive of journalistic fears that they were 'ahead' of their listening public.[22] Lennon did not become involved in political action until later in the decade.[23] The association here between drug use and involvement in the counter-culture is crucial.[24] This is particularly dramatised by the circumstances surrounding the composition of 'A day in the life' and the line 'I'd love to turn you on'. Despite McCartney's claim that it referred to a 'spiritual' turning-on (carried in *Melody Maker* on 27 May 1967, i.e. prior to the album's release), this line has always been read as an exhortation to hallucinogen use, and has led 'A day in the life' to be regarded as a song which had meaning in the context of countercultural values: the meaningless death of Tara Browne in a car crash, at which onlookers just 'turned away', the meaningless counting of holes in 'Blackburn, Lancashire', all in turn signifying the meaninglessness of bourgeois existence and, in turn, the necessity to escape bourgeois practices in order to discover meaning. And yet, as the accounts of both Davies and Martin imply, the Beatles' approach was simply to work, rather than painstakingly to encode hidden meanings to be disinterred by those at the forefront of social change. From this point of view, to the extent that *Sgt Pepper* is a window on sixties' culture, that window is very much on an upper storey, disengaged from the traffic below. It contains no programme for civil rights or subcultural formation. It was an individualistic enterprise in which the Beatles were simply exploring the limits of their own creativity at the time. In its type of autonomy in relation to social processes lies perhaps a degree of success in its aim for legitimisation of the kind enjoyed by the music of the European high-art tradition.

In his introduction to this volume, Arthur Marwick proposes some eight characteristic features of cultural products of the period. *Sgt Pepper*, at the forefront of contemporary popular music, evidences a number of these, to differing degrees. The issue of cross-over seems self-evident. The search for legitimacy is, even if only obliquely, an attempt to test the barrier between 'elite' and 'popular' forms. In the realm of aesthetics, this issue finds explicit expression in at least five of the songs. The orientalism of 'With or without you' was, in 1967, popular only among listeners familiar with psychedelia (the proto-hippie audiences for the Yardbirds, Jimi Hendrix and Pink Floyd, for instance). The changing metres of 'Good morning good morning', and the use of 'atmospheric' samples were both foreign to popular music (and the former have remained so in almost all popular styles other than 'progressive rock'). The strings of 'She's leaving home' and the import of freelance musicians both suggest 'classical' paradigms, even if the style of the string writing is closer to Mancini. The 'cut-and-paste' technique of the carillon interlude to 'Being for the benefit' clearly originates in avant garde tape music. Finally, the orchestral crescendi on 'A day in the life' were an overt attempt to exhibit the influence of the avant garde, explicitly that of Stockhausen. In this context, we should note the early review by musicologist Wilfrid Mellers, who found echoes of Stockhausen in the use of taped audience noise on the opening track.[25] Although this is not a widely accepted connotation, there is irony inherent in the fact that the instruments we can hear tuning up are strings, rather than the brass who will play on the opening number. This again points to a lack of planned narrative. And yet, we must remember that this was still a pop album: the identity of the performers (not the composers) was vital (making the *Pepper* illusion work); it was marketed and displayed via the mass media (rather than up-market or specialist publications); it was intended for home (or perhaps communal) use and re-use rather than being the trace of an unrepeatable live event. In these areas, there was no sense of cross-over. The barriers were as strong as ever. Indeed, in this respect, such a notion of cross-over would have to await the appropriation of mass marketing techniques for classical music attendant on the circulation of compact discs.

The employment of indeterminacy as a compositional strategy was widespread among avant garde composers of the time (the very varied examples of Cage, Ligeti, Stockhausen and Cardew come immediately to mind) but is not usually expected in popular music. Neither is it apparent on *Sgt Pepper*, although there are intimations of its presence. The most audible of these are the two unnotated orchestral passages on 'A day in the life'. McCartney reports having determined the structure (i.e. the length, which was left empty while the remainder of the song was being recorded) and the outer extremities of the pitch range to be traversed, leaving it to the musicians to create the necessary effect.[26] On two other songs, 'Being for the benefit of Mr Kite' and 'Good morning good morning', we find similar examples. The tape carillon on 'Being for the benefit' was created from tapes cut up and reassembled randomly.[27] At the end of 'Good morning good morning', a cock crow is replaced by the opening guitar tone of 'Sgt Pepper (Reprise)'. The match was fortuitous, but capitalised upon.[28] Although these examples show indeterminacy in the strict meaning of the term (the use of an event due to chance, the precise outcome of which could not have been foreseen), this is very far from a thoroughgoing employment of what we might call an aesthetic of indeterminacy which, it appears to me, can have no substantial place within popular music due to the latter's requirement for repeatability.

Although largely defeated by the costs it would have incurred, traces remain of McCartney's initial desire to produce a 'package'. Peter Blake's cover art and gatefold sleeve give the album an identity rare at the time (and recognisable even today), while early aims to make a film to coincide with the album were overtaken both by other projects (particularly *Magical Mystery Tour*) and by the understandable failure on the part of the Beatles to realise that *Sgt Pepper* would come to outlive its time.[29] It seems to me that the album can be regarded as spectacle only in the imagination. Within a month of its release, of course, the Beatles would be in the television studio taking part in an early global satellite broadcast, with the live recording of 'All you need is love'. Here was spectacle indeed, although again with viewers partaking vicariously: the live audience (fellow pop musicians and all) appears to have been carefully chosen.

The dominant position of the 'meaning' of *Sgt Pepper* is problematic, both in determination of what it is, and also of how it is to be received (insofar as the two can be separated at all). As I have already argued, the music-stylistic diversity apparent on the album hardly encompasses a coherent world-view. Much the same can be said for the lyrics. Nonetheless, one powerful strand of interpretation of the album has focused on its apparent aesthetic unity. There is a certain irony in this, for hitherto pop albums had largely been collections of unrelated, individual songs, while avant garde conceptions (particularly notable from 1967 were Pousseur's *Votre Faust* and Foss's *Baroque Variations*, with Berio's *Sinfonia* and Maxwell Davies's *Eight Songs for a Mad King* following before the end of the decade) were learning to create aesthetic expressions of Lyotard's infamous 'incredulity toward metanarratives'.[30] But *Sgt Pepper* was notable for its unity. Advance notice of the album in *Melody Maker* of 6 May announced that the record would play in a 'virtually continuous fashion', while Jack Kroll's early review praised its 'organicism'.[31] Richard Middleton's view seems more apt: he noted that on the album the

> cultural techniques of the blues are broadened in scope, as befits the wider, indeed global context in which the music exists... *Sergeant Pepper's Lonely Hearts Club Band...* is explicitly about the very theme with which the synthesis itself is concerned. tradition and rebirth, the conflict and relationship of cultures and hence of generations... ['A day in the life'] thus sums up the 'message' of all the preceding songs: we can no more run away from our civilisation than we can be content with it as it stands.[32]

That this requires interpretation is clarified in Middleton's later view, in which he came to understand the album as 'undercoded'.[33] The illusory nature of this 'unity' was identified in William Mann's early essay. He argued that three songs ('Sgt Pepper', its reprise, and 'Being for the benefit of Mr Kite')

> ... give a certain shape and integrity to the two sides, and if the unity is slightly specious the idea is... worth pursuing. Sooner or later some group will take the next logical step and produce an LP which is a popsong cycle...[34]

In the way it was taken to provide a narrative, *Sgt Pepper* laid the groundwork for the plethora of 'concept' albums which were to plague the following decade. Such a history begins from the Pretty Things' *S.F. Sorrow* of 1968 and the Who's *Tommy* of 1969, continues into punk through Sham 69's *That's Life* (1978), and even the work of punk leaders The Clash, whose *London Calling* (which appeared in 1979) asserts a unity both through its tone and its related key-scheme. At the end of the century, the idea retains some currency as demonstrated by Pulp's *This is Hardcore* (1998).

Back in 1967, it was already being recognised that the degree to which *Sgt Pepper* utilised technological means was setting new standards. The Beatles themselves (and particularly McCartney) were acutely aware of the challenge posed by the Beach Boys' *Pet Sounds*, which had itself been recognised as an advance on their own *Rubber Soul* and *Revolver*. The Beach Boys' working practices were rather different: the vast majority of their material originated in Brian Wilson's constant, unfocused 'play' in the studio, whereby songs grew from grafting together whole series of what began as little more than doodles. The somewhat autocratic nature of Wilson's leadership was, in part, the reason the Beach Boys were unable to better *Sgt Pepper*.[35] But in the case of the Beatles not only were studio manipulations applied to songs the kernel of which existed prior to studio work, but such manipulations were largely in the hands of an external agent, George Martin. Although not averse to making suggestions, his role appears to have been very much one of realising the somewhat imprecise feelings Lennon and McCartney tried to express. The imprecision may well be due to the difficulty of finding adequate sonic analogues for internal states. MacDonald reads the heavy echo in which much of the album is bathed to be the most complete communication of the psychedelic experience, thereby harnessing the technology of recording to the technology of drug production.[36] The invention of stereo recording and the improvement in quality of home hi-fi was, of course, necessary to make such a communication audible. There are difficulties in the view that *Sgt Pepper* actually evokes such states.[37] How, for instance, can such meanings arise for listeners without prior experience of LSD? It is likely that such an experience was beyond many who had access to the album. Presumably, such meaning can arise only by reading such meanings into the lyrics. There is of course no doubt that members of the band worked under that influence, and it may even be that the failure of easy narrative in some of the songs ('Good Morning good morning', 'A day in the life'), still an unusual textual strategy in 1967 (although previously turned to good effect on *Revolver*'s 'Tomorrow never knows') can be accounted for in this way. However, to claim that the experiences of the musicians became magically encoded on vinyl in order to evoke analogous experiences in (unspecified) listeners is, in the wake of Barthes, no longer credible.[38]

SGT PEPPER AS POSTMODERN ARTEFACT

The difficulty, and contradictions, found in attempting to discern the 'meaning' of *Sgt Pepper* certainly resonates with Barthes' call for the 'birth of the reader',[39] although this comment hides two very important features. The first is the extent to which this ambiguity can be aligned with a postmodern, post-structural interpretation. Various authors have put forward strong arguments for the isolation of particular aesthetic identifiers of postmodernism. Although my treatment here is inevitably brief and superficial, I would not argue strongly for such an interpretation of *Sgt Pepper*. We have isolated instances of Jencks' 'double-coding', where references to competing style codes can be found (eg the 'She's leaving home' strings, or the 'A day in the life' crescendo), but these are insufficient to create an adequate degree of interest on the part of an elite audience, in the way Jencks seems to intend.[40] Nor can we clearly identify instances of Jameson's 'blind parody'.[41] Neither 'Within you without you', nor 'When I'm 64', the songs clearest in their calls on recognisably formulated styles, are intended parodistically (although one can guess that the latter would have been received that way among early hippies, while the preaching tone of the former was read that way by some contemporary critics). Pete Manuel's 'exhilaration of surfaces'[42] might resonate with the indulgent studio treatments and the variety of instrumental forces employed, but the absence of structural integrity in the music implied in Manuel's discussion cannot be substantiated for *Sgt Pepper*.[43] I have already expressed doubts about the representation of a collapse of the distinction between 'popular' and 'elite' art forms in *Sgt Pepper*: Andrew Goodwin argues that debates within postmodernism on this issue give different answers, depending on whether such a debate focuses on aesthetic form, on cultural capital, or on technique.[44] The most pressing identifier of 'postmodernism' is that enshrined in Barthes' call. McCartney's and Lennon's abdication of authorial position (in the invention of Sergeant Pepper) might be cited. This would be countered by the fact that nobody was actually fooled into believing in the existence of the bandleader, but the refusal of an easy narrative for the album might lead to such a reading.

The second, and arguably more important, feature questions whether music can ever be thought to acquire the sort of fixed meaning that in literature was under attack from Barthes. Issues of referentiality in music have been subject to heated debate in recent years, from the dehistoricised, essentialist position adopted by Deryck Cooke[45] for music (for which read 'European art music'), to the relativist positions necessitated by a strict sociological approach.[46] While audiences clearly do use music to refer outside itself, the argument for negotiated meaning made by Barthes and by Eco[47] is, perhaps, closer to the way music in European civilisation has always operated, rather than representing a programme for the re-evaluation of musical meaningfulness.

This failure of explicit reference frequently leads to the identification of music as some sort of 'universal language'. But one problem with this position is that of the failure of unequivocal reference: it clearly is not universally understood in the same way. Since it does not refer unambiguously, its realm of signification is available to all listeners. But, then, it probably shares this feature with all cultural products and events.[48] A second problem reminds us that there is no uniform 'music', just as there is no uniform 'language': listeners acquire competences not in music *per se*, but in particular musical styles. Aficionados of Mozart will recognise that 'Sgt Pepper', for instance, contains chords which imply tonal functions, but unless they have a competence for rock, they will fail to recognise the overt references to the blues contained in the sequences in which those chords appear (and thus the deflection of their tonal functions), and will not therefore recognise the connotations of an important site of meaning. To understand music as a language, therefore, is not immediately open to all listeners. All understanding is mediated through competence, and thus experience.

The potential for rock to act as a universal means of communication certainly existed at the time of *Sgt Pepper*: the music was available to all with access to a gramophone and the cash to buy the record; a degree of competence could be acquired through repeated exposure; the print media carried multitudinous references; communities of listeners existed wherein meanings could be negotiated. This communication was rather unidirectional, however. The participatory aspect of rock's power, as experienced directly by the Beatles, might be symbolised by their final live gig in San Francisco's Candlestick Park in August 1966, where a hysterical audience were so intent on their own communication as to be oblivious to the questionable coordination exercised by the band on stage. (Subsequent television appearances of mimed performances surrounded by hordes of fans only supports this interpretation.) The Beatles had, of course, originated in a community – early Liverpool shows enabled a sense of participation on the part of the dancing audience – while McCartney (at least) had experienced the participatory psychedelia being developed at this time by Pink Floyd and Soft Machine at the Roundhouse and UFO Club.[49] The interminable studio jams indulged in by the Beatles later in 1967 (and which remain unreleased) may have been an attempt to (re-)capture this participatory facet, but any evidence of it on *Sgt Pepper* (the audience noises) was simply fanciful. What also existed were communities of listeners aggravated by the delineations (most specifically, of sex and drugs) of what was then, still, just 'pop music'. After all, 'A day in the life' was banned from BBC Radio, specifically for the call to 'turn you on'. And even within affirmed communities, as we have seen, there was no general agreement.[50] After 1967, the listening public tended to become fragmented as styles multiplied and new genres evolved. *Sgt Pepper* was, therefore, perhaps the nearest popular culture has come to a universal expression in music. And yet, as Grossberg argues, this 'universal' expression, at least as read in the USA, failed to challenge the racism inherent in contemporary industrialised society.[51]

This expression, of course, was made from a position within youth culture, and in this lies rock's most problematic feature: it remains the music of those whose youth culture coincided with its rise. The equation of popular culture with youth culture, intrinsic to the construction of popular culture as a culture of resistance, can be seen to have roots in this moment, a recording open to appropriation by all, even if that equation had to await punk rock (which, at the other extreme, was closed to a majority) for its own logical expression. The usurpation of popular ('everyday') culture by youth was signalled by British Prime Minister Harold Wilson's politically convenient awarding of MBEs to the Beatles in 1964, acknowledging that the rebirth of British popular music coincided with the election which returned a Labour government for the first time in 13 years.

Parallels with the curious contemporary lionisation of 'Britpop' by 'cool' 'New Labour', and the coincidental and unexpected musical influence of the Beatles on bands as diverse as Oasis, Blur, the Boo Radleys and Ocean Colour Scene are unfortunately beyond the scope of this essay.

SGT PEPPER AS A SIXTIES ALBUM

What, then, does *Sgt Pepper* teach us about life in the 1960s? It does not speak for the marginalised or the provincial, even though the Beatles incorporate their own experiences of the mundane. It does not illustrate a unified counter-culture, even though many have yearned to interpret it that way right from its inception. It does not destroy the rigid aesthetic divisions between low and high culture, even if it marks an early (and rather inconsequential) point in this ongoing strategy. It speaks, really, for the richness of everyday culture, its gaudiness, perhaps, its loss of unequivocal direction but its desire to find the same. It articulates the discovery of individual pathways to finding 'an answer', even without being able to articulate that answer (or even whether one exists). It is at the forefront of creative expression, but without (at the time) providing the means for others to follow. Most of all, it amplifies how heady, how unrepeatable, and ultimately how irreducible that summer of 1967 was.

NOTES TO CHAPTER 7

1 Quoted in MacDonald, *Revolution in the Head*, (London, 1995, Pimlico), p 198.
2 *New York Times*, 18 June 1967.
3 Robert Christgau, 'Symbolic Comrades', in E. Thomson and D. Gutman (eds), *The Lennon Companion* (Basingstoke, 1981, Macmillan), p 227.
4 Allan Moore, *Sgt Pepper's Lonely Hearts Club Band* (Cambridge, 1997 Cambridge University Press).
5 Allan Moore, *Rock: The Primary Text* (Milton Keynes, 1993, Open University Press), pp 62–3.
6 Mark Lewisohn, *The Beatles Recording Sessions* (London, 1989, Hamlyn/EMI).
7 Richard Middleton, *Pop Music and the Blues* (London, 1972, Gollancz), p 167.
8 Moore, *Sgt Pepper's Lonely Hearts Club Band*, op. cit., p 58.
9 MacDonald, *Revolution in the Head*, op. cit., p 186.
10 George Martin, *Summer of Love: The Making of Sgt Pepper* (London, 1994 Macmillan), p 148.
11 Hunter Davies, *The Beatles*, (London, 1985, originally 1968, Cape), pp 345–9.
12 The Beatles, *Anthology 2* (London, 1996, Apple).
13 Steve Turner, *A Hard Day's Write* (London, 1994, Little Brown), p 130.

14 David Pichaske, 'Sustained Performances: "Sergeant Pepper's Lonely Hearts Club Band"' (1972) in Charles P. Neises (ed.), *The Beatles Reader* (Ann Arbor, 1991, *Popular Culture Ink*), p 61.

15 Turner, *A Hard Day's Write*, op. cit., p 125.

16 Michael Bracewell, *England Is Mine: Pop Life in Albion from Wilde to Goldie* (London, 1998, Flamingo), p 133.

17 Moore, *Rock*, op. cit., pp 83ff.

18 Derek Taylor, *It Was Twenty Years Ago Today* (New York, 1987, Bantam), p 24.

19 Ibid., p 25.

20 Jonathon Green, *Days in the Life* (London, 1988, Heinemann), p 190.

21 Ibid., p 191.

22 Moore, *Sgt Pepper's Lonely Hearts Club Band*, op. cit., p 22.

23 Robin Denselow, *When The Music's Over* (London, 1989, Faber), pp 102–7.

24 Moore, *Sgt Pepper's Lonely Hearts Club Band*, pp 60–1.

25 Wilfrid Mellers, 'Lonely Beat', *New Statesman*, 2 June 1967, pp 770–1.

26 Taylor, *It Was Twenty Years Ago Today*, op. cit., p 28.

27 Martin, *Summer of Love*, op. cit., pp 90–2.

28 Ibid., p 25.

29 Moore, *Sgt Pepper's Lonely Hearts Club Band*, op. cit., pp 71–2.

30 Jean-Francois Lyotard, *The Postmodern Condition: A Report on Knowledge* (Manchester, 1984, Manchester University Press), p xxiv.

31 Jack Kroll, 'It's Getting Better', *Newsweek*, 26 June 1967.

32 Middleton, *Pop Music and the Blues*, op. cit., pp 243, 245.

33 Richard Middleton, *Studying Popular Music* (Milton Keynes, 1990, Open University Press), p 173.

34 William Mann, 'The Beatles Revive Hopes of Progress in Pop Music' in E. Thomson and D. Gutman (eds), *The Lennon Companion* (Basingstoke, 1981, Macmillan), p 93, originally in *The Times*, 29 May 1967.

35 Daniel Harrison, 'After Sundown: The Beach Boys' Experimental Music' in John Covach and Graeme M. Boone (eds), *Understanding Rock: Essays in Musical Analysis* (New York and Oxford, 1997, Oxford University Press), pp 37–46; and Barney Hoskyns, *Waiting for the Sun: Strange Days, Weird Scenes, and the Sound of Los Angeles* (London, 1997, Bloomsbury), pp 104–7.

36 MacDonald, *Revolution in the Head*, op. cit., p 199.

37 Sheila Whiteley, 'Repressive Representations: Patriarchy and Femininities in Rock Music of the Counterculture' in Thomas Swiss, John Sloop and Andrew Herman (eds), *Mapping The Beat: Popular Music and Contemporary Theory* (Oxford, 1998, Blackwell), pp 161–2.

38 Roland Barthes, 'The Death of the Author' in *Image-Music-Text*, trans. Stephen Heath (London, 1977, Fontana Collins), p 148; originally 'La mort de l'auteur', *Mantéia* V, 1968.

39 Ibid.

40 Margaret Rose, *The Postmodern and the Post-Industrial* (Cambridge, 1991, Cambridge University Press), p 119.

41 Frederic Jameson, 'Postmodernism, or the Cultural Logic of Late Capitalism', *New Left Review*, 146, July-August 1984.

42 Peter Manuel, 'Music as Symbol, Music as Simulacrum: Postmodern, Pre-Modern and Modern Aesthetics in Subcultural Popular Musics', *Popular Music*, 14/1,

May 1995, p 233.

43 Moore, *Sgt Pepper's Lonely Hearts Club Band*, op. cit., pp 26–57.

44 Andrew Goodwin, 'Popular Music and Postmodern Theory', *Cultural Studies*, 5/2, 1991, p 177.

45 Deryck Cooke, *The Language of Music* (Oxford, 1959, Oxford University Press).

46 Peter Martin, *Sounds and Society: Themes in the Sociology of Music* (Manchester, 1995, Manchester University Press), pp 63–74.

47 Barthes, 'The Death of the Author', op. cit., and Umberto Eco, *The Role of the Reader* (Bloomington, 1979, Indiana University Press).

48 Robert S. Hatten, *Musical Meaning in Beethoven* (Bloomington, 1994, Indiana University Press), pp 246–57.

49 John Platt, *London's Rock Routes* (London, 1985, Fourth Estate), p 148–50.

50 Lucy Green, *Music on Deaf Ears: Musical Meaning, Ideology and Education* (Manchester, 1988, Manchester University Press), p 36.

51 Lawrence Grossberg, *We Gotta Get Out of This Place* (New York, 1991, Routledge), p 147.

8 *Panorama* in the Sixties

Robert Rowland

INTRODUCTION

An eye-witness has only one perspective. Valuable, illuminating, alive… but it can only be the view of experiencing a scene, or an occasion, or an institution from the position of seeing it, living with it. This chapter will seek to temper the experience of living with one of the most significant television programmes of the late fifties and sixties, through some of its achievements and turbulence, with the benefit of hindsight and the archive records. As the eye-witness and participant, I have to try to be the historian. But, as with any author, it is difficult to present a dispassionate critique of work which you have written and offered to the public. So I hope that some of the views and (no doubt) prejudices which are implicit in this chapter will be useful for those who want to try to get some understanding of at least one person who worked on a major television programme of the sixties. The reader may question why *Panorama* has been selected for this book. The reason is simple. My colleagues in the Open University Sixties Research Group asked me to do so – recognising that little has been written from within television production about this period, and that some 'prime-time' programmes in the sixties occupied an important place in the nation's understanding or awareness of events.

It is difficult to describe *Panorama* as a 'text'. It ran for 48 weeks a year every year throughout the period defined by Arthur Marwick as 'the long sixties'.

Old programmes are not publicly available like a book. Television, for all its supposed impact, is ephemeral. Access to BBC film archives depends on credentials and money. So I cannot assume that the reader will have an ability to consult the 'text'. This chapter is, inevitably, selective and subjective. I was only one of a team of around eight producers (at any one point in time), and for some of this period a very junior member. *Panorama* editions across the period number just under 800 – around 700 hours of airtime. Many people were involved with the programme over Marwick's 16-year stretch of the sixties, so this can only be, at heart, a personal view of a project which this participant found fulfilling and exciting – both at the time and in retrospect. I shall endeavour to describe the context, discuss some of the arguments about cost and structure, explore some of the influences, describe the production process, and sketch in some audience perspectives.

THE CONTEXT

Marwick's broad definition of the sixties as running from 1958 to 1974 fits my 'patterning' of professional life. 1958 was my first year at Oxford, after National Service, as one of the grammar school generation emancipated by the Butler Education Act of 1944. 1974 was my first year running the BBC's partnership with the Open University – one of the great monuments of the sixties and the Wilson administration of 1964–70. In between, I was a BBC General Trainee, a film producer around the world for *Panorama* and Deputy Editor of the programme, becoming Editor in 1971 after running *The Money Programme* on BBC2 and helping to start *Nationwide* on BBC1. So 1958–74 marked the long transition from student to senior management. It also marked, in television terms, a pathway from 'majority' productions to 'minority' productions. The sixties were certainly a high-water mark of the mass media, with great attention given to relatively few outlets. At the beginning of the decade, there were only two channels – and still only three in 1974. The sixties had no cable or satellite capacity. The Open University was one of the first acts of 'narrow casting' or 'target broadcasting' that was devised. It was, in its way, the precursor to the more 'niche' production which has developed in the 1990s and will develop with great pace with the advent of digital broadcasting. (Broadcast satellite television, professionally produced, is now used for internal communications by major companies such as British Airways, Shell, Sainsbury's and ICI.)

I believe that the definition of the sixties as running from 1958 to 1974 also fits the television world generally. Any cut-off is arbitrary, and another time bracketing could be from 1953 to 1969 – from the coronation to man on the moon. Equally, it could be from 1955 to 1969 – from the beginning of ITV to the beginning of the Open University. But I am happy to agree with Marwick's definition because, to someone who was a young person of the time, it feels right. From the Munich air disaster to the Miners' Strike, perhaps, or 'Macmillan after

Eden' to 'Wilson after Heath', or Eisenhower's second Administration to Nixon's resignation.

Panorama certainly exemplifies, I believe, the process described by Marwick as 'permeation' assisted by 'measured judgement'. To this participant in the *Panorama* process and the many debates about the future in Lime Grove, 'measured judgement' would describe the way many producers and programme editors saw their role. The capacity to surprise, to be original, to break new ground was vital – but all in the context of feeling part of a great institution based on Reithian principles of fairness, tolerance, balance and improvement. Respect was tempered by irreverence. All the main programmes – *Monitor, Tonight, Panorama, Sportsnight, The Money Programme, Gallery, Face to Face, The Sky at Night, That Was The Week That Was, Zoo Quest* – came from Lime Grove. Producers met each other across a wide range of output and felt part of the BBC family. We were not entrepreneurial in the true sense of the word, supported as we were by the licence fee (or 'protected' as the Thatcher/Murdoch axis would describe it). We wanted good audiences, we fought for good airtime, we wanted the best crews and film editors. There was felt, in those days, to be a real and true distinction between the BBC and its commercial television (ITV) rivals.

Marwick's thesis that there was no sharp dialectical divide between a commercialised, mainstream culture and a socialistic non-profit-making alternative culture is, as far as broadcasting is concerned, open to challenge, because it could be argued that it fails to capture the real dichotomies. There was thought to be a mainstream non-profit-making culture, vigorously proclaimed by the BBC (which was certainly not socialistic). This culture fought in the popular marketplace with its commercial rival, without losing those distinctive attributes which proclaimed its purpose: no advertising, a commitment to education, careful and mixed scheduling, a 'public service' attitude to staff and staff development, a relatively fair reward system with no 'fat cats' at the top. To this extent, the sixties were balanced more towards public service broadcasting than was the case in the eighties. The BBC achieved the remarkable double of being (in current jargon) national and global brand leader – while paying its staff between a half and two-thirds of the going rate paid by its commercial competitors, an achievement which could be worth closer scrutiny by today's business and management theorists.

I have always found the concept of 'public service' commercial television jarring. The fact that the BBC was such a strong competitor meant that commercial television had to put on some of its rival's mantle to gain audience affection – but it was, at heart, as Lord Thomson memorably said, 'A licence to print money'. The coining of the phrase 'independent television' to describe the commercial alternative to the BBC was a brilliant stroke of spin-doctoring – claimed to me by the late Norman Collins (the founding father of ATV and an ex-BBC senior executive) to be his idea.[1] At a stroke, it suggested that liberty was on the side of the commercials and lack of freedom the personification of the public sector. As the early wisps of Thatcherism drifted across the mid-seventies skies, so the commercialised culture grew and the debate subsided, so that by the end of the period there was beginning to be some force in Marwick's observation.

There was, at the turn of the decade, a fierce and forgotten debate about the advent of commercial television – and radio. Some Labour MPs vigorously opposed the activities of the pirate radio station 'Radio Caroline', trying to protect the BBC's radio public-service monopoly. Many BBC people refused to leave the BBC for the richer pastures of commercial television because they 'believed in' public service broadcasting. It was, almost, a faith. Advertising was thought to be pernicious and damaging as well as getting in the way of the programmes. In the 1959 general election the use by the Tory Party of an advertising agency called Colman, Prentis and Varley was sneered at by all supporters of the Labour Party – I can hear, to this day, Dennis Potter curdling the names in his mouth as he spoke in an Oxford Union debate. Lord Reith, in opposing the arrival of commercial television, said, 'Somebody once introduced the Black Death and the bubonic plague...'[2] It was a heavy parallel to lay on the merry jingles for 'Murraymints, the too good to hurry mints'.

But who can say what the effect has been on society, over three decades of what Marwick suggests was 'an ambience in which nothing succeeded like excess', of the incessant images of consumerism and messages based, at the best, on half truths and, frequently, on distortion and hyperbole? What has been the effect, on us all, of the parade of high lifestyles, glossy hair and fast cars? In the early sixties, the debate about mass television advertising was lively. Now, with the deeply-rooted market economy, it is a subject little discussed in media debates. Advertising on television is thought to be more creative than corrosive. It is thought in the nineties to be in the vanguard of visual fashion – and regards itself as such. But to many producers in Lime Grove between 1958 and 1974 it was a real problem, and to some a reason for working for the BBC. Some left for higher rewards in the commercial world, of course. But many stayed, to exercise their public service role of 'measured judgement', and to oppose what was seen as the all-consuming juggernaut of the hard sell. There was a mission not to be commercial in those days.

PANORAMA: A BRIEF HISTORY IN THE SIXTIES

When television came into its own with the live coronation broadcast of 1953 (with Richard Dimbleby as the commentator), it became, almost overnight, the nation's entertainer, news provider the family hearth. *Panorama*, which started in 1955 (soon after the breaking of the BBC's television monopoly), rapidly became the vehicle of authoritative opinion, with very little competition. Its reporters were highly valued: Christopher Chataway, Woodrow Wyatt, Robert Kee, Ludovic Kennedy, James Mossman, Robin Day and, later, John Morgan, Michael Charlton, Michael Barratt, Richard Kershaw, Robin MacNeil. Like so much in the BBC, it was run (broadly) by the kind of person who, some decades earlier, could have landed up being district commissioners in the British Empire. With only a few exceptions, staff and reporters were ex-public schoolboys, many Oxbridge and mostly men.

Though the *Panorama* programme was regarded as heavyweight, this must be seen in the context of limited competition, limited audience choice and the 'freshness' of everything to television. The world was the programme's oyster, and *Panorama* was able to open its 'Window on the World' through the speed and freedom conferred by the revolution of the passenger jet. It was a magazine programme, and took itself seriously, with a band of fine, world-class reporters. It was a programme based on well authored reports and special interviews, linked by the physically heavyweight Richard Dimbleby. But it also had light items to entice and amuse the viewers. When Richard Dimbleby went to Italy to report on the Italian spaghetti harvest on 1 April 1958, many believed him, such was the power of the programme and the innocence of the audience. It established a tradition of journalistic April fool's day jokes which continues to this day.

Towards the end of the fifties, *Panorama* was locked in rivalry with the BBC's *Tonight*, an early evening programme edited brilliantly by Donald Baverstock (in his early thirties). *Panorama*, under the editorship of Michael Peacock, became the heavyweight flagship, with *Tonight* its cheekier, brighter relative. *Panorama* producers were sober-suited. *Tonight* producers wore dark glasses and sports jackets. Alasdair Milne, who succeeded Baverstock as editor of *Tonight* (and who later became Director General of the BBC at a time when the Thatcher years were in full flood), recently described *Panorama* in those years as 'rather self important and faintly tiresome'.[3] Both programmes engendered tribal loyalties, and mixed little in the Lime Grove bar, or the canteen. We fought our journalistic corners, believing that the distinction between us expressed that 'creative tension' which was proclaimed to be the essence of what Huw Wheldon called 'excellence'. Occasionally, there was miscegenation. A fine reporter, John Morgan, moved from *Tonight* to *Panorama* at the turn of the decade and brought a touch of irreverence and wit to the programme. Duplication was rare, and when it occurred it was a source of real concern. Alasdair Milne complained, early in 1962, that Keith Kyle's trip for *Tonight* to cover the famine in Kenya and RAF aid was made fruitless because Paul Fox, editor of *Panorama*, had dispatched Robin Day to cover the same story. He said that 'it had not been on the *Panorama* schedule'. Milne agreed to withhold the story but wanted financial compensation: 'Naturally, I understand Fox's predicament with only one story per week,' he added, spicily.[4] Sometimes, there was co-operation. I remember Anthony Jay, a later luminary of business management video training, calling in to the *Panorama* offices early one morning in July 1963 to say that if *Tonight* was on the air they would be looking for the grave of the London-based rent racketeer Rachman, and what was *Panorama* planning to do? It was the closing years of a Tory administration which had been overwhelmed by the Profumo Affair in 1963 and also the scandal of rent racketeers exploiting the new immigrant communities in Notting Hill – with the mysteriously disappeared property owner

Peter Rachman being the focus of concern. We took Anthony Jay's hint, and it resulted in a *Panorama* 'exposé', which went into a second report the following week at the specific request of Director-General Hugh Greene. The reports, presented by Michael Barratt and John Morgan, were influential in the general election of 1964. 'Rachmanism' became a focus of attack by the left. On Wednesday 17 July 1963, two days after the first broadcast, Lord Stonham, for the Labour opposition, drew the attention of the Lords to the programme. A week later, on 22 July, in the House of Commons the new Leader of the Opposition, Harold Wilson (who had succeeded Hugh Gaitskell after his death in January 1963), led the Rachman debate with an attack on 'Shabby gangsterism'. He said that the people of the country had been gravely shocked by what they had read in the national press and seen on *Panorama*:

> The Rachman story is a lurid version of a story which goes on in more sombre sepia tones in other slum empires and cities other than London. I think that in the Rachman headquarters, if we could find them, there must be honoured places for portraits of Macmillan, Sandys, Brooke, Hill and Joseph.[5]

A week after this blistering attack on Macmillan's cabinet, a committee of inquiry, under Sir Milner Holland QC, was set up to make a survey of housing in London so that the government might learn what pressures were being brought to bear on tenants by unscrupulous landlords. Labour lost a censure motion on housing against the government by 94 votes.

BBC producers were very young. Michael Peacock was editor of *Panorama* at twenty-seven. Alasdair Milne was editor of *Tonight* at the same age. Paul Fox, Jeremy Isaacs, Brian Wenham, Peter Ibbotson, myself and many others were editors in our early or mid-thirties. Great responsibility was given very early by an organisation which had powerfully discovered the art of devolution of authority in a way which could be instructive to many less well run organisations of the late nineties. That aside, the BBC Lime Grove Studios of the sixties certainly demonstrated what Marwick describes as 'the rise to positions of unprecedented influence of young people'. The Beatles were our music, jostling with Sinatra and the Rolling Stones.

When Richard Dimbleby's death occurred in 1965, *Panorama* was in the midst of one of its upheavals. A new editor, Jeremy Isaacs, had been appointed from commercial television. To this eyewitness, he vouchsafed that though sad and too early, Richard Dimbleby's death was a kind of liberation from the programme's past, allowing him to change the nature and structure of the programme to fit the changing times. Interviewed at the time by the *Daily Telegraph*, he was described as 'witheringly critical' of aspects of the present *Panorama*, which he described as 'a class programme with little contact with ordinary people'. The report said that 'his determination to produce longer items and more film reports will have the interesting consequence of considerably lessening the role of the eternal link-man Mr Richard Dimbleby'.[6] Curiously, Jeremy Isaacs's changes (to lengthier, better researched, more considered items) were the beginnings of *Panorama*'s move into a journalistic solemnity which outdid anything undertaken during the Dimbleby years (with three earlier outstanding editors, Michael Peacock, Paul Fox and David Wheeler under the, respectively, shrewd and inspirational heads of department, Leonard Miall and Grace Wyndham Goldie). *Panorama*'s place in the nation's heart began to shift. In the late sixties, under another fine editor from commercial television, Brian Wenham, the programme became much more 'single subject' and it was lengthened to one hour (instead of 50 minutes). As editor (with Alastair Burnet as 'presenter'), I made attempts to reintroduce a magazine style in the early seventies, and returned it to a 50-minute length. But by then there were more current-affairs television programmes prowling the screens and there was also fierce scheduling competition from BBC2 (which ran *Alias Smith and Jones*, a 'western' series, against *Panorama* at eight o'clock). *Panorama*'s role as a 'news creator' was nibbled by *Weekend World*, operating on the fringes of audience perception in a lunchtime Sunday slot on LWT. But the new programme had a feisty PR streak which meant that it punched above its weight – watched by few but reported by many. Peter Jay, its presenter, was a lively publicist for the programme and all those who sailed in it. But the big audience, with all its demands and expectations, was not there.

So Marwick's long sixties (1958–74), which began with *Panorama* at the centre of the television world, finished with *Panorama* struggling against new competitors, uncertain of its future but still maintaining its place in the schedules as a major statement by the BBC of its commitment to good journalism in prime-time. Its place was maintained by various BBC Director Generals: Charles Curran, Ian Trethowan and Alasdair Milne.

The decade of the sixties began with a programme which was self-defining of *Panorama*'s role. The publicity – and its contents – showed remarkable self-confidence and an ability to 'cast' a programme which in the nineties would be hard to emulate. The *Radio Times* billing for the first Monday of 1960 read:

> The 1950's are finished. As they close, 2880 million people are alive on Earth. At the end of the next ten years, there will be 3460 million – an increase of one fifth. This is one of the staggering facts on which *Panorama* bases its special edition on Monday – 'The Challenge of the Sixties'. The question it seeks to answer is 'What kind of world can we expect to be living in 1969?' Almost certainly, the sixties will see the growing emergence of Africa. Mr Julius Nyerere, who is leading Tanganyikan progress towards self government talks to Robin Day. He speaks for Africa and is interviewed in Dar Es Salaam. What of Asia's millions? How will the struggle for influence over them between China and India develop? In Delhi, Prime Minister Nehru contributes an exclusive interview with James Mossman. How will we in the Western World react to the growing world of the sixties? In New York, Adlai Stevenson, twice Democratic Presidential candidate warns of the dangers of a prosperous but materialistic society, while in Paris, the French writer, Bertrand de Jouvenal looks ahead to the problems of the new Europe. Will the Cold War with Soviet Russia go on? How will Russia respond to the growing strength of Communist China? Edward Crankshaw, expert on Soviet affairs, and Robert Kee try to look at the sixties as they might appear to Mr Khrushchev. And what new knowledge

– in space and on Earth – will science bring to the sixties? At the Institute of Advanced Studies in Princeton New Jersey, Dr Robert Oppenheimer, who headed the team which made the World's first Atom Bomb, talks to *Panorama* on this theme. In Britain, there will be prophecies for the future by Professor Bernard Lovell, Director of Jodrell Bank Audio Telescope and Dr Jacob Bronowski.[7]

Hardly a modest programme, but fulfilling a high political role which defined the core of *Panorama*'s activity. With a big and consistent audience, frequently over ten million in prime-time, it took root in the nation's mind, I believe, as the place to hear what important people had to say. It developed the political interview, through the work of Robin Day, Michael Charlton and James Mossman, away from the deference of the fifties to the sharp and hard style of the late sixties, without becoming hectoring or discourteous or loud. Grace Wyndham Goldie, who helped to establish *Panorama*'s authority by supporting, inspiring and trenchantly criticising the production team, said,

> What distinguishes one television magazine programme from another is its style. Style must be consciously created. It depends upon consistency in the choice of items, the way in which these are linked, and the personality of the compere who presents them. All these depend upon the quality and outlook of the Editor of the programme. The style of *Panorama* was to be authoritative. Like any serious weekly, it could not afford to omit major developments at home or in international affairs. And, on television, if at all possible, to interview those making vital decisions in regard to them. Such interviews frequently made news. What was said in *Panorama* on Monday evening came increasingly to be headlined in Tuesday's morning papers. And an interview on *Panorama* was soon accepted by politicians, including Prime Ministers and Leaders of the Opposition, as a suitable method of communicating with the nation.[8]

The early sixties were ushered in by the editorship, after Michael Peacock, of a television sports producer, Paul Fox. It was an appropriate start to a decade of social and cultural fluidity. He had made a success of *Sportsnight* with his close friend and colleague, Ronnie Noble. Leonard Miall and Grace Wyndham Goldie saw the powerful grain of the competitive instinct in him, and he took over the reins of the BBC's most prestigious programme and built its reputation with his strong sense of popular journalism. He encouraged young ideas from a young team. He developed outside broadcast anchor locations for Dimbleby from time to time. He wanted stories, recognising that television is a narrative rather than an analytical medium. Eventually, he was promoted in the BBC to the controllership of BBC1, and left to become a commercial television mogul, before returning, as the prodigal son, to the BBC in the late eighties.

The regular weekly 'billing' in the *Radio Times* in 1963 (at the beginning of Arthur Marwick's 'High Sixties') said,

> *Panorama*. The Window on the World... introduced by Richard Dimbleby, with reports on People, Places, Problems in the news with Richard Dimbleby, Robin Day, Michael Barratt, Michael Charlton, Roderick MacFarqhar, John Morgan.

Associate Producers David J. Webster [later Director of Corporate Affairs for the BBC] and Richard Francis [later Director General of the British Council]. Assistant Editor, Chris Ralling, and Editor David Wheeler.[9]

The BBC's excellence in what has been begun to be described as its 'Golden Age of Television'[10] was based on a real understanding of devolved responsibility and authority, within a system of 'upwards reference'. This was rarely defined, but all producers were expected to have an instinct for knowing when they needed advice, or when those senior to them needed to know that a course of action would be initiated which might need approval. BBC staff selection processes probably underpinned the relative security of the system, together with that sense of pride in working for *Panorama* and the BBC which many of us felt and which we would not abuse. Great freedom was given 'down the line'. With that freedom went great trust. And that trust was rarely unaccompanied with a sense of responsibility to the wellbeing of the corporation. Trust given down the line was reciprocated by a transactional loyalty.

PRODUCTION METHODS

The production process for *Panorama* from 1961 centred on a weekly meeting every Tuesday morning in the Editor's small office on the third floor of the office block in Lime Grove (before the programme's move to different accommodation in the late sixties). It was attended by those producers and reporters who were 'at base', together with (until the summer of 1965) Richard Dimbleby. Ideas were discussed, future events and their relevance to *Panorama* considered, films and reports in the pipeline were deployed to their most appropriate week for transmission, approaches for interview with this or that leading politician were decided and apportioned. The role of the Editor was central, and he was expected to lead the discussions and make quick decisions of story choice and staff deployment.

Film crews were never more than three-man units: cameraman, assistant cameraman and sound recordist. The crews were full-time BBC staff and were dedicated to the programme. To edit the film material there were three cutting rooms, again with film editors dedicated to the programme (the late Ian Callaway worked on *Panorama* as a film editor for over ten years). Everything was shot on 16-millimetre film black and white (until 1969) with separately-recorded sound. Film stock came in 400-foot rolls, which lasted ten minutes. Everything had to be sent to the laboratories for developing and printing. Sometimes, *Panorama* used 'one man bands', where the cameraman acted as his own sound recordist – people such as the South African Ernie Christie or the Austrian/Canadian Erik Durschmied. Some natural film pairings occurred: the reporter James Mossman with the producer David Webster, John Morgan with Chris Ralling or Revel Guest. A film trip at home or abroad consisted (usually) of five people: reporter, producer and camera crew. We never took production assistants on location, except where there was a live outside broadcast element from outside London or from Europe or America (after good satellite links were established).

The programme content was usually finalised during the course of Sunday evening – where film reports might be finally approved by the editor as late as midnight. All film dubbing took place on the afternoon of transmission, while the studio was being rehearsed. The schedule was always very tight and depended on a team of people with different skills who knew each other well and who identified themselves with the programme in a very personal way.

Foreign film trips were undertaken on the cost effective basis that every trip should generate at least two, and often three reports. Frequently, the first two films were transmitted before the producer and reporter returned to base. This meant that every shipment of film had to be accompanied by an accurate and detailed shot list of the content of every roll of film. The final batch of film would be accompanied by a detailed running order and a commentary (often recorded in a hotel bedroom). There were no viewing monitors. Nothing could be reviewed on location. So the producer/director had to have a clear knowledge of what was being shot, and needed to explain very closely the purpose of each sequence to the camera crew. The 'shape' of a film would develop during the shooting. The final commentary had to be written in such a way that the film editing suite in London could have opportunities to change the length or shape of the film, so every report had to include optional sections which could be removed if necessary to allow the film to fit into the 50-minute length of the programme and take its place with other items. Time, and the best use of it in a limited space, was the feature which always dominated the final processes of completing and preparing the programme for transmission. The reporter had to know what images had been collected, so that the words of the commentary would enhance the film, and work with the pictures. The interdependence of the team 'on the road' was paramount.

The choice of stories on a film trip was often left to the reporter and producer in the field. The job was to find a way of illuminating an issue which might have been the reason for the investment. Researchers rarely went as advance parties, and everything was usually done 'on the hoof'. The programme was created on the principle that reporter and producers could be entrusted with the responsibility of deciding on the spot what should be offered back to London and how to tackle it.

Throughout most of the decade of the sixties, there were no union-agreed manning levels in the BBC. It had not been gripped by the ACTT in the same way as commercial television, which had developed and continued inefficient manning levels which could only be financed by the shining coffers of commercial income. *Panorama*'s rival programme on commercial television in these years, *This Week*, operated with eight-man film crews, all travelling first class. At the BBC there were no overtime payments, until the 'cameramen's agreement' in 1968.

COSTS

On 20 June 1960, Michael Peacock, then Editor of *Panorama*, wrote to the Head of Talks, Leonard Miall:

> The situation in Japan and the Far East in general cries out for *Panorama* coverage… as usual, there is one fly in the ointment – money. Any filming in the Far East is an expensive proposition. We are looking into the possibility of hiring a Japanese crew. The total cost will be £3500… at the moment, we have no money in the kitty and I could only save at the rate of £200 per week. So I could accommodate £2000. Could you ask Controller Programmes TV for £1500?[11]

The request was refused.

In 1961, the Controller of Television expressed worry about *Panorama*'s 'hospitality' costs of £30 per week, at a time when the overall programme budget allowance was £1625 a week (£600 of which paid for the prestigious reporters: Richard Dimbleby earned £105 per programme, Robin Day received £4500 per annum, James Mossman £3500, John Morgan £2750, Ludovic Kennedy £4900, at a time when senior producers were earning around £1500 per annum).[12] The notion that the BBC was never cost-conscious is a myth peddled by some of the senior managers from commercial television who were given key responsibilities in the BBC during the Thatcher years and after, and who have persuaded some of their well-established BBC colleagues that their past was profligate. The BBC archive files on *Panorama* are littered with arguments about cost. A note from the editor, David Wheeler, to all staff on 4 October 1963 said:

> Travel must be economy, and all foreign trips must be costed before there is a go-ahead… any estimate must not be exceeded and there will be no First Class travel under any circumstances… shooting ratios are too high… three recently aborted stories cost £250, £500, and £525 at a time when producers in other Departments are expected to turn out half hour shows for these budgets.[13]

On 14 July 1965, the Controller of BBC1, ex-*Panorama* editor Michael Peacock, gave reluctant agreement to budget increases for *Panorama* and *Tonight*. *Panorama*'s budget went up to £3000 per week (including £345 for foreign travel and £255 per week for the hire of outside film crews). *Tonight*'s budget went up to £5500 per week.[14] By this time *Panorama* was facing strong competition from ITV's *This Week* and *World in Action*. In the first quarter of the year, *Panorama* averaged audiences of 8 million, *World in Action* six-and-a-half million, and *This Week* seven-and-a-half million. Audience analysis for the end of 1964 showed that *Panorama* was watched regularly by a sixth of the population every week: nine million people (one third of the 'middle class', one quarter of the 'lower-middle class' and one seventh of the 'working class'). The 'middle class' made up 40 percent of the audience while being 30 percent of the population. Half of the audience was over 50 and only a tenth were teenagers: a fifth were aged between thirty and forty.[15]

In June 1966, Jeremy Isaacs urged forcefully for a third film crew to be established with the other two regular crews for *Panorama*. (Stephen Hearst, a long-established BBC producer and later Controller of Radio 3, told Isaacs that if he were to achieve his ambition of an effectively-researched single and relevant topic approach to *Panorama*, he would need to achieve a dramatic re-structuring of the programme production and resource support). Isaacs's request was refused by BBC management. 'God Blast and Damn Them All to Hell,' he scrawled frustratedly on the memo which rejected his argument.[16]

STRUCTURES

The arguments about the programme structure of *Panorama* after the death of Richard Dimbleby in December 1965 became almost theological in their complexity, and generated great heat. The BBC archive smoulders with memos pulling this way and that. They all centred around a perception that *Panorama* was a major public institution. They continue to this day.

A new style was discussed in 1965, before Dimbleby's death. On 19 March 1965 Paul Fox, then Head of the Current Affairs Group, wanted a new shape 'in response to the continuing challenge of *This Week* and *World in Action*'.[17] *This Week* had centred on single-subject programmes, such as 'Abortion' on 2 February 1965. In that same week *Panorama* scheduled a programme with three items: the aircraft industry, Vietnam and Lord Beeching on British Transport policy. At the beginning of March 1965, *Panorama* had five items: Spain, computers, Malcolm X, 'The Making of the Prime Minister' and a film shot in Italy and the Vatican based on the newly-published diaries of Pope John XXIII, 'The Journal of a Soul'.

The single-subject debate was at its peak under Jeremy Isaacs. He said, when he took over, that there were two important tests for a current affairs production: 'does It matter?' and 'can we add something new?'

Late in 1966, Robin Day asked wistfully in a memo, 'Is there no place in television for anything between the quick fire journalism of *Twenty Four Hours* and the forty minute documentary? There are many subjects which merit 15–20 minute coverage.' He went on to say that 'the single subject has destroyed *Panorama*'s credibility and breadth of appeal and reduced the BBC's ability to give peak time coverage to big issues at short notice... *Panorama* used to be a big event of the week with something worthwhile for everyone'.[18] John Grist (Assistant Head of Current Affairs) was critical of Isaacs' approach and style in a private memo to Paul Fox. Later that year, 1966, when Grist had taken over from Isaacs as editor, Fox sent this mission statement: 'What is needed is to restore the authority and identity of the BBC's major Current Affairs programme – to make it a top programme again'.[19] Another note in the archive, dated 8 September 1967, from David Webster to John Grist, is concerned about the challenge of ITV competitors, who are doing some 'sure fire easy stories'. David Webster says, 'If *Panorama* is to play a world role, and if other people are going to lap up the cream of the cheaper options, it is going to be expensive for us'.[20]

All this was an echo of 1964, when Richard Francis, then a senior producer on *Panorama*, wrote to Paul Fox and John Grist in a note dated 11 August:

> '*Panorama* is losing its status... faced with increasing competition, we are no longer indispensable... we should drop the four story concept and plan for a major feature every week... we must get more contracted experts as reporters – in the fields of Defence, the Communist Block, Science etc.[21]

There is a blistering critique of the programme from Derrick Amoore, then Assistant Head of Current Affairs (and a member of the *Tonight* tribe in Lime Grove), written in July 1968. As ever ahead of the game, this very clever producer proposed a *Panorama* research and production unit:

> Complex stories often have to be started from a state of utter ignorance. Therefore, coverage is often superficial – coverage rather than a probe – a pull-together of the generally known, rather than a revelation of the unknown but significant. Too often, it seems to me, *Panorama* stories, though indisputably the work of civilised and literate men, tell the similarly literate and civilised nothing they didn't know before. The programme tends to be concerned with those issues which become explicit and can be covered through existing representative bodies... it is in this sense that *Panorama* may be damagingly identified as a 'political' or 'establishment' programme. The programme should take factual positions, as distinct from merely acting as a high powered vehicle for the often mutually exclusive positions of other authorities.[22]

Amoore argued for a new unit to concentrate on long-term investigations with a low strike rate, 'to discover what is the case – rather than what is thought to be the case'. He pointed to the fact that sanctions over Rhodesia were regularly discussed, but the fact that they were being regularly broken was not exposed. This was the voice of its times, challenging anything that might smack of received opinion. Brian Wenham, when he became Editor in 1969, took the programme some way down this road, back into a single-subject and more 'investigative' mode.

When I was Editor in the early 1970s, the arguments continued: single subject versus magazine; flexibility, authority, relevance, analysis, depth, superficiality, forward planning. The words continued to reverberate around the Editor's chair. Over at *Weekend World*, John Birt and Peter Jay coined the phrase 'mission to explain', thought by some to be an ultimate expression of television journalistic hubris.

For this study, it is the words that matter: 'authority', 'world role', 'indispensable', 'status', 'identity', 'credibility'. They describe the way many of those involved with the programme and its management saw *Panorama*'s role in the sixties. Some may disagree, but these words (used by those who argued for the role and purpose of the programme) were central to some internal attitudes to the programme – so they have a contemporary validity, even though the passage of time may tend to trim them down a little in some selective memory processes.

AUDIENCES

A television programme does not exist without its audience. From the late fifties, *Panorama* became for almost a decade the most respected and valued vehicle for high-quality television journalism in the UK and, arguably, in Europe (or so those who worked on it believed). It was highly admired in the USA. It was, it proclaimed, a 'window on the world'. To work for it was to be conscious of being in an elite media squad. It was watched, every Monday night, by audiences frequently over ten million people, following the very British *Z Cars* series or the very American *I Love Lucy* series. The audience was vast, and the authority of the presenter, Richard Dimbleby, unmatched by any successor. For a period of time, until his early death in 1965, he was almost a tribune of the people. *Panorama*'s special programme on the Cuba crisis in 1962, 'Flashpoint Cuba', put Dimbleby at the heart of the nation's anxieties, and his tone soothed the watching millions. In a period of debate and questioning, his iconic status began to be seen as an 'establishment' tool – even though he had been, in the late pre-war period, a BBC iconoclast, upsetting what he saw as a stuffy news management style. Dimbleby was seen by some as 'pompous'. The programme's success in getting to the heart of affairs had imbued it with a sense of being 'important' – and to the questioning style of the sixties, it had become the voice of 'authority'. An article giving the 'inside story' of *Panorama* in the *Daily Sketch* in 1964 said of Dimbleby:

> He has become an institution of the television age, a comfortable, rotund embodiment of security and promise, the Town Crier of the Telly whose very appearance seems to bring an assurance that it's 8.25 and all's well. He has become the visible incarnation of something essentially British as the chimes of Big Ben, warm beer, and the flag on Buckingham Palace.[23]

Audience reaction to *Panorama* was always very varied and diverse, reflecting the size and disparate nature of the audience. I produced a special profile of Sir Oswald Mosley in 1968. We were attacked from all sides for being biased against and for him. He was a controversial figure, and his appearance stimulated all the preconceptions, memories, distrust, admiration and revulsion that his political career had stimulated. James Mossman interviewed him fairly, we thought. To some, he was too aggressive and sceptical to his subject, while to others he was too courteous. A delegation from the Board of Deputies of British Jews came to express their distaste for the broadcast *per se*. The audience was over ten million.

Earlier audience research for the programme on 4 June 1962 showed a similar picture. The programme included an interview with the Australian Prime Minister, Robert Menzies, on the Common Market, the situation in Thailand by James Mossman, a report on the Dalai Lama and Tibetan refugees by Ludovic Kennedy, and a report on the West Derbyshire by-election by John Morgan. It was watched by 13 percent of the population, with the different social categories being A+ 32 percent, A 43 percent, B 20 percent, C 4 percent and C- 1 percent.[24]

Another audience analysis of a *Panorama* programme later in 1962 showed the same picture, where the items were a report from Bulgaria, a story on Soviet cosmonauts, a film on the Berlin Wall and a feature on tourism in Berchtesgaden (Hitler's Bavarian home). A retired civil servant wrote of this programme that 'it is of great importance to viewers to have events of international importance brought to their notice'. A teacher wrote, 'I believe Richard Dimbleby and his colleagues are successful because they give the impression that they have put serious hard work in the preparation of their commentaries – and this is much appreciated'. A less appreciative member of the audience panel said '*Panorama* is always a "must" for me, but my enjoyment is marred by the man who introduces it. He always gives me the impression that he is doing me a favour by being on the programme, not vice versa – as it should be.'[25]

PANORAMA FROM LIVERPOOL, APRIL 1964

Another example of a patchwork audience reaction was the *Panorama* 'special' from Liverpool, transmitted on the opening night of BBC2 on 20 April 1964 (there was a power failure in the Lime Grove area, so all the film items due to be 'injected' into Dimbleby's live presentation from Liverpool had to be transmitted from Alexandra Palace). The programme included a special report by John Morgan on the famous section of the Liverpool football crowd at Anfield massed on the 'Kop', filmed with three camera crews on the last match of the season (when Liverpool defeated Arsenal 5-0 to win the league championship). Another item covered architecture and attempts to regenerate the inner city area. It was at the height of Liverpool's fame as the home of the Beatles and great football.

'When will we get a true picture of Liverpool?' asked the *Liverpool Echo*. A letter to that paper from Eileen Banks said, 'I feel I must congratulate the BBC on their magnificent efforts to leave no stone unturned in order to produce such a crop of beastly ugliness which assailed our eyes and ears on *Panorama*'.[26] She was referring, no doubt, to the extraordinary scenes on the Kop, where an almost entirely male crowd, packed shoulder-to-shoulder, swayed together like a cornfield in the wind to the rhythm of 'She Loves You, Yeah, Yeah, Yeah'. Another critic said, 'More time should have been devoted to culture on Merseyside... the squalor was over emphasised'. Mrs Young wrote to the *Echo* and said, 'Strangers would get the impression that we all live in slums, and do nothing but watch football. We saw nothing of Liverpool's life-line, the docks – or the lovely parks.'[27]

The Chief Architect, Walter Bor, attacked the programme, writing, 'It was more important at this point in time not to hark back to the well known poverty and slums of Liverpool, but to produce a forward looking image of a progressive city'.[28] (All this was nearly 20 years before Michael Heseltine's initiatives under Margaret Thatcher to help to regenerate Liverpool's inner-city area.) On the other hand, the national press said that *Panorama* had painted the fashionable view that Liverpool is a fine place and didn't show what it is really like. And the film on the Kop was immensely popular, with pirated copies of the sound track becoming a cult and highly marketable property among the Liverpool supporters (there were no home video recorders in those days).

Looking at it today, the Kop film shows a crowd of extraordinary unity, good humour and wit, well dressed with ties, suits and jackets, and very neat, about as threatening as a tiger cub. Perhaps some could see that it might grow up into the beast of the Heysel Stadium, but we couldn't. It was all on the cusp of change. Big money had not invaded football, as it began to by the end of the decade, leading to the grossly-inflated rewards of the late nineties – arising from the huge performing rights paid to the leading clubs by the television industry and its new satellite and cable players such as Rupert Murdoch. Crowds and players appeared to be closer in spirit in the less well-rewarded sixties. *Panorama* paid the Football League £75 for the afternoon's shoot at Anfield, on condition that we used no more than three minutes of football in the film. I sent a special £25 facility fee to Bill Shankly, the Liverpool Manager.[29]

INFLUENCES

Panorama was rarely told what to do, though Jeremy Isaacs (who was Editor in the mid-sixties) suggested recently that the BBC hierarchy was sometimes affected by the 'political steers' of the Foreign Office and MI5.[30]

The BBC archive shows that Paul Fox received a suggestion from the Board of Governors on 6 April 1961 that he should produce an item for the programme on why Italian labour is imported to Bedford for the nearby brickworks instead of labour from areas of chronic unemployment in the UK such as Northern Ireland. It was also suggested that *Panorama* should consider another item on a recent report by the National Institute of Industrial Psychiatry on the attitudes of workers to takeover bids. Fox rejected both suggestions; he expressed robust opinions on the first idea:

> Foreign labour is recruited into places like Bedford because the work is too nasty and too badly paid to attract British workers... it is virtually impossible to get them to pull up their roots to move them... it does not stand up to *Panorama* treatment.[31]

Pressure to run items from above was unusual, and Editors had very considerable freedom and autonomy.

Just as high commercialism had not yet seized sport, so had the spin-doctors not yet invaded politics, business and industry. In the 1960s there were few powerful public relations people, and fewer Directors of Corporate Affairs. The field for *Panorama* was relatively uncluttered by competition, and there were fewer barriers to direct access to prominence. At the other end of the scale, cameras were still a novelty in the streets and on the shop floor. They were greeted often with pleasure, usually with great co-operation, with little of that mist of suspicion which hovers around camera crews in the 1990s.

Even so, the Wilson administration leaned heavily on the BBC, with an abrasive relationship in the 1966 general election (a fast turn-around from the friendly relations established in the 1964 general election). The relationship with the Wilson leadership reached rock bottom with the transmission of a programme called 'Yesterday's Men' after the Labour defeat of 1970, a satirical programme which nobody actually 'owned' editorially, and which was grafted through the Lime Grove editorial methods with some elegance. It was supposed to be a product of a nightly programme called *Twenty Four Hours*, but the then editor, Anthony Smith, reasonably disclaimed any responsibility. It had not been on his budget and it could not, in his view, be seen as a counterpart to a more measured programme from his stable about the Conservative front bench. It was an inventive and lively programme but it caused long-lasting political offence and scarred the BBC's relationships with Harold Wilson's Labour Party.

To this observer, the Heath administration was very clear and unskewed in its relationship with Lime Grove. When the BBC made its valedictory programme about Lime Grove in 1991 (before the BBC's abrupt departure from the studios under a new management unmoved by what the buildings represented in BBC and broadcasting history), Sir Edward Heath insisted on coming to the studios themselves to pay his tribute. As he sat in one of the hospitality suites on a twilight evening, he said he wanted one last look because he had valued the relationships with television production and the conversations that took place after live programmes such as *Panorama*. He believed it had helped the broadcasters to understand the politicians – and vice versa. He paid tribute to the fact that 'nothing ever leaked'.[32] It was, in its way, intended as a compliment. But it could be seen as underlining a cosiness between politicians and the media, which might have got in the way of the full picture. To some extent, it is inevitable that those 'in the know' will always take pleasure from their intimacy with power centres. The discreet sharing of knowledge – 'who knows what first' – is central to most political journalism.

Panorama pushed the boat of powerful independence of spirit very far into the stream. In 1968, Prime Minister Wilson and Leader of the Opposition Heath both agreed to come to Lime Grove to be questioned live on *Panorama,* after being seen in the studio watching a filmed report which they had not previously seen, and of whose contents they were unaware. They were expected to respond to a 20-minute film 'on the hoof', as well as fielding sharp questions from James Mossman, Michael Charlton and Robin MacNeil (an ex-NBC reporter who eventually returned to the USA to become the doyen of American political television commentators on his daily Channel 13 programme *The MacNeil Lehrer Report*). It was perhaps as far as any programme has ever gone in interviewing politicians. No Prime Minister has ever done such a thing again.

PANORAMA SMETHWICK REPORT (GENERAL ELECTION 1964)

There was one very curious earlier incident in the run-up to the general election of 1964, where it could have been the case that the BBC bowed to external pressure in a way which belied the Director General Hugh Carleton Greene's ringing pronouncements about independence. Because of strong corporate loyalty, half the story was never told at the time. The facts are simple. Their interpretation is more difficult. It could have been the moment when Wilson thought that he could have his way with the Corporation – if he really chose to – when the chips were down. Or it could have been an aberration. In any event, it was very odd.

The highly experienced Editor of *Panorama*, David Wheeler, had decided that the programme would deal with major issues of the campaign during the election period. One of the topics chosen was 'Immigration and Race'. As a well respected producer from *Panorama*'s earliest days, David Wheeler knew the ways of the BBC. After some discussion, it was agreed that I should go to Smethwick in Birmingham to produce a report on the campaign in that constituency, where the issue of race was dominant. The defending Labour candidate was Patrick Gordon-Walker, a major figure in the Labour Party. His Conservative opponent was Peter Griffiths, who was to win the seat, and who was described by Wilson as a 'parliamentary leper' on account of what was thought to have been his racist campaign. The Liberal candidate was David Hugill. The reporter, Michael Barratt, and myself filmed interviews with all the candidates and with people in the constituency.

When we had completed our filming, we were contacted by the *Panorama* office and told that it had been decided that we should film in another Birmingham constituency where race was an issue, but where the political balance was the opposite of Smethwick – where there was a sitting Conservative challenged by Labour. Michael Barratt and I thought that this was a strange request, because it would be repetitious of what had already been filmed. Leslie Seymore, the sitting Conservative MP for Sparkbrook, was contacted, and Roy Hattersley, the young Labour challenger, agreed to co-operate. Filming began quickly, and interviews with the candidates in Sparkbrook began, together with constituency background material.

Before the extra filming had been completed, we were informed that the item had been cancelled. Michael Barratt and I had little time to tell all the contributors, and were puzzled and dismayed by the decision. Our concerns were heightened by the fact that the BBC, through a 'spokesman', told the national press that this was not done at the behest of any political party but because it was 'realised' that the item would exacerbate racial feelings. The spokesman's statement said:

> We took a look at it, and in the circumstances up there, we thought we had better not do it. The reason for this decision is that we feel in our treatment of it, we could not help giving rise to some racial feelings.[33]

The statement sounded measured and fair, and in line with the Director General's image of the BBC. The difficulty with it, and the reasons given, is that none of the film judged to be so inflammatory had been sent to London. Every can of exposed film was still in our possession in Birmingham – it had not been sent to Kay's Laboratories for processing. So nobody other than myself, Michael Barratt and the camera crew knew the contents of our proposed film and treatment. No final script had been written, no editing shape had been proposed, no interview had been seen or heard. There had been no discussion with Michael Barratt or myself. We were consulted at no stage and given no opportunity to outline the final shape or content of the film. The Birmingham *Evening Mail* suggested that the programme had been referred to Hugh Greene himself.[34] If it was, he never sought any information which could have informed his decision.

Why the Smethwick film was withdrawn is a mystery. The BBC archive is almost totally silent. All that exists is a letter from Peter Griffiths, the successful Conservative candidate, written to Greene on 21 September 1964 asking for an explanation as to why he had learnt of the decision in the press and saying:

> Surely it is not necessary to carry out the interviews before deciding if they will be screened... Immigration is a vital issue in many constituencies. To ban the reasonable discussion of the matter on the BBC is a failure on the BBC's part to report the campaign accurately. Such action favours the Labour Party which would prefer not to discuss the matter.[35]

The Director General replied on 25 September 1964, saying,

> The reasons for withdrawing the item for *Panorama* were quite clear and very widely publicised. No discourtesy to you was intended on our part by not writing to you in   advance to tell you of our decision and the reasons for taking it: there was, in fact, no time for this and the best way, it seemed to me, to inform all concerned was to announce at once the decisions and the reasons for taking it. This decision does not mean that the immigration question will not be discussed or reported. As you will perhaps have heard, a number of questions on this subject have already been put to Party Leaders in our 'Election Forum' broadcasts and answered by them. Lastly, the decision was taken for the reasons given and with no regard for the advantage of any political party.[36]

Patrick Gordon-Walker went on to lose Smethwick at the general election on 15 October, and was defeated again at the Leyton by-election soon afterwards. This second election was specially engineered for him to get him into the House of Commons, because Wilson (unprecedentedly) had appointed him Foreign Secretary after the Smethwick defeat. Was the BBC leant on? Did it succumb to pressure from the Labour Party? There are no answers, and the archive is oddly empty of references to a controversial decision about an important programme. The fact that the BBC and the Director General distorted the truth in its explanation leaves me to believe that this could have been the moment when Wilson thought 'in extremis' he could manipulate the BBC if he (or someone) exerted sufficient pressure. If that is the case, it set the scene for some bumpy moments ahead.

What was also remarkable in that election period was the decision by the Director General to remove the immensely popular comedy series *Steptoe and Son* from its 8.30pm slot in the schedule on polling night on October 15. Harold Wilson had urged the Director General to do so, because it could be a factor in getting the final stages of the Labour vote to the polling stations.[37] The polls closed at 9pm, and *Steptoe* enjoyed an audience of over 12 million. In the event, Wilson won by a tiny majority of four seats. It could be argued, therefore, that the BBC's decision to re-schedule an episode of *Steptoe and Son* was a factor in the ending of thirteen years of Conservative government.

ASPECTS OF *PANORAMA* IN AMERICA

Racial conflict may have been a delicate subject for *Panorama* treatment in the 1964 general election, but it was a regular feature of American coverage in the sixties. *Panorama* reported regularly on the troubles in the Deep South and then in the northern big cities: in Birmingham, Alabama, and during the 'long, hot summers' of the mid-sixties as American society faced up to the consequences of years of prejudice. It was all rolled in with regular (and often very brave) reporting on the Vietnam War by reporters such as Michael Charlton and Julian Pettifer. This was another soul-searching experience for the American people as it acted out the fearsome logic of John Foster Dulles's domino theory about the spread of Communism in South East Asia, which he urged when he was Eisenhower's Secretary of State in the fifties. Under Kennedy and Johnson, who inherited the theory, the troops for Vietnam were America's reply to what was seen as the rising tide of Communism, so feared by American politicians reared in the intolerant climate of the fifties. There is a thesis that television coverage of the Vietnam conflict helped to weaken American national resolve and international support for the conflict. War, with cameras present, could never be glorious again; perhaps it is television's greatest achievement (in its short life) that there will be fewer statues to generals.

America, to this observer who made many visits as a journalist in the sixties, seemed to be in an uncertain state of mind. I went to film the protesting students on the Berkeley Campus of the University of California in 1966, and interviewed (with John Morgan) at Los Angeles airport the very courteous and friendly Ronald Reagan, who was standing for Governor of California. He knew about cameras and camera crews, and was disarming in his co-operation in a busy schedule. His Hollywood tone and style belied his public hostility to the students. In him, the American Hollywood dream became tangible. He talked about his days as a Democrat and the relationship between acting and politics. He rejected accusations of police brutality in the Watts 'negro ghetto' and, when questioned about the student protests at the Berkeley campus, said,

> 'I have documentary evidence that things have taken place which are in such a violation of the normal ethical and moral codes that I couldn't begin to disclose

them here in a television programme. I have always figured that liberty and freedom of speech is a two-way street and I figure that I have no right to say that
someone can't use, for example, vulgar language. But I do have a right, if he's
at the next table and saying it loud enough for my wife and children to hear – I
have a right to ask him to lower his voice. The Constitution prescribes he has a
right to speak – but the Constitution doesn't prescribe that I have to listen... I
think we have something of a moral crusade that's required here. We have a
crime problem in California in which 9 percent of the people of our nation live
in our state – but 17 percent of the crime is committed in this state. When the
increase in arrests for youngsters under 18 for narcotics crimes last year was up
33 percent I think it's time to do something about it.'[38]

The counsel for the defence of the Berkeley students involved was an American
lawyer called Bob Treuhaft, who was married to a famous and honourable rebel
of the thirties, Jessica Mitford. We filmed them also, linking the radicalism of
Jessica Mitford to what was then a more modern cause than her fight against
European Fascism and its seduction of some of her siblings.

We mounted a special programme after the assassination of Martin Luther
King live from Atlanta on his funeral day in 1968. Robin MacNeil, the reporter,
filmed the funeral in the morning, processed the film, edited it, dubbed a commentary and transmitted it live from Atlanta into *Panorama* at 8pm London time
(2pm Atlanta time). For those days, this was fast. The funeral followed days of
rioting in the northern cities. I filmed with Richard Kershaw in Washington the
day after Martin Luther King's death. A famous black entertainer, Dick Gregory,
spoke to an angry crowd in a park:

> You'all turn your television sets on and watch our cities burn... then you turn
> down the volume on the set and you invite your Mom and your Dad, your
> Grandpa and your Grandma watching those cities burn and you begin to recite,
> loudly, the Declaration of Independence: 'We hold these truths to be self evident,
> that all men are created equal, and that all men are endowed with certain
> inalienable rights which include life, liberty and the pursuit of happiness'.

It is without question that, through an often terrible crucible, 'crucial moves
from segregation to multiculturalism took place during the 1960s', as Marwick
asserts in his introduction. I first visited the southern states as Marwick's 'long
sixties' began in 1958 as a student. I went to Little Rock, Arkansas, and was
hustled away from the High School (famous as the place where racial integration
was resisted by the then Arkansas Governor Faubus) by a caretaker wielding a
gun and calling me a 'Nigger lover' for wishing to look at the scene of recent
racial tension. In those days, black people had no vote, sat in the back of
Greyhound buses, and were refused entrance to certain hotels and restaurants.
It was like South Africa. The distance travelled by American society between
1958 and 1968 was remarkable. The British were responsible for creating
(through the slave trade which was central to the eighteenth century urban
economies of London, Bristol and Liverpool) the culture of discrimination and
servitude which permeated American society for so long. In my view, we should

have looked at the racial conflicts in America with a much greater sense of a national historic responsibility than we ever mustered. The teaching of history to students of the fifties centred on the way Britain had stopped the slave trade. There was little emphasis on the vast ethnic restructuring of a global population in which Britain played a central part in the seventeenth and eighteenth centuries. (Perhaps to the post-war generation of history teachers, the slave trade could have been a confusing competitor with the Holocaust?)

Racial intolerances in Britain were also eased in this period (as I have suggested, the 1964 campaign had a strong commitment to better race relations from the Labour Party). They are still in many ways deeply unresolved, but voices of fairness, liberty and goodwill have not been silenced. Laws have been passed to provide a framework for integration, and the sixties saw positive steps to beginning to recognise the positive and creative benefits brought to Britain by a more multicultural society.

Just a year before Martin Luther King's assassination in Memphis, I went with Michael Charlton to Cleveland, Ohio, to spend a week with King on his 'Operation Breadbasket', an attempt to raise the prospects and hopes of the inhabitants of Cleveland's black ghettos after a period of rioting, and to help to break down barriers of white prejudice. We filmed him in halls and homes, with his advisers. Michael Charlton interviewed him at length on a little lawn outside a chapel. To this observer, he had great courtesy – and the deepest and most sensitive eyes. In his special interview for *Panorama*, he proclaimed his faith in his style of non-violence, while recognising the clamour of the dispossessed:

> 'We can't win the struggle here in America without bringing white America to the point of being just, and seeing the negro as a human being and treating him that way. The problem with the riot is that it pushes this problem into the background. It intensifies the fear of the white community on the one hand, and relieves their guilt on the other. After all, the riot is the language of the unheard, and America has failed to hear that the plight of the negro has worsened over the last few years; and that justice and equality have not come to the negro. Large segments of the white society are more concerned about tranquillity and the status quo than about humanity, justice and equality.'[39]

'CALIFORNIA 2000', JUNE 1966

Some years earlier, in 1966 (under the Editorship of Jeremy Isaacs) *Panorama* decided to devote a complete edition to explaining the way people in California saw the future. We called the programmme 'California 2000'. It was one of the first of Jeremy Isaacs's 'single-subject' editions, which were the cause of that fierce debate and discussion in the Lime Grove hothouse. We went to California because, in those days, it was where it all seemed to be happening. Chips and silicon were beginning to revolutionise the world, and California's 'think-tanks', and its youth, led the way. The Head of Current Affairs, John Grist, said,

'We specifically chose California because there is great wealth, enormous development in the last few years, enormous appetite for new things and – in Watts –
the breakdown of the modern city... and, also, in the drug taking etc, and the
jumbo universities, indications of the world to come'.[40]

The programme included pre-echoes of the future, rather like fuzzy signals from
a distant galaxy. Just as inter-galactic signals help to locate our place in the
cosmos, future predictions often help to define the nature and feel of the present,
with all its hopes and fears. In the 'California 2000' film, Jimmy Sherman, a young
black man from the Watts 'ghetto' area of Los Angeles (which suffered serious
riots in 1965) recited a poem he had written:

> I was working real hard on my job one day,
> When my boss came on the scene.
> He said, 'Son, go in and get your pay,
> And make way for the working machine'.
> I rolled my eyes, I sure was sore.
> My boss, he sure was mean.
> He said, 'Son, you know I don't need you no more,
> You're fired, because I got a machine'.
>
> Well, I got another job the following day,
> Working harder than you ever seen,
> 'Til I heard my boss, in a loud voice say...
> 'Look out' – it was another machine...[41]

No cameraman would film in Watts with us at that time – it was thought to be so
dangerous. 'B -B -B' ('Burn, Baby, Burn') was the slogan on street corners. One
man agreed to drive the car, because he knew the area, while I filmed from the
window. The driver would not stop anywhere in Watts, and we wore hard hats.

In the same programme, Thomas Paine, then the head of the General
Electric think-tank Tempo, had his own related visions. He went on to be head
of NASA, and is reputed to have written the words spoken by Neil Armstrong on
21 July 1969 as he set foot on the Moon: 'One small step for [a] man, and a giant
leap for Mankind'. Thomas Paine's predictions for Panorama were:

> 'By the year 1990, we shall see a delay of the entry of the work force into the
> labour market, and people will start work at about 25. Then we think the retire-
> ment age will occur at around 50. And in the 25 years of the working life, peo-
> ple will work half of what they do today. We see a partnership developing
> between the heuristic role of management and the computer. The computer will
> replace much of middle management and all the need to store paperwork... it
> will replace a large segment of the white collar middle management staff.[42]

For 'California 2000' we filmed a new group called the Grateful Dead at the
Fillmore Auditorium, with a crowded hall of misty-eyed people lit by psychedelic effects projected onto the dimly-lit walls (they were achieved by squeezing
rhythmically together two glass dinner-plates smeared with tomato ketchup and
olive oil lit by an overhead projector: such was the prosaic basis of a mesmeric

world). Flower power and pot were the answers of young Americans to Vietnam and the creaking timbers of the inner-city areas. We were invited to a party by Jerry Garcia and the Grateful Dead held at a ranch in Marin County, across the Golden Gate Bridge, on a hot Sunday afternoon. Everybody was naked apart from the reporter (John Morgan), myself and the cameraman. Being well trained by the BBC, and knowing the limits of television, on prime-time, we put the camera away. I remember being introduced to a ginger bearded and pubic haired thin man holding a flute. Somehow, this forlorn figure is an image of an age of aggressive uncertainty. It was just months before Timothy Leary's 'be-in' in San Francisco (known as Psychadelphia... Tripsville) where people were enjoined to 'Turn on, tune in and drop out'. The *Panorama* 'California 2000' film was in the centre of Marwick's 'High Sixties'. It was an attempt to define the present by divining the future – a feature of the times which were, as Bob Dylan's song told us, 'a-changing'.

In the same film, Linus Pauling (twice Nobel-Prize winner), speaking at a conference at the Centre for the Study of Democratic Institutions in Santa Barbara, gave his vision of the future:

> We are changing from the old world where people struggled for income, to be properly fed and housed to a time when we will have resources available to all human beings to live full and interesting and varied lives relatively free from the sufferings caused by economic injustices and the suffering caused by a lack of variety and intellectual curiosity.[43]

For him, and the academic soothsayers at the conference, it was a time of hope for a better and fairer world, which they believed technological advances would bring to the last quarter of the twentieth century.

The audience for the programme was 10 percent of the UK population. The BBC Audience Research Report stated:

> Some older viewers were inclined to count themselves fortunate that the year 2000 lies at a comfortable remove from their own probable lifespan and were thankful that the prognosis that humanity will become increasingly influenced by automation would not affect them personally.
>
> Some viewers were horrified by a sequence showing a group of schoolchildren for whom computer 'know-how' in solving mathematical questions is a familiar part of schooling.[44]

NORTHERN IRELAND

While *Panorama* in the sixties covered the consequences of bigotry and racial conflict all over the world – Vietnam, Rhodesia, USA, South Africa – we failed considerably to report the festering difficulties of Northern Ireland. I remember, as Editor of *Panorama* in the 1970s (when it seemed we reported little else), talking with John Hume in Belfast, who said he believed that if the media had reported the treatment of the Roman Catholics in Northern Ireland earlier a boil might have been lanced before it burst. In the mid-sixties, he had sent an article to the *New Statesman*. It had been rejected. He felt that had the article been published it would have alerted what are now known as the 'chattering classes', with considerable political effect. He thought that British lack of knowledge of the situation in Northern Ireland contributed to the force of the trouble when it burst.

It is certainly the case that the Wilson administration of 1964–70 did little to anticipate the catastrophe that exploded at Burntollet Bridge, leading to the violent days of Ulster in August 1969, a woeful feature of British history in the last quarter of Marwick's 'Catching Up' period (in Northern Ireland's case, catching up on 300 years). The BBC was equally silent. But there were pressures at Lime Grove for the activities of Ian Paisley to be fully reported. A young producer, Phillip Whitehead (later Editor of commercial television's *This Week* programme before being elected Labour MP for Derby North and later MEP for Staffordshire East and Derby) urged that filming should take place during the 'marching season' in a memo dated 26 January 1967, when it appears that a film was being considered. He said that if filming takes place outside the marching season:

> We shall be able to film eloquent Irish chat about discrimination and bigotry, but no action. Will people be convinced the situation has the explosive potential that we know it has: I think it would be a shock to the people of Britain to see the extreme violence of religious passions in this part of the UK.[45]

This is a prescient note, linked to another in the BBC Archive saying that the Director General wanted a major report on Northern Ireland with Robin Day as the reporter[46] (few were better as 'on-the-road' reporters in those days). But nothing emerged, and *Panorama* never focused on Northern Ireland, as we should have done. One of the difficulties for Lime Grove in reporting on Northern Ireland was the iron grip maintained on all coverage by the BBC Controller's office in Northern Ireland. There was a view that, as part of the Protestant hegemony, the Controller's control was pretty absolute. Voices of dissent, cries of concern about the position of Roman Catholics were stifled by the Northern Ireland editorial system – even though senior BBC voices elsewhere urged reporting freedom. 'Because of these tight editorial controls, our inability to report on the growing difficulties in Northern Ireland was our biggest journalistic failure in the sixties,' said Sir Paul Fox.[47] Richard Francis, as Controller Northern Ireland in the early 1970s, in a speech to the Royal Institute of International Affairs at Chatham House in 1977, said,

> When the first BBC Northern Ireland Advisory council was introduced in 1947, at the very first meeting, the Chairman ruled that the question of partition and the Border was out of order. A solemn directive was issued by the Regional Director in 1947 stating that BBC policy was 'not to admit any attack on the constitutional position of Northern Ireland'... Up to 1968, the accent on the positive, coupled with the periodic denial of air time to people outspoken in their criticism of the status quo, failed to convince the public of the troubles which were just over the horizon. By accentuating the middle ground, the BBC

unwittingly may have lulled people into a sense of security which subsequent events were so rudely to shatter.[48]

Another pre-echo of constitutional change came from Robin Day in the same year. He proposed, on 8 November 1967, that *Panorama* should record a debate in the House of Lords for use in an entire *Panorama* devoted to Lords reform. 'It would, in no sense, be intended to "jump the gun" on the delicate issue of televising either House'. He proposed recording from 2.30pm to 6.30pm. He went on to say, '*Panorama* is a programme which their Lordships could trust to transmit their proceedings with dignity, authority and clarity'.[49] It was an idea which Robin Day urged consistently for years, and he must take great credit for the eventual decision to allow the broadcasting of parliament, denied to all television broadcasters until 1985. And he was right about *Panorama*'s faith in its own dignity, authority and clarity. Though the programme was never deferential, those with responsibility for it did regard it as a major television institution of the Sixties – with responsibilities to balance, fairness and impartiality.

LIME GROVE

Panorama came from a romantically impractical building in Shepherd's Bush, West London. By the side of the towering Lime Grove Studios (where Charles Laughton and Margaret Lockwood and many others starred in British feature films) was a row of modest terraced Edwardian houses. The BBC acquired these as television production in the Lime Grove Studios expanded in the early fifties. Later in the period in question, *Panorama*'s offices were in the sitting room, front room, bedrooms and front hall of one of these houses – complete with the original tiles and stained glass in the front door. From outside, *Panorama*'s office looked exactly like a typical London home of one of its target audience. The editor's chair had its back to the bay window of the front room which looked on to the street. *Panorama* had started 'in the houses', as it was always called (next door to *Tonight*). It moved, for a period in the sixties, to the third floor of the studio block in another little warren of offices. The modesty and cramped nature of the surroundings for *Panorama* were in sharp contrast to what was felt by the producers and reporters to be the national and central importance of the product. The only 'luxury' centred on the wood-panelled hospitality rooms – called S8 and S9 – so much admired by Edward Heath. Here programmes were often fiercely discussed immediately after transmission, with guests, producers and Heads of Department contributing. These rooms were in what was called the 'Polish corridor' because this is where the old bosses of the film studios had their offices, and where (some said) they had their casting couches. It has now all gone. On the Lime Grove site are new houses, and it is all as if the studios, with their constant swarm of film and television activity, had never existed.

CONCLUSION

Panorama was central to the process of what Marwick describes as television's capacity to render the private quickly public. But the programme was not investigative. Jeremy Isaacs's questions 'does it matter' and 'can we add anything new?' were, I believe, the basis of our journalism. We rarely asked, 'Is there anybody out there who doesn't want this told?' – except in our probing of the political debate. We 'scooped' on news value, not on sensation. We were never 'tabloided'. To that extent, *Panorama* was a fairly sober beast in the television jungle of the sixties. Metaphorically speaking, we wore suits throughout the period. But the programme did break many new and influential stories: the rigged elections in the electrical trades union in the late fifties, the Rachman rent scandal in 1962, a special programme on the great taboo, cancer, after Richard Dimbleby's death (he had fought cancer with great bravery for the last five years of his vigorous life, and it was known to very few), and the first four-letter word on television (from Ken Tynan) in Marwick's 'First Stirrings of a Cultural Revolution' period.

Panorama certainly mattered, if comment on world affairs and high-quality on-the-spot reporting matters. It added something new often by just 'being there' and helping the audience to understand what was happening by offering the perspectives of highly experienced and literate reporters. The world is now cobwebbed with satellites and instant communication: 'live from New York' is no longer surprising, as it was in the sixties. Throughout most of this period, foreign reporting arrived in cans of film, which needed processing before editing, and which took time. That time allowed for judgement. The nature of terrible pictures from Vietnam or Northern Ireland could be considered before transmission. To this day, cameras are far less intrusive on personal suffering than they could be – except where there is famine or natural disaster, where television plays a central role in telling the world and stimulating help. *Panorama* helped to create that lexicon of style and editorial judgement which continues today.

Arthur Marwick asks us to be cautious of saying what a wonderful time the sixties were. He is right, of course. It was a time of great trouble in America, in the Middle East, in Vietnam, in Africa, in the Soviet Bloc. But for some of the generation born in the United Kingdom just before the Second World War, it presented extraordinary opportunities to those fortunate enough to have swum through the tight meshes of the educational system. It gave great responsibility very early. A colleague on the programme, Paul Hodgson, said recently, 'It was great fun'. And, in all honesty, it was – though so much of our programme content was thought to be very serious. The internal arguments could be fierce, but the companionship and the sense of doing something worthwhile was central. It was a vibrant team effort, and stands as a monument to an era when what you did mattered more than what you earned, and who you were was more important than who you knew.

The sixties were evanescent – but what isn't? They had an influence, of course. But as a street slowly changes as shop functions change, so they have slipped away. But the period did hear new voices, it did tackle new issues, it shrank the world – and *Panorama* was central to all that in the United Kingdom. At the end of Marwick's 'High Sixties' television offered, on 21 July 1969, the supreme icon of the age: a man standing on another heavenly body for the first time in the history of mankind, looking back at our beautiful blue planet. And television was there, a window on the world in a literal sense.

NOTES TO CHAPTER 8

1 Norman Collins to the author at Alexandra Palace, November 1976.
2 Lord Reith, House of Lords debate on Government White Paper on Broadcasting Policy (CMD8550), 22 May 1952.
3 Alasdair Milne to the author, 29 May 1998.
4 BBC WAC (Written Archives Centre), T32/1191/8, October 1962.
5 Quoted in *Daily Telegraph*, 23 July 1965.
6 *Daily Telegraph*, 27 June 1965.
7 BBC WAC, T32/1248/1.
8 Grace Wyndham Goldie, *Facing the Nation* (London, 1977, Bodley Head), p 192.
9 BBC WAC, T32/1191/8, January 1963.
10 Paul Hoggart, *The Times* ('Digital Television' supplement), 1 October 1998.
11 BBC WAC, T32/1272/1, Michael Peacock to Head of Talks Television (Leonard Miall), 20 June 1960.
12 BBC WAC, T32/1191/8, Talks contracts, 27 March 1962.
13 BBC WAC, T32/1191/8, David Wheeler (Editor of *Panorama*) to production staff, 4 October 1963.
14 BBC WAC, T58/265/1, note from Michael Peacock, 14 July 1965.
15 BBC WAC, T58/265/1, BBC Audience Research analysis of *Panorama* audience, weeks 45–8 1964, dated 10 February 1965.
16 BBC WAC, T58/265/2, scribbled on memo dated 9 June 1966.
17 BBC WAC, T58/265/1.
18 BBC WAC, T58/265/2, Robin Day to Huw Wheldon, 15 November 1966.
19 BBC WAC, T58/265/2, Paul Fox (Head of Current Affairs Group) to John Grist, 5 December 1966.
20 BBC WAC, T58/265/3, David Webster to John Grist, 8 September 1967.
21 BBC WAC, T32/1191/9, Dick Francis to Paul Fox and John Grist, 11 August 1964.
22 BBC WAC, T58/265/2, Derrick Amoore proposal for *Panorama* research and production unit, July 1968 (also ref T58/265/4).
23 The Inside Secrets of *Panorama* by Anthony Bristow, *Daily Sketch*, 6 April 1964.
24 BBC WAC, T32/1340/1, Audience Research, 4 June 1962.
25 BBC WAC T32/1340/1, Audience Research, 13 August 1962.
26 *Liverpool Echo*, 23 April 1964.
27 Ibid.
28 BBC WAC T32/1362/1, Walter Bor, letter to the author, 1 May 1964.

29 BBC WAC T32/1362/1, agreement with Alan Hardaker of Football League.
30 Sir Jeremy Isaacs (Editor of *Panorama*, 1965/66) to the author, 16 June 1998.
31 BBC WAC T32/1191/9, suggestion from Board of Governors, 6 April 1961, and response from Paul Fox, 23 May 1961.
32 Sir Edward Heath to the author, 15 July 1991.
33 *The Times*, 18 September 1964.
34 *Birmingham Evening Mail*, 17 September 1964.
35 BBC WAC T16/716/4, Peter Griffiths to Director General Hugh Greene, 21 September 1964.
36 BBC WAC T16/716/4, Hugh Greene to Peter Griffiths, 25 September 1964.
37 Sir Paul Fox to the author, 15 March 1999.
38 Transcript of interview, 1966, in possession of the author.
39 BBC *Panorama* Report, 1966
40 BBC WAC T58/265/2, John Grist to the BBC Secretary, June 1966.
41 BBC *Panorama* Report, 1966.
42 Ibid.
43 Ibid.
44 BBC Audience Research Report, 1966, in possession of the author.
45 BBC WAC T58/265/3, memo from Phillip Whitehead to John Grist, 21 January 1967.
46 BBC WAC T58/265/3, memo from Paul Fox to John Grist.
47 Sir Paul Fox to the author, 15 March 1999.
48 'Broadcasting to a Community in Conflict – the Experience in Northern Ireland', speech by Richard Francis to Royal Institute of International Affairs, 22 February 1977.
49 BBC WAC T58/265/3, memo from Robin Day to editor of *Panorama*, 8 November 1967.

Conclusion

Arthur Marwick

Perhaps there was a touch of the sledgehammer about the ten propositions, six tasks (or questions), and 16 characteristic features – appropriate as a digest of my own enormous book on *The Sixties*,[1] but obviously less so for short specialist chapters on individual texts – set out in my Introduction. This Conclusion will be confined to three sections: methods and approaches; areas where contributors go beyond points made in the Introduction, or, indeed, disagree with them; points made which seem to support the general analysis offered there.

All of the contributions are basically historical in methodology, that is they are all careful to make references to precise pieces of evidence in support of their arguments. Chapman stands out in his fruitful use of some of the language of cultural studies, but is always rigorous in his citation of the primary sources. Moore deploys the specialist techniques of the musicologist, particularly effectively when pointing out that those who emphasise 'the social construction of the text' fail to take account of the differences which are present within music. Rowland stands a little apart from the other contributors in that he was a participant in and, as he puts it, 'eye-witness' to the production of the texts he is discussing. But Rowland has made an impressive, and successful, attempt to be a historian as well, seeking out the records in the BBC archives and, where they fall silent, pressing hard to obtain oral testimony from such a key figure as Sir Paul Fox. As a result, all contributions most satisfyingly answer that most important question of how a particular cultural artefact came to be produced (as distinct from simply taking the text as a given and striking off brilliant thoughts from it, or using it to support some predetermined theory). As the contributors are specialists also in film, television or popular music, they confidently address the question of genre (I leave readers to make their own assessment as to my success, or lack of it, with the branch of literature I chose for myself, where I speak of 'the comedy of manners' and 'the campus novel'). Agajanian brings out how *A Hard Day's Night* combines the genres of documentary and musical, reinforcing her point through the comparison with the documentary, *The Beatles: The First US Visit*. So also the question of reception is very thoroughly discussed: particularly illuminating is the fact brought out by Aldgate that *This Sporting Life*, which many of us would regard as one of the greatest of all British films, had a mixed critical reception and little commercial success, suggesting that indeed attitudes and values in Britain were already changing by the time the film was released.

The remainder of this Conclusion will be concerned with the two more purely historical questions contributors were asked to address. A major part of my own thesis is that transformation came through permeation, rather than dialectical conflict. Rowland challenges this with specific reference to broadcasting, seeing a dichotomy between 'a mainstream non-profit making culture' and its commercial competitor. As I see it, both the BBC and ITV fell within what we might call 'established culture', but both, with the BBC leading, became affected by countercultural elements which themselves formed no part of a unified dialectical agenda. This is a topic ripe for discussion and debate. Periodisation, and even sub-periodisation, in my view essential to historical study, must always be a trifle inexact. The point I have just picked up from Aldgate, linked to the fact that the rumbustious *Tom Jones* was released in June 1963, might suggest that what I term the 'High Sixties' had already begun before 1964. However, Agajanian insists that *A Hard Day's Night*, of 1964, belongs to 'The First Stirrings of Cultural Change', not to the 'High Sixties'. I see no problems here: periodisation is not prescriptive, but should stimulate critical analysis. Coyne, in introducing a relativist note, is perhaps the least happy of our contributors with my sub-periodisation. Certainly he announces himself a firm supporter of the thesis (challenged in my ninth proposition) about sixties' developments entailing an unravelling of American society – I should recognise that this view, widely held by American authorities, has been confirmed in a most important recent collection.[2] Coyne also bring outs something critically missing from the Introduction (though, in fact, I strongly agree with it), the way in which a text can refer to, or represent, an enduring tradition, rather than simply relating to the immediate historical context. He reveals how *Seven Days in May* integrates with a basic element in political consciousness, the fear of the power of the military within American democracy. In fact our contributions provide a rich array of references which fall outside even the period covered by my 'long sixties'. Agajanian refers to early comic films (the Keystone Kops, Laurel and Hardy, and the radio programme of the fifties, *The Goon Show*), Leab refers to the postwar British film *Brief Encounter*, Moore points out that 'When I'm sixty-four' was based on a song written in the fifties for Paul McCartney's trumpeter father, I myself point out Lurie's debt to Jane Austen and the English novel generally. Chapman opens up a very interesting area when he refers to *The Avengers* as a 'cult': is this something specific to the sixties, to the contemporary world, or is it in fact timeless?

Where my Introduction most definitely feared to tread was into the realm of postmodernism. Chapman uses 'postmodernist' very precisely and explicitly as a style label, and copiously supports his argument for identifying *The Avengers* as the first postmodernist television series. Obviously, the sixties was the era of the founding postmodernist philosophers: Foucault, Barthes and Eco. Was the 'High Sixties' also the moment when postmodernism appeared as an artistic style (the analogue, in its own way, of, say, the Baroque)? Certainly, in my *The Sixties* I identify early hints of postmodernism in architecture.[3] Moore addresses the matter more comprehensively, calling in Barthes, Eco, Jameson and more recent postmodernist commentators. While finding instances of what the great authorities have decreed to be 'postmodernist', he 'would not argue strongly for' interpreting *Sgt Pepper* as a postmodern artefact.

Generally, the contributors provide rich and detailed evidence in support both of the periodisation and the propositions and characteristics set out in the Introduction. Leab's consistent theme is of *The Apartment* standing on the 'cusp' of change, looking both backwards and forwards. He stresses not only what was done in this particular film, but what became possible quite soon after. The image of a rather stuffy, conformist, unexciting fifties (with which the sixties can be sharply contrasted) comes through in the chapters by Leab, Coyne and Rowland – Rowland refers to the 'courteous interviews' which characterised broadcasting in the fifties. It is in the nature of our texts that they do not directly testify to the transformations in the lives of ordinary people which I claim lies at the heart of the 'cultural revolution' of the sixties. However, there is at least indirect evidence of changes in sexual attitudes (Leab and Agajanian), the status of women (Marwick and Chapman), of Jews (Leab) and blacks (Coyne and Rowland), Rowland explicitly stating that 'crucial moves from segregation to multiculturalism took place during the 1960s', though, as he says, 'through an often terrible crucible'. Chapman, incidentally, notes the almost total absence of blacks from *The Avengers*. One of my biggest claims is that the changes of the sixties were enduring, not simply a temporary period of excess fit only for provoking nostalgia. Both Moore and Agajanian testify to the enduring influence of The Beatles, Chapman to that of postmodernist style, and Leab to that of cultural change generally.

Each contribution in its way provides evidence of the sixties as a time of the emergence of new movements and subcultures: fleetingly, but tellingly, Rowland refers to the touch of 'irreverence' entering the BBC. The importance of youth has perhaps already become a cliché, but valuable discussions by Agajanian and Rowland go beyond the cliché. Technology is often also referred to, but too little explored. Rowland mentions the obvious television, and the rather less obvious jet plane, which enabled Panorama both to get out to the trouble spots and back again much more quickly and easily. The technology of both television production and musical production are analysed, respectively, by Chapman and Moore. Quite definitely, the crucial significance of technology to sixties developments is brought out clearly by these three contributors.

Two of my own pet themes, of the place of 'spectacle', and of personal appearance, self-presentation, and 'beauty', in the sixties, not unnaturally, are not strongly represented (interestingly, Agajanian does not single out the sexy good looks of Paul McCartney). Am I pushing it a bit if I associate Chapman's focus on Honor Blackman's 'kinky' costumes and the way *The Avengers* became 'a phenomenon which permeated the wider realms of popular culture more generally' with the notion of 'spectacle'? Moore has some wise words on the elasticity of the concept. Ponder this:

> It seems to me that the album [*Sgt Pepper*] can be regarded as spectacle only in the imagination. Within a month of the album's release, of course, The Beatles would be in the television studio taking part in an early global satellite broadcast, with the live recording of 'All you need is love'. Here was spectacle indeed, although again with viewers partaking vicariously – the live audience (fellow pop musicians and all) appears to have been carefully chosen.

On 'beauty', Chapman, in discussing Diana Rigg, does directly quote some words of my own on mini-skirts.

Much more obvious is the phenomenon of international cultural exchange: both Chapman and Agajanian refer to the international nature of the production teams behind, respectively, *The Avengers* and *A Hard Day's Night*, and the latter explicitly refers to the incorporation of *nouvelle vague* techniques into The Beatles' film. Even more obvious are the changes in popular culture, the greatly enhanced role it assumed, and, in particular, the status of rock/pop music as universal language. The first two points come through strongly in Chapman's chapter; Moore, once again, has some careful words on rock as a universal means of communication – he does suggest that *Sgt Pepper* was 'perhaps the nearest popular culture has come to a universal expression in music'.

Moore agrees with me that cross-over was a characteristic of cultural products in the sixties. However, he stresses the limited extent of cross-over in *Sgt Pepper*. I, for my part, am in total agreement with him: cross-over is actually much more marked in high culture than popular culture.[4] On what is perhaps one of the most controversial aspects of my interpretation of the sixties, Rowland, at least, is unambiguous:

> *Panorama* certainly exemplifies, I believe, the process described by Arthur Marwick as 'permeation' assisted by 'measured judgement'. To this participant in the *Panorama* process and the many debates about the future in Lime Grove, 'measured judgement' would describe the way many producers and programme editors saw their role.

Equally forthright is Aldgate, who concludes his source-based analysis of the censorship procedures to which *This Sporting Life* was submitted by saying of the Secretary to the British Board of Film Censors, John Trevelyan, that he manifested 'what Arthur Marwick has best described as "measured judgement"', adding:

> He was, in effect, an arch exponent of that flexible, tolerant, liberal response shown by many in positions of authority to the new cultural developments permeating British society during the course of the 1960s.

This brief Conclusion has merely indicated a few issues which you, the reader, might wish to follow up in detail. It would be wasteful to view, listen to, or read, the texts discussed in this book without at least considering what the contributors have had to say about them – and in some cases, particularly, as Rowland points out, that of *Panorama*, you may well not be able to get hold of the texts. But our aim has certainly not been to tell you what to see, or what to think; apart from, we hope, expounding and encouraging sound methodology, it has been to stimulate discussion and debate.

NOTES TO CONCLUSION

1   Marwick, *The Sixties*, op. cit.
2   Alan Brinkley, '1968 And The Unraveling of Liberal America' in Carole Fink, Philipp Gassert and Detlef Junker, *1968: The World Transformed* (Washington, DC and Cambridge, 1998, German Historical Institute and Cambridge University Press), pp 219–36.
3   Marwick, *The Sixties*, op. cit., p 337.
4   Marwick, *The Sixties*, op. cit., pp 316–40.

Index